A HIS

ETON CLLEGE

BY

LIONEL H. CUST

PREFACE

It would seem as if some apology were due for the publication of this book. Eton has been a fruitful, perhaps too fruitful, source of inspiration to writers of all ages in the nineteenth century. The attractiveness of the subject cannot be gainsaid; but it may fairly be asked, Why write another book when there is nothing new to be said, no new record to be discovered; why try and glean in a field which has been reaped close, and swept clean, moreover, by other gleaners before?

Yet the series of English Public Schools in course of publication by Messrs. Duckworth & Co. could hardly be complete without the inclusion of some account of Eton College; hence the present work.

The general history of Eton College has been completed and added to from time to time by Sir Henry Churchill Maxwell-Lyte, K.C.B., Deputy-Keeper of the Records, than whom no one by inclination or experience could be better fitted for his task. A third edition of his work has just been issued to the public. It should be clearly understood that no writer can hope to add anything of importance to the history of Eton College, as set forth in Sir H. C. Maxwell-Lyte's monumental work.

The history of the buildings of Eton College—a most interesting subject in itself—has been set forth in minute detail, and with the greatest care and accuracy, by Mr. John Willis Clark, Registrary of the University of Cambridge, in the chapters on King's College and Eton College, which are embodied in the *Architectural History of the*

i

University of Cambridge, compiled by Mr. Clark and the late Professor Willis. It is to be hoped that this valuable contribution to the history of Eton and King's may some day be issued in a separate volume.

The general history of King's College, Cambridge, so closely associated with that of Eton College, has recently been set forth, in what will probably prove a final form, by the present Provost of King's, the Rev. Augustus Austen-Leigh.

The biographies of famous Etonians have been collected by various writers, such as Mr. J. Heneage Jesse and Sir Edward S. Creasy, to say nothing of so famous a work as Harwood's *Alumni Etonenses*. They are now about to be put into a final shape in the sympathetic hands of Mr. Arthur C. Benson. Mr. Chetwynd-Stapylton's *Eton School Lists* have, in spite of many inaccuracies, proved an inexhaustible mine of information.

The various books in which stories have been collected of Eton and Eton boys are very numerous, and continue at the present day to multiply their progeny. The same may be said of those in which the doughty deeds of Etonians on the river, the cricket-field, and elsewhere are recounted with Homeric enthusiasm, and perhaps also with something of Virgilian piety.

With all these books on Eton the present volume does not hope or wish to compete. An attempt has been made to give a short narrative touching on the most important features of the history of Eton College, without however making it any the less necessary to refer to the more important works of Sir H. C. Maxwell-Lyte and Mr. J. W. Clark; and also to make such allusion to the various books of reminiscences, such as *Etoniana* and others, as may create in the stranger, not only in the Etonian, a desire to become more closely acquainted with the peculiar intimate atmosphere which envelops Eton and Eton boys, and converts apparently trivial and commonplace occurrences or sayings into events as important as any recorded in Herodotus, Livy, or the Student's Hume.

Thanks are specially due to Mr. Arthur C. Benson and Mr. Ingalton Drake for permission to use some of the negatives taken in view of Mr. Benson's forthcoming work; to Mr. Philip Norman for the use of the beautiful drawings here reproduced; to Mr. Thomas Carter for the use of some new photographs taken by him at Eton; to Earl Waldegrave for permission to reproduce the portrait of the fifth Earl; and also to Mr. W. Essington Hughes for permission to reproduce the curious portrait of the founder, Henry VI., which was copied from the original in the British Museum at Mr. Hughes's expense.

The author has also to thank Mr. Reginald J. Smith, Q.C., for his kindness in reading the proofs, and for much sympathetic advice.

The author has also to thank Mr. Reginald J. Smith, Q.C., for his kindness in reading the proofs, and for much sympathetic advice.

ETON COLLEGE.

I

FOUNDATION AND EARLY HISTORY OF ETON COLLEGE

To have founded a great public school, which has continued from the date of foundation to the present day to be the principal place of education for the sons of the governing classes in this country; to have furnished this school with buildings conspicuous for their beauty, unique in some respects in their construction, and for centuries sufficiently adapted to their original purpose; to have drawn up with his own pen a series of statutes which remained in force with but slight alterations for a period of four hundred years—these are achievements which might have been expected of a strong and lawgiving monarch such as Edward I. or Henry VIII., a scholar such as Erasmus, a zealous Churchman such as Wolsey or Laud, rather than of a delicate, somewhat feeble-minded youth but little more than nineteen years of age. Yet the foundation of Eton College was entirely due to Henry of Windsor, sixth of the name, 'the good and holy youth,' whom a turn of fortune's wheel had brought, when but an infant in arms, to occupy an unstable throne at the outset of a cruel and internecine dynastic struggle.

From his earliest youth Henry VI. had been brought up in an atmosphere of religion and learning. He had been baptized by the great Henry Chichele, Archbishop of Canterbury, whose services in the cause of education are well known. His early youth was passed under the influence of his uncle and first guardian and protector, the scholar-statesman Humphrey, Duke of Gloucester, the Good Duke Humphrey as he was called, more perhaps from his munificent benefactions to scholarship and learning than from his general moral character, which is one of the most perplexing problems in the Middle Ages. Subsequently Henry had fallen almost entirely under the control of his great-uncle, Henry Beaufort, Gloucester's enemy and rival, who, when not engaged on militant politics, may be presumed to have not neglected his position as a Cardinal of the Church. Beaufort was a more powerful mind and a better counsellor than Gloucester; but the bitter contest for supremacy between the two must have been a source of trouble to the infant-king, and a bad augury of further difficulties to come. Henry's mind was one ill constituted to cope with the tempests and buffets of fortune with which he was fated to contend. From his earliest childhood he was inclined to works of piety and devotion. In Windsor Castle he was accustomed to associate with the youthful heirs of the nobility, so much so that Windsor became known even in those days as an 'academy for the young nobility.' "There was not in the world," writes Polydore Vergil, the historian, "a more pure, more honest, and more holy creature." Such were the qualities, it may be surmised, which Henry would be most desirous to transmit as a legacy to his scholars at Eton and Cambridge.

As early as 1439 Henry had planned in his mind the foundation of Eton College. He had acquired certain properties upon the site, and obtained leave from the Bishop of Lincoln to appropriate the advowson of the parochial church of Eton and convert it into a collegiate church. He was guided in his plans by the older foundations of William of Wykeham at Winchester and New College, Oxford, and also in all probability by the foundations of Archbishop Chichele at Higham Ferrers and All Souls', Oxford. It has been stated that it was John Langton, Master of Pembroke College, Cambridge, and afterwards Bishop of St. David's, who first suggested to the boy-king the idea of similar foundations at Eton and Cambridge. At all events, in 1440 Henry paid more than one visit himself to Winchester, in order to make himself personally acquainted with the details of Wykeham's foundation and its actual working in practice. It is clear that, although the colleges at Eton and King's College, Cambridge, were founded simultaneously, it was not the King's original intention to make them dependent upon each other, as in the case of Winchester and New Collie, Oxford. Whatever Langton's influence may have been at Cambridge, it seems certain that, as far as Eton College was concerned, the King's principal adviser was Thomas of Bekynton, a Wykehamist scholar.

In September 1440 letters patent were issued by the King for the constitution of a college of Fellows, priests, clerks, choristers, poor scholars, and old poor men, with one master or governor, "whose duty it shall be to instruct these scholars and any others who may resort thither from any part of England in the knowledge of letters, and especially of grammar, without payment."

This was followed on October 10 by a Charter of Foundation, in the preamble to which, after a panegyric on the Church, "the Mother and Mistress of all who are born again in Christ," the King states that "at length, while we were thinking over these things with the most profound attention, it hath become a fixed purpose in our heart to found a college in honour and in support of that our Mother, who is so great and so holy, in the Parochial Church of Eton near Windsor, not far from our birthplace." By this charter the 'King's College of our Lady of Eton beside Windsor' was constituted into a corporate body, consisting of a Provost, ten Fellows, four clerks, six choristers, a schoolmaster, twenty-five poor and indigent scholars, and twenty-five poor and infirm men. It thus comprised the elements of a college, a grammar-school and an almshouse. The Provost was to have been educated at Eton College or King's College, Cambridge, to have been born in England, to be a Bachelor of Divinity, Doctor of Canon Law, or Master of Arts, to be in holy orders, and not less than thirty years of age. The Fellows were to be selected from the Fellows or former scholars of King's, or from present or former chaplains of the college, or, failing both these sources, from the other colleges or anywhere else, according to the discretion of the existing Fellows. They were to be in priest's orders, Bachelors of Divinity, Masters of Canon Law, or Masters of Arts. They were not to own property of more than £10 a year, or be absent from college longer than six weeks at a time without special leave. The Provost was to receive £75 a year (including an allowance for tithes), twelve yards of cloth at 3s. 6d. a yard, and 3s. a week for commons. He was to keep three servants (*quorum unus generosior domicellus, alii vero duo valecti*) who were partly paid for by the College. The Fellows received £10 a year, six yards of cloth, eighteenpence a week for commons, and all dieta were at first paid in kind. A Provost was at once appointed, an honour which the King seems to have intended for his trusty friend, John Stanbury, afterwards Bishop of Hereford, but which he finally conferred upon Henry Sever, his chaplain and almoner, then Chancellor of St. Paul's Cathedral. One of the first Fellows, with the title of Vice-Provost, was John Kette, who had resigned the Rectory of Eton in order to further Henry's scheme of foundation. At that date, in order to carry through so important a scheme, and one so nearly connected with the Church, it was absolutely necessary to obtain Papal sanction for anything involving the foundation of a new religious institution. Henry VI. was not likely to neglect his duty in this respect. Frequent messages passed between Windsor and Rome, until in January $144^0/_1$ a Bull was issued by Pope Eugenius IV. giving sanction to all the King's intentions. Upon receipt of this Henry proceeded to endow the new colleges at Eton and Cambridge with some of the estates in England which the alien priories in France and elsewhere had been compelled to surrender to the Crown. At Eton also he bought up all the private houses and fields which lay within the intended precincts of the college. After making these and other careful provisions, Henry proceeded to lay the first stone of the new collegiate church, as the most important of the new buildings already carefully planned out in his mind. This event seems to have taken place on or about June 5, 1441.

There are few more picturesque incidents in the history of England than the foundation of Eton College. It is easy to imagine in the mind a bright leafy day in June, with a procession issuing from the gates of Windsor Castle, descending the hill under the shadow of the castle walls, and crossing the wooden bridge over the Thames on its way to the parish church of the hamlet of Eton. In the centre would be riding the youthful, beardless King, while the unusual number of prelates and clergy in the procession would suffice to denote the sacred character of their errand. Cardinal Beaufort, then the all-powerful Bishop of Winchester; William of Alnwick, then Bishop of Lincoln, in whose diocese Eton lay; William Ayscough, Bishop of Salisbury; Richard Andrews, Dean of York and first Warden of All Souls' at Oxford; William Lyndewode, most learned and trusted of councillors; and, probably nearest the King, Thomas of Bekynton, the King's secretary and most confidential adviser, would have been conspicuous in the train. Near the King, also, would have ridden the most puissant William de la Pole, then Earl, but afterwards Marquess, and eventually Duke of Suffolk. In such state might the King have laid the first stone of "the college roiall of our Ladye of Eton by Windesore," the stone which still remains under the altar-steps of the present chapel.

The King's plans for the college buildings were drawn up, after two or three preliminary drafts, in a document, still preserved in the college, known as the Will (or Intention) of King Henry VI. Had the King's original plans been carried out, a traveller arriving by the road from Slough (*via que ducit versus le Sloo*), after passing the 'Shooting Fields,' then not yet acquired for the college, and crossing the bridge, known later on as 'Fifteen Arch Bridge,' would have arrived at the corner of the stone wall, which was intended to form the boundary of the college, enclosing the 'Kinges Werde' between the road and the river Thames. A little farther on he would have come to the gate of the college, and on entering would have found himself in an outer court, with the college service buildings on his left and the almshouse on his right. Crossing this court, towards the right hand he would have come opposite the turreted gateway of the college buildings, within which would have been the chief quadrangle, considerably larger than the present cloister. Round this would have been rows of chambers, one storey high, a schoolroom, a library, and on the south side the dining-hall and the Provost's residence. On the western side of the quadrangle a postern door would have led into a cloister, corresponding somewhat to the present schoolyard. On the south of this cloister would have risen the collegiate church, approached from the cloister, in the western side of which would have risen a high tower. Outside the cloister the stone boundary wall, mentioned before, would have been continued up to Baldwyn's ('Barnes') Bridge, passing the old parish church on the site of the present churchyard, and turning at the bridge over the stream, which flowed thence rapidly into the Thames, would have passed round the kitchen and ended on the bank of the back-water, surrounding the ground now known as 'Fellows' Eyot.' Special provisions were made for 'enhancing' certain buildings as a protection against floods, then, as now, the cause of much perplexing trouble and inconvenience.

Of this plan, or Intention, the only portions to be carried out were the dining-hall, the kitchen, and, to a certain extent, the church. No record has been preserved of the King's amended plans for the existing buildings, or the actual date at which he changed his mind. The building accounts have been preserved, and are unusually complete. They commence on July 3, 1441. June 5, 1441, is spoken of in the accounts as 'Dedication Day,' and may perhaps for this reason be accepted as the date on which the first stone was laid by the King. The general superintendence of the buildings was entrusted to William de la Pole, Earl of Suffolk. Full details are given in the accounts of the stone, bricks, timber, and other materials employed in the construction of the buildings. The timber, much of which was transported by the river, was stored in a field opposite the college, then known as the 'timbrehawes,' a name still surviving in 'The Timbralls.' One Jourdelay is named among those employed upon the works, and he is paid "for brede and hale and chese for workemen and laboras, taking the groundes of the college thorow the pondis in to the college." This house seems to have been used as a hostelry for strangers and their horses, and his name still survives in 'Jordelay's Place,' one of the houses at present occupied by an assistant-master. The building accounts contain many interesting particulars concerning the master of the works, the clerk of the works, the masons, carpenters, smiths, purveyors, and others, with their wages, hours of work, rules, fines, &c., for which those curious in these matters must be referred to the careful extracts and abstracts given in the account of Eton College, which is embodied in Willis and Clark's *Architectural History of the University of Cambridge.*

Under the revised plans, the buildings were arranged very differently to those given in the King's 'Will.' They were practically reduced to a cloistered quadrangle for the Provost and Fellows, with a library, dining-hall, and necessary offices, a collegiate church, and a detached building containing dormitories for the boys, school-rooms, and residences for the Master and Usher. By the summer of 1443, if not earlier, some considerable portion of these buildings was far enough advanced to admit of occupation. As early as the Papal Bull of January 1441 the names are given, in addition to those of the Provost and Vice-Provost, of two Priest-Fellows, two clerks, four choristers, two scholars, and two bedesmen, who must have been quartered upon the neighbouring inhabitants. The Founder now paid further visits to Winchester, and in consequence took a step fraught with the utmost importance for the history and welfare of Eton College. He persuaded William of Waynflete (William Patyn, born at Wainfleet, in Lincolnshire, about 1395), the Master of Winchester College, to remove to the new college at Eton as its first Master. Waynflete brought with him five Fellows and thirty-five scholars to form a nucleus for the school; this is the number recorded by tradition, though it does not agree with the Registers at Winchester itself. Waynflete had been a fellow-pupil of Bekynton at Winchester, and was on terms of great personal friendship with him. In 1443 Henry VI. re-cast his whole foundation in order to bring the numbers more into conformity with those at Winchester. Sever relinquished the post of Provost to William of Waynflete, and was rewarded in February 145^5/$_6$ with the Wardenship of Merton College, Oxford, where he died, and was buried in 1471. The numbers on the foundation were fixed at a Provost, ten Priest-Fellows, ten chaplains, ten clerks, sixteen choristers, seventy poor scholars, a Headmaster, an Usher, and thirteen bedesmen.

At the same time the Founder took a new step with regard to the sister foundation at King's College, Cambridge, dedicated "to the honour of almighty and immaculate Virgin Mary, mother of Christ, and also of the glorious confessors and Bishop Nicholas, patron of my intended college, on whose festival we first saw the light." It is touching to note the solicitude with which Henry connected his foundations at Eton and Cambridge with his own life. He laid the first stone of the buildings at Cambridge on April 2, 1441, two months before the similar ceremony at Eton. With the subsequent history of King's College and its glorious chapel these pages cannot, however, deal. In 1443, however, Henry, acting no doubt under the advice of Waynflete, decided to connect the colleges of Eton and King's College, Cambridge, together, like those of Winchester and New College, Oxford, in order to provide for the safe progression of the best of his Eton scholars to the University. With these new departures the actual history of the school at Eton may be said to begin.

In November 1443, during the progress of the new buildings at Eton, an interesting ceremony took place in the parochial church. Thomas of

Bekynton, the King's secretary, and without doubt his most confidential friend and adviser in the plans of the College and its foundation, was consecrated Bishop of Bath and Wells. At Bekynton's special wish the ceremony took place at Eton, the Bishops of Lincoln, Salisbury, and Llandaff officiating. The new collegiate church stood unfinished hard by, and a temporary altar was prepared under an awning and directly over the foundation stone. Thither Bishop Bekynton proceeded after his consecration in the parochial church, and celebrated his first mass in full pontificals. After the service Bekynton entertained his visitors in the new school buildings, *et in nova fabrica collegii ibidem ex parte boriali dum adhuc cameræ non erant condistinctæ subtus tenuit convicium*. It is not quite clear in what room this banquet was held. The text of the entry in his register leaves it doubtful whether the room was on the ground floor or above. 'Long Chamber' bears traces of completion at a later date, but may have been planned out among the first buildings. In this way a series of Etonian bishops was inaugurated from Bekynton of Bath and Wells in 1443 to Welldon of Calcutta in 1898.

In the following December another ceremony took place in the same choir, the first after its completion, and one of deeper import to the college. At this ceremony Bekynton officiated with the Earl of Suffolk as the King's commissioners. William of Waynflete was solemnly installed as Provost in accordance with the revised statutes, and received the oath of allegiance from the Fellows, scholars, and other existing members of the foundation. For four hundred years and more the corporate body, formed on this occasion, remained practically unaltered in its scheme, if not maintained in its entirety. The tie thus formed between the foundations of William of Wykeham at Winchester and Oxford and these of Henry VI. at Eton and Cambridge was further cemented by a covenant (*Amicabilis Concordia*) drawn up between them for their mutual support and assistance in the case of need.

During the progress of the buildings at Eton, Henry VI. continued to make numerous provisions for the endowment and welfare of the College. Bekynton was his chief agent in the matter. In September 1443 Bekynton obtained leave from the Bishop of Lincoln to invest the Provost of Eton with special archidiaconal jurisdiction in the parish of Eton, on condition of a small annual payment to the Archdeacon of Buckinghamshire, which was, until lately, paid annually by the College. He then proceeded to solicit the Pope, on behalf of the King, for further and special favours. In order to attract strangers to Eton, indulgences of a very special nature had been granted by the Pope to all penitents visiting the collegiate church of Eton at the Feast of the Assumption, each penitent being expected to contribute towards the maintenance of the College, and advised to offer prayers for the Founder. In May 1444 a fresh Bull was issued, considerably extending, while confirming, the indulgences already granted to Eton College. In consequence of this and subsequent advantages the number of pilgrims to the new college was very large. Their contributions, however, to the cost of the buildings hardly seem to have covered the expenses of their entertainment. To provide for the food and lodging of visitors on such occasions, in addition to an annual gift of red Gascon wine from the King, an annual fair was established to last during the six days after the Feast itself. A similar fair was instituted during the three days succeeding Ash Wednesday for a similar reason. Both these fairs were entirely under the control of the Provost of Eton, and survived in modified forms until quite recent days. The College also was allowed a weekly market, a very exceptional privilege. The College was besides exempted from subsidies and other imposts. Furthermore, as the Provost was compelled to make frequent journeys to London to consult with the King, he was granted the Hospital of St. James, then used for lepers, and standing apart in the fields near Westminster. Books, ornaments, vestments, relics, and the like were provided for the College on the petition of the Provost and Fellows.

On April 11, 1447, Cardinal Beaufort, Bishop of Winchester, died, leaving in his will legacies of money, with valuable jewels and relics, to Eton College. These legacies were, however, of less import to the college than the actual event of Beaufort's death, and the vacancy caused by it in the important see of Winchester. Henry VI. hurriedly nominated William of Waynflete to the see, anticipating not only the wishes of the Chapter at Winchester, but even the right of nomination exercised by the Pope. The latter difficulty was easily arranged; but Waynflete himself seems to have shown no desire to leave Eton and break off the work which he had been the first to set in motion. It is recorded that the commissioners came from Winchester with the royal *congé d'élire*, and found the Provost at prayers in the old parish church. Some persuasion was necessary to make him obey the command. In July 1447 the

Provost was consecrated Bishop of Winchester in the church at Eton, and afterwards, by special permission of the Bishop of Lincoln, held his first ordination on the same spot.

The removal from Eton of so important an individual as William of Waynflete might have been disastrous to the future of the college. It proved, however, the reverse. As Bishop of Winchester, and afterwards as Lord High Chancellor, Waynflete became one of the most powerful men in England, so long as the Lancastrian cause was in the ascendant. Even during its eclipse his position in the Church remained unshaken. Eton College thus obtained a champion and protector more powerful under the circumstances than even the Founder himself.

Meanwhile the Founder had made an important alteration in the plans for the buildings at Eton College. Whether it was the growing importance of Eton as a place of pilgrimage and a centre of religious thought and practice, or nothing more than an increasing desire to expand and further a pet hobby, Henry was dissatisfied with the plans of the new collegiate church, and substituted for them a plan on a vastly extended scale. Perhaps the real moving cause was a wish to bestow on the Church, to which he was so much devoted, an edifice which would be one of the glories of Christendom, and obtain for its founder the thankful prayers of future generations. Roger Keys, then master of the works, was instructed to draw out new plans. Had these been carried out the new church would have been, so far as its simple construction of nave and choir allowed, greater in size and dimensions than any church in England save York Minster and the present St. Paul's Cathedral.

The new church was to be erected in the Pure Perpendicular Style, of which the portion completed remains such a conspicuous and typical example. A choir, with a Lady Chapel at the eastern end, would have opened out into a nave with aisles. It is impossible to say whether any additions would have been made to this simple plan, since the only part to be completed was the choir, which, without the Lady Chapel, forms the present well-known 'Chapel.' Had the nave been completed, the church would have extended a considerable way down what is now known as Keate's Lane. It is noteworthy that among the benefactors to Eton, William de la Pole, now Marquess, but soon to be Duke of Suffolk, contributed a sum towards building the church exceeding at the moment the contributions of the other chief contributors—the King, Waynflete, and Bishop Ayscough of Salisbury—all put together.

Another favour conferred by the Founder on his colleges at Eton and Cambridge was the grant of armorial bearings. The flower most connected with the Virgin Mary, to whom Eton College was dedicated, is the lily, and a combination of white lilies with the royal arms of France and England, and in the case of King's College with the crozier of St. Nicholas, seems to have been in use in Waynflete's day. The actual grants of these armorial bearings were not issued until January $144^7/_8$. In these the Founder explains the significance of the charges. The sable ground denoted the perpetuity of the foundation, and the three white lily-flowers (without stalks or leaves) the service of God and the blessed and immaculate Virgin Mary, Mother of Christ. "The chief of the shield was to contain a portion of the royal arms of France and

16

England, in order to impart something of royal nobility, which may declare the work truly royal and illustrious." In the case of King's College, the sable ground was charged with three white roses, as "bright flowers redolent with every kind of learning." Similar roses form part of the armorial bearings of Winchester College.

In such a way did the new college at Eton rise and flourish under the very eye of the Founder himself.

Clouds, however, began to rise upon the political horizon, though few could have prognosticated the terrible storm which was to break upon the land, and the cruel dynastic struggle which, besides devastating England, swept away the Founder of Eton College. In fact the College narrowly escaped being cast into the same gulf of destruction as the hapless Henry himself. In 1452 Margaret of Anjou gave birth to a long-desired son. She sent two messengers to Eton College to announce the news, which was received with joy there, probably as an augury of a continuous enjoyment of royal favour. In the following year Henry's mind gave way, and he became incapable of managing his affairs. His cousin, Richard, Duke of York, who had been until the birth of the prince the next heir to the throne, was appointed Protector. The rivalry between him and Queen Margaret had already been shown in more than one way. From this time, however, it was converted into open hostility, which formed a short prelude to the disastrous Wars of the Roses.

During this terrible time the works at Eton were carried on with great difficulty, and eventually suspended altogether. The choir of the new church had been nearly completed, but the nave not even commenced. The quadrangle and cloister were nearly completed save on the western side. The dining-hall was finished by 1450. The scholars' buildings opposite the church with the Master's house were nearly finished, although only some portions seem to have been in use. The supply of money had ceased with the capture and incapacity of the Founder and the execution of the Duke of Suffolk. The whole future of the college depended on the whim of one man, Edward, Duke of York, whose hand was on the crown. Was it likely that during so heated a struggle as that of the Yorkist and Lancastrian causes any of the specially wealthy foundations or possessions of the latter should escape spoliation?

Fortunately for Eton College Waynflete had been succeeded, first as Master and then as Provost, by a man who was equal to the crisis. William Westbury came from Winchester to Eton to succeed Waynflete in the management of the school. He was elected Provost in November 1447—Waynflete's actual successor, John Clerk, having died five months after his election—and may be presumed to have been the heir and recipient of Waynflete's intentions with regard to the future of the college. When it was evident that the Lancastrian cause was ruined, Westbury showed unexpected powers as a diplomatist. In February $146^0/_1$ he sought direct protection from Edward, then still Duke of York, who signed a deed to protect the Provost and Fellows of Eton, in which he is described as "by ye grace of God of Englande Fraunce & Irlande way and just heire." This seems a surprising act of tergiversation on the part of a college whose Founder was alive and a captive in the hands of the usurping prince. The line taken by the Provost and Fellows seems, however, to have been politic, for in a few months all Lancastrian grants were revoked except those to Eton. The danger, however, was not yet past. Edward had established himself at Windsor Castle, and having no particular interest in Eton, which he probably regarded as Henry's special hobby, he made up his mind to annex the whole foundation to one in which he took a personal interest, that of St. George's Chapel in Windsor Castle. The Dean and Chapter of St. George's were only too willing, and with their help Edward had little trouble in obtaining a Bull from Pope Pius II. to carry the amalgamation into effect. The Chapter of St. George's at once laid hands upon all the portable wealth at Eton College and removed it to Windsor.

The lion was, however, roused in Provost Westbury. Before the Papal Bull was received he went to London and proclaimed his lawful claim to the Provostship, and claimed thereby the special protection of the Pope. To the Pope he declared that as Provost he would never be a consenting party to the suppression of the College. In this action he was of course supported by Waynflete, who, although his political influence had waned, still held one of the most commanding positions in the Church. Clement Smyth, who, after being Master of Chichele's school at Higham Ferrers, had succeeded Westbury as Master, and been transferred to the more lucrative post at Winchester, returned to Eton and resumed his post to support Westbury at this critical time. Westbury's efforts were crowned with success. He seems to have expended much time and energy in assiduous court to the great nobles and the highest dignitaries of the Church. Edward was easy-going and indolent, careless of both religion and politics, and ready to cancel one day any order or grant which he had made the day before. His position on the throne was precarious, and depended on the support of the great nobles, who had already begun to look upon Eton as the obvious place of education for their sons. At all events, he was induced to ask the Pope to revoke the Bull on the plea of erroneous information. As the Bull uniting the foundations of Eton and Windsor was issued by his predecessor and not by himself, Pope Paul II. thought himself able to give a cautious though sufficient assent. Westbury's triumph was almost complete, though the legal business connected with the revocation of the Bull seems to have been immense. Matters were complicated by the unexpected restoration of Henry VI. to the throne, which must have been the cause of great rejoicing to Eton College. The Provost and Fellows seem to have acted diplomatically in the matter, and, while being true in their devotion to their royal Founder, they managed to avoid giving offence to his enemy and the usurper of his crown. The Founder was, however, soon dethroned again, and had been but a few weeks in his grave when Edward IV., now recognised as King, paid with his Queen the first of frequent visits to Eton.

It is difficult to account with certainty for the change in Edward's treatment of Eton College. Tradition, never a safe guide, but one which should not be entirely ignored, has attributed it to the influence of the beautiful Jane Shore, Edward's mistress, and her memory has been cherished at both Eton and King's for this reason, and her frailty excused by the extent of the benefits obtained from her intercession. There is indeed no reason for discrediting this particular tradition. Sir Thomas More says, that "where the King toke displeasure she could mitigate and appease his mind; when men were out of faver, she could bring them in his grace." The Provost and Fellows of Eton were not likely to neglect any means of influencing Edward IV. It would seem, however, quite possible that the influence exerted upon Edward was much more legitimate, namely, that of his Queen, Elizabeth Widvile. Elizabeth accompanied Edward on several of his visits to Eton. Her brother, Anthony, Earl Rivers, was a scholar and a patron of learning, and is known to have taken an active interest in the welfare of the college. His services to the College were sufficient to ensure a daily mass, at which prayers were said for Edward IV., Queen Elizabeth, their children, and for Earl Rivers, and even his parents and other relations.

Whether through the influence of 'Shore's wife,' or of Elizabeth, the 'upstart' Queen, Eton College was preserved from destruction. It suffered, however, severely in lands and revenues. The building operations, so grievously interrupted, were resumed in 1469, but funds were very short. It remains to be stated that but for the generosity of Bishop Waynflete they would in all probability never have been completed at all. This is all the more remarkable, inasmuch as Waynflete was at the time engaged on his own foundation at Magdalen

College, Oxford. It was, if not hopeless, at all events undesirable that the church should be completed on the scale designed by the Founder. The portion completed was finished off, and an ante-chapel added in the place of the nave. The church as completed now took the place of the old parish church, which was demolished. The school buildings were also completed, and a boys' chamber is mentioned as early as 1470, which was probably, but not certainly, identical with Long Chamber. The impoverishment of the College enabled the Provost and Fellows to dispense with some of the original members of the foundation, such as the bedesmen and the almshouse, and the somewhat unnecessary large number of chaplains.

Provost Westbury died in 1477. The Fellows nominated as his successor a late Vice-Provost, Thomas Barker, who, however, gave way to Henry Bost, the nominee of the crown. It has been stated that it was to the time of Provost Bost that the legend of Jane Shore should be applied. His epitaph, however, distinctly alludes to his having used his influence to obtain sums from the legitimate consort of the King.

Richard III. during his short reign, in spite of his hatred of the Widvile family and their friends, such as the Etonian Archbishop Rotherham, and his specially vindictive persecution of Jane Shore, does not appear to have troubled his mind much with the affairs of Eton College.

The union of the Houses of York and Lancaster under Henry VII. was the signal for an epoch of prosperity for Eton College. Henry VII. is stated, but on very doubtful authority, to have actually been himself a scholar in Eton College. This would hardly seem to have been possible, for until 1470, his fourteenth year, Henry was brought up in Wales. He only came to London during the short restoration of Henry VI. to the throne, when the King may have wished to place him at Eton. A few months later, however, Henry was a refugee in Brittany, where he remained during the whole of Edward IV.'s reign. Shortly after the accession of Henry VII., in 1486, William of Waynflete died. With his death the first epoch in the history of Eton College may be said to have come to an end.

II

THE EARLY PROVOSTS

When the Houses of York and Lancaster, the White and Red Roses, were at last united under the sway of Henry VII., Eton College and other similar institutions enjoyed a few years of tranquil prosperity. The vicinity of Eton College to Windsor Castle has always rendered it peculiarly susceptible to the varying breezes of royal favour. Seizing their opportunity the colleges of Eton and King's presented a petition to the King, and explained therein the losses which they had sustained during the Civil Wars. They were successful in recovering some of the possessions of which they had been despoiled by Edward IV., and as the re-establishment of peace once more unloosed the fountains of private beneficence, they received further endowments by gift or bequest. The Church became rich with jewels, plate, and sacred images. Visits were paid to the College by the King, the Papal Legate, the Bishops of Lincoln and Chichester, and other eminent persons, who were handsomely entertained in *esculentis et poculentis* by the Provost. Beyond this and the succession of Roger Lupton as Provost upon the death of Provost Bost, there is little to record in the history of Eton College under Henry VII.

Henry VIII. visited Eton soon after his accession, and the repute and importance of the College was shown by visits from the Duke of

Buckingham, the Lord Chancellor Audley, and other dignitaries of State or Church. This very importance was in itself a source of danger. During the general appropriation of ecclesiastical endowments and revenues, which marked the establishment of the reformed religion in England, the endowments and properties of Eton College, though duly scheduled and valued, were exempted, as were those of Winchester, the two schools being regarded as part of the two Universities. The danger, however, was a real one. Thomas Cromwell, the King's secretary, was only able to maintain himself in the royal favour by supplying the King with money. Provost Lupton did his best to keep on good terms with the King and with the all-powerful arch-enemy, Cromwell. Henry's appetite for the spoils of the Church was too omnivorous, his wallet too capacious, for so fat a prize as Eton College to escape. In 1531 Cromwell extorted from the College the valuable property of St. James's-in-the-Fields at Westminster, consisting of some one hundred and eighty or more acres of land "between Charing Cross and Aye Hill." The College was allowed to retain some property in the north of London at Hampstead, and received in exchange lands in Kent and Suffolk, the value of which could never, even at that date, have been an equivalent to that of the land between London and Westminster. The College still retains the property in North London, and its value is now sufficient to make the College sadly rue the day when Provost Lupton surrendered to the King the Hospital of St. James. The College, however, probably incurred further peril by falling under the royal displeasure. Edward Powell, a noted preacher at Court, had been Head-master of Eton for two or three years at the end of the fifteenth century. He took a prominent part in opposing the divorce of the King from Katherine of Arragon, and in refusing to acknowledge the royal supremacy in the Church. Powell therefore shared the fate of Sir Thomas More and Bishop Fisher on the scaffold at Smithfield. The goods and property of the College were again all duly valued and scheduled for seizure if required in the Act for the Dissolution of Colleges, Chantries, and Free Chapels at the King's Pleasure, and the endowments would have shared this fate had not the King died before he had an opportunity for carrying out his rapacious intentions. *"Ferus omnia Jupiter Argos Transtulit"* writes sadly the author of a survey of the College property in 1545.

Under Edward VI., another boy-king like the Founder, and also a reputed saint, it might have been supposed that Eton College would have been specially favoured with royal patronage. As it was, the danger of sequestration became more acute. The Protector, Edward, Duke of Somerset, and the King's other advisers were so violent and bigoted in their desire to enforce the reformed Church upon the country, that they determined in the King's name to seize and suppress all existing schools and colleges, and after purging them of any taints of monasticism which might linger about them, to reestablish them as new schools "to good and godly uses," in which the Church could have no power. Eton and Winchester were again saved by their connection with the Universities. It may, however, be conjectured that it was the support and strenuous opposition of the nobles which saved Eton and

Winchester from the boy-king's pious desire to remodel everything upon his own little dry and narrow plan, with a neat little bust of himself over the principal entrance, as the Defender of the Faith and patron of true learning and knowledge. Though Eton was saved, the King's hand was felt heavily in the College. The dedication of the College to the Virgin Mary was expunged, the Feast of the Dedication and other prominent saints' days abolished, the altars, relics, images, and other ornaments in the church destroyed or appropriated, and the library purified of all superstitious books. If the scholars and other students were to be allowed to receive their education at Eton and Cambridge in the way intended by their Founder, Edward VI. was determined that they should do so under a system of his own. During the short reign of Mary Tudor and the reprisals inflicted by the Catholic Church in return for the oppressive bigotry of the preceding reign, much was restored and replaced in the chapel, and the old ritual revived. The Provost, nominated by Mary, stood high in the Queen's favour. More than one prominent Etonian went to the stake during the miserable religious war which ensued, but the College appears to have been safer in the hands of Mary Tudor than in those of her father or brother. With the accession of Elizabeth, whose view of all ecclesiastical questions was broad and liberal, Eton College was relieved from any further danger. The Queen was cautious and deliberate in promoting the cause of the reformed religion into England, and accomplished its eventual supremacy by a policy of slow and gradual infusion, instead of a violent and polemic insistence.

During this period of the history of Eton College, its outward history is mainly that of its Provosts. It has always been a contested point, whether the Founder by his statutes invested the Fellows with the right of electing their own Provost, or whether this privilege was retained by the Crown. The Founder during his own lifetime certainly exercised the right of appointment to this post, and his successors on the throne claimed the same power. The Fellows always contested the claim of the Crown, and on nearly every occasion made an effort to assert and establish their right. The Crown, however, usually got its way, with the result that the Provosts of Eton for some generations, as the nominees of the Crown, were continually brought into personal contact with the sovereign. The safety of the College revenues during these checkered times may be attributed in a large degree to the influence of the Provost in person.

Provost Bost undoubtedly exercised a great personal influence at the court of Edward IV. and Elizabeth Widvile, and later of Henry VII. and Elizabeth of York. He died on February 7, 1503, and was buried in the antechapel; a monumental brass for many years marked his grave, but was in recent years removed, incorrectly repaired, and fixed to the wall of Lupton's Chapel. Bost was succeeded by Roger Lupton. Lupton had founded a grammar school at Sedbergh, in Yorkshire, which had been improved away by the pious Edward. He was a Fellow of the College, but it remains uncertain whether he was elected Fellow only one day prior to his election, as generally recorded, so as to enable him to hold the Provostship, or whether he may not be identical with the Roger

Sutton (*sic*) elected Fellow in March 1488. Lupton was more remarkable for what he did than for what he was as Provost, although excuse may be made for the way in which he was harried by Secretary Cromwell. He seems to have been of a pliable disposition, and to have yielded in every way, perhaps wisely, to the pressure of circumstances under Henry VIII. In July 1534 Provost Lupton and the Fellows acknowledged the royal supremacy and repudiated the jurisdiction of the Pope. Lupton too surrendered to the King the valuable London property, alluded to before, and narrowly escaped being swallowed up himself, College, Fellows, and all their revenues, in the greedy maw of the new Defender of the Faith.

Provost Lupton, however, left an enduring mark upon the College, whereby his name will ever remain linked with its history. Up to his time the college and school-buildings had remained much in the same condition as when left by Waynflete. The church, as has been stated, had been hastily completed by the ante-chapel in place of the projected nave; the cloister-quadrangle was complete on the north, east, and south sides, but the western side had remained unfinished. In the school quadrangle the rooms of the masters and scholars, with school-rooms beneath them, occupied a detached building on the north side. A new chamber for the boys in college is mentioned in the Audit Book for 1507-8. Perhaps Long Chamber was remodelled or rebuilt; for although it resembles the earlier buildings of Henry VI., and seems to be certainly the room mentioned in 1468, it may have been remodelled by Provost Lupton. A new school is mentioned as built in 1514-15, the exact position of which is uncertain. Lupton's chief addition to the college buildings was the completion—begun in 1500, and finished in 1520—of the western side of the cloister-quadrangle, forming the eastern side of the present schoolyard. Externally, the chief feature was the insertion of the great square tower, known as Lupton's Tower, breaking into the line of the quadrangle; internally, his alterations involved the removal of the Provost's apartments to the northern part of the western side, instead of its old location with an approach from the hall, and the construction of a fine suite of apartments for the accommodation of the Visitors at Election time, and also for the College library. The large room, known as the 'Provost's Hall,' or 'Election Hall,' seems to have been originally intended for the library. Among other minor additions to the school buildings, Lupton built at his own cost the well-known chantry in the chapel, between two of the great buttresses on the northern side towards the east end of the chapel. A rebus of his name, a *tun*, or barrel, bearing the letters *Lup* upon it, forms part of the decorations of this chantry. In this chantry Lupton himself was buried after his death at the age of eighty-three or more, in February 1540, he having resigned the Provostship some five years before. He bequeathed certain sums of money to the Foundation of Eton, to be paid on the anniversary of his death, part of which bequest still survives in the annual payment to the King's Scholars on 'Threepenny Day,' February 27. Lupton was succeeded as Provost by a former Head-master, Robert Aldrich. Aldrich was a man of note in his day. He was an Eton man, and proceeded to King's College, Cambridge, in 1507, and became Master of

Eton in 1515. As a scholar he was a friend of Erasmus, who describes him as *juvenis blandæ cujusdam eloqttentiæ*, and, as a diplomatist, he was selected by the King as one of the Commissioners sent by Henry VIII. to the Pope in 1533, on the question of the divorce of Katherine of Arragon. He was Canon of Windsor and Chancellor of the Order of the Garter, and compiled the famous Black Book of the Order, which has been kept up and continued to the present day, and is now in the custody of the Dean of Windsor. Aldrich was Almoner to Jane Seymour, and in high favour at Court. Subsequently he was made Bishop of Carlisle, and held this post jointly with the Provostship, until he resigned the latter in 1547. Aldrich was more of a courtier than a divine, and his tenure of the Provostship was more remarkable for dignity and splendour than for any tangible benefits conferred upon the College. Shortly before his resignation there was interred in the chapel the body of John Longland, Bishop of Lincoln, and in that capacity Visitor of Eton College. Longland had taken a strong personal interest in Eton, and by his will was a benefactor to the College, especially to the library. His affection for the College was shown by his directions that his body should be taken there for interment in the chapel, while his heart was to be buried in Lincoln Cathedral, and his entrails at Woburn, where he died in 1547.

Upon the resignation of Provost Aldrich the appointment fell into the hands of the Protector Somerset. It was too valuable and influential a piece of patronage to be thrown away, and Somerset did not hesitate in his decision. Although the Fellows claimed a nominal right of election, it was under a *congé d'élire* from the Crown. Somerset, in Edward's name, in defiance of the Founder's statutes, requested them to elect Thomas Smith, a learned man and scholar, then Master of Requests, the King in his letter giving his special dispensation for the breach of the statute; the said Thomas was 'not priste or doctor of divinitie.' As a matter of fact Smith seems to have been ordained a priest in 1546, and was even made Dean of Carlisle at the same time as his election to the Provostship of Eton. Nevertheless he became Secretary of State and was knighted, and therefore had many other interests than those of Eton to preside over. He was a devoted adherent of Somerset, and under his superintendence the College was carefully purged of its Roman Catholic ornaments and appanages. Sir Thomas Smith was married, and lived in great state in the Provost's lodge. On the strength of the Provost's marriage some of the Fellows followed suit, in spite of the express direction in the statutes. In some ways Smith was well fitted for his post, although he seems to have never been on good terms with the Fellows. He is principally remarkable for his having introduced into England a pronunciation of Greek in accordance with the views of Erasmus. The Greek language has been pronounced accordingly at Eton and throughout England. The correctness of this pronunciation was hardly questioned until the resuscitation of Greece as a living country, and the actual use of the language as a means of conversation, showed that the pronunciation as fixed in schools was an artificial convention. When Edward VI.'s short life and reign was ended, and his sister Mary had secured the throne, Sir Thomas Smith, besides supporting the cause of Lady Jane Grey, held too conspicuous a post as Provost of Eton, and a zealous Reformer withal, to make it likely that he would remain unmolested, even if he was not in more actual peril. He was prudent enough to resign before any inquiry was instituted into his tenure of the Provostship and his compliance with the statutes as to priesthood and marriage. Henry Cole, Archdeacon of Ely and Canon of Westminster, was thrust upon the College as Provost, a fervent Catholic 'more earnest than wise,' who did his best to obliterate what he considered the ravages of the Reformers. Otherwise Cole left but little mark upon Eton. The one historical incident connected with his Provostship was his selection to preach the sermon at St. Mary's, Oxford, which was to precede the execution of Archbishop Cranmer, resulting in a scene which may be said to have been literally burnt into the history of the Church of England. Cole was afterwards Dean of St. Paul's, Vicar-General to Cardinal Pole, and a zealous hunter of heretics. Less prudent than Sir Thomas Smith, Cole did not resign his Provostship on the death of his patrons Queen Mary and Cardinal Pole, holding it until at last he was deprived for contumacious behaviour and committed to the Fleet Prison, and to subsequent oblivion. In the room of Provost Cole the post of Provost of Eton was conferred by royal command, though ostensibly by election of the Vice-Provost and Fellows after admission as Fellow, on July 5, 1559, upon William Bill, D.D., a man of wisdom and experience, who had already been Master in succession of St. John's and Trinity Colleges at Cambridge, until the accession of Queen Mary, when he had been deprived. Provost Bill stood high in the favour of the new Queen, Elizabeth. In addition to the Provostship of Eton, he was appointed Dean of Westminster and Chief Almoner to the Queen, and was also restored to the Mastership of Trinity College, Cambridge. Elizabeth, oreover, entrusted to Dr. Bill the re-foundation of Henry VIII.'s school at Westminster. Provost Bill was cautious in introducing fresh ecclesiastical changes into the great institutions under his charge, but his careful policy seems to have been the starting-point for the gradual diffusion and establishment of the Protestant faith as the dominant religious power in England. His period of office at Eton was too short to allow of any great or sweeping changes in the administration of the College. It is to be regretted that the chief action which can be attributed to him was the whitewashing of the interesting fresco-paintings in the chapel, which had escaped even the reforming zeal of Edward VI. and the Duke of Somerset.

Provost Bill died in 1561. Under his easy rule the Fellows had had it much their own way, and they thought the election of a new Provost an opportunity for attempting to assert their rights. Without waiting for the royal command they chose and elected to be Provost Richard Bruerne, a Fellow of Eton and Canon of Christ Church, but one 'of whom there is disperst very evil fame,' as his enemies alleged. The Drown took up the challenge. By the Founder's statutes the Archbishop of Canterbury was appointed Visitor of the College in addition to the Bishop of Lincoln. Matthew Parker, then Archbishop of Canterbury, and the Bishop of Winchester, Home, were therefore sent down to make a visitation of the College in September 1561. The opposing forces were easily routed. Bruerne resigned, thereby escaping expulsion, and afterwards became a Canon of Windsor and Rector of Mapledurham. Three of the Fellows, Kyrton, Ashbrooke, and Pratt, with one of the chaplains, Legge, were expelled, and another, John Durston, was only allowed to remain until the ensuing Michaelmas.

Several candidates were submitted by Archbishop Parker and Bishop Grindal for the Queen's consideration. She selected William Day, an Eton and King's scholar, and a pronounced advocate of the reformed religion. Day, after being admitted as Fellow in order to abide by the statutes, was therefore elected Provost on December 18, 1561.

Provost Day resumed the work of reform initiated under Edward VI. by Provost Sir Thomas Smith. He cleared out of the chapel any traces which still remained of the Roman Catholic ritual, including what must have been a rood-loft of particular beauty. He introduced some broad and sweeping reforms into the College establishment itself. He married, although a priest, and thereby incurred for some time the Queen's displeasure. He obtained from the Queen in 1565 a very important dispensation, whereby the Fellows of the College were allowed to hold, in addition to their Fellowship, one benefice above the value of ten pounds *per annum*, but not exceeding the value of fifty marks. This dispensation remained a charter of liberty for the Fellows, though its actual scope was called into question and finally settled as late as 1815. Some religious observances, fast becoming of an obsolete nature, were also dispensed with. Day enjoyed the advantage of having as his Vice-Provost, and as such the chief manager of the school, a man who was not only his brother-in-law, but also one of the leading Churchmen of Elizabeth's reign, William Wickham, afterwards Bishop in succession of Lincoln and Winchester.

Queen Elizabeth visited Eton College, and was entertained by Provost Day on more than one occasion. Other exalted personages were also his guests in the College. A doubtful honour was conferred on the Provost when the French Ambassador, who had been placed under compulsory restraint, was lodged in the College. Much scandal and disorder ensued, and the Provost was not only grievously annoyed, but was even subjected to personal insult, by his unsought-for foreign guests. Provost Day, in spite of his Puritanism, ruled the College well. He is spoken of as 'our good old Provost,' and as affable, courteous, a good and intelligible preacher, and noted for learning as well as for piety. He held the Provostship for thirty-four years, and from 1573 the Deanery of Windsor as well. In November 1575 he was elevated to the Bishopric of Winchester, when he resigned the Provostship, but survived his new dignity only a few months.

Elizabeth had some difficulty in filling the post, not, however, for want of candidates. Mr. Secretary Cecil therefore wrote in the following January to the Vice-Provost and Fellows, ordering them to suspend for a time the election to the vacant Provostship. The most eager applicant was Henry Savile, Warden of Merton College, at Oxford, who had formerly been the Queen's instructor in the Greek language, and stood high in her estimation. However much Elizabeth may have wished to advance Savile, she did not show the same readiness as her brother

Edward to violate the Founder's statutes and appoint a Provost who was not, or was only nominally, a priest. Savile, however, importuned her for the post, and eventually through the influence of the Earl of Essex and of Lord Burghley, he was successful. He was made Provost in May 1596, "any statute, act, or canon to the contrary notwithstanding." Savile's appointment was very successful. He had been a strong and severe ruler at Oxford, and brought the same system to Eton. In 1604 he entertained James I. at Eton, and was knighted by the King. Savile made Eton the centre of a learned company of scholars. Having devoted his leisure to an edition of the works of St. John Chrysostom, he determined to print it under his own supervision. A new range of buildings had lately been erected on the western side of the Provost's stable-yard abutting on the highroad to Slough. In this building, which still remains as one of the most picturesque in Eton, and was until lately the residence of the Head-master, Provost Savile, the 'Lay-Bishop' as his contemporaries called him, set up his printing-press. He obtained a special fount of type from Holland known as the 'silver letter,' engaged the services of the King's printer, John Norton, and commenced his work. A few smaller Greek works were issued in addition to the famous edition of St. John Chrysostom, which was issued in eight folio volumes, and took three years to produce. Savile also had a share in the translation of the Bible, which still remains the authorised version.

Under Sir Henry Savile Eton College occupied a very high position among learned societies in Europe. This was mainly due to the Provost's personal influence. Both Oxford and Eton owe much to his learning, his munificence, and his wise and experienced government. It is to Savile probably that the study of Greek at Eton owes its first signs of progress, together with the introduction of the Greek Grammar originally compiled by William Camden the historian, and known later as the *Eton Greek Grammar*. Savile died at Eton on February 1621-2, and was buried there. James I. had no intention of letting this important piece of patronage slip through his hands. He had, in fact, promised the post to Thomas Murray, a Scotchman, who had been tutor to Charles when Prince of Wales, and whose nephew, William Murray, afterwards Earl of Dysart, is said to have acted as 'whipping-boy' to the young prince. Murray seems to have had no particular qualifications to succeed a man like Sir Henry Savile. He was an alien moreover, had no university degree, and was no priest. The famous Lord Keeper Williams was then Bishop of Lincoln and Visitor of the College, and objected strongly to Murray's appointment. He could not, however, withstand the royal mandate, although he managed to secure the rights of the Fellows to a voice in the election. Murray, however, only retained the post into which he had thus been thrust for one year, and would have left no mark on the history of Eton College had not a fine and sumptuous Jacobean monument been erected to his memory in the Chapel, as the Collegiate Church at Eton seems to have been styled from about this date.

During the illness of Provost Murray intrigues were busy and frequent with regard to his successor in this valuable post. Two

38

prominent diplomatists, neither of them Etonians—Sir Dudley Carleton, who had married Provost Savile's step-daughter, and Sir Henry Wotton— had angled for the post before Savile's death. They again became candidates. The post had been practically promised to one Sir William Beecher, clerk of the Privy Council. The King was disposed to give it to Sir Robert Ayton, a Scotchman like Murray, who had been secretary to Queen Anne. Ayton's application was addressed to James I. in verse, which may have been the origin of that sage monarch's approbation, apart from his notorious penchant for Scotchmen. Murray's widow also appears to have intimated her willingness to remain in the lodge as Lady Ayton. Other candidates were Sir Ralph Freeman, Master of Requests, who was connected by marriage with Buckingham, Sir Robert Naunton, Secretary of State, and Sir Albertus Morton, an Etonian, step-nephew to Sir Henry Wotton, secretary to Princess Elizabeth at Heidelberg, and clerk to the Council. Most formidable, however, of all the candidates was the great Francis Bacon, Viscount St. Albans, so sadly fallen from the high estate of Lord High Chancellor of England. That Bacon eagerly desired the post is evident from his letters to Sir Edward Conway, then Secretary of State. Bacon says that the Provostship 'were a pretty Cell for my Fortune,' and particularly suited to him, 'specially in the spent houreglass of such a life as myne.' It is characteristic of the history of England at this moment that, among all these candidates James was unable, or did not dare, to decide in the absence of the Duke of Buckingham, who was then with the Prince of Wales in Spain. Bishop Williams in fact wrote

39

himself to Buckingham, as the person in whose power wholly the nomination lay. Buckingham, however, was not going to hurry home for such a trifle, and the candidates were obliged to wait in uncertainty for Buckingham's return. Somehow or the other Sir Henry Wotton, who had aspired to the higher position of Secretary of State, importuned or cajoled Buckingham the most successfully, and obtained the Provostship, to which he was elected on June 24, 1624, nominally by royal mandate, but really by the mere favour of Buckingham.

In spite of the somewhat ignoble circumstances of the struggle for the Provostship, Sir Henry Wotton has left a fragrant memory at Eton. Wotton was in many ways the ideal English gentleman. He was an elegant scholar, and a successful dabbler in literature. As a diplomatist at Venice and elsewhere he was the precursor of the best kind of ambassador; at Venice especially his name is still cherished with affection. Perhaps much of the pleasant romance which surrounds Wotton's name is due to his friendship with Izaak Walton, the 'Angler,' beloved of all true Englishmen, and the inimitable biography which Walton wrote of his friend. At Black Pots, a bend in the river now desecrated by the bridge of the South-Western Railway, the two friends are said to have sat and angled, and to have written verses by the peaceful gliding river.

Wotton was conscientious enough to conform to the Founder's statutes by entering holy orders. He was thus enabled, as he himself writes in a letter to Charles I., "for the point of conscience . . . to hold my place canonically, which I held before but dispensatively, and withal

40

I can exercise an archidiaconal authority annexed thereunto, though of small extent, and no benefit, yet sometimes of pious and necessary use." He was also ready "for the next good Deanery that shall be vacant by Death or Remove."

"I comfort myself also," adds Wotton, "with this Christian hope, that Gentlemen and Knights' sons, who are trained up with us in a Seminary of Churchmen (which was the will of the Holy Founder), will by my example (without vanity be it spoken) not be ashamed, after the sight of Courtly Weeds, to put on a Surplice." For fifteen years Wotton held the Provostship, and exercised a kindly and fruitful influence over the College. It is impossible in these pages to do justice to the charm of Wotton's character. Much has been written about him, and remains to be written still. Etonians will, however, turn to the pages of Izaak Walton, not only for the sake of Wotton himself, but also for the picture drawn therein of a Provost's life at Eton in his day.

III

EARLY STATUTES, HEAD-MASTERS, AND ETONIANS

In the original scheme for the foundation of Eton College, as stated in the first chapter, the Founder's body corporate consisted, according to the charter of October 1440, of "one Provost and ten priests, four clerks and six chorister boys, who are to serve daily there in the celebration of divine worship, and of twenty-five poor and indigent scholars, who are to learn grammar; and also of twenty-five poor and infirm men, whose duty it shall be to pray there continually for our health and welfare so long as we live, and for our soul when we shall have departed this life, and for the souls of the illustrious Prince, Henry, our father, late King of England and France, also of the Lady Katherine, of most noble memory, late his wife, our mother, and for the souls of all our ancestors, and of all the faithful, who are dead; and also of one master, or teacher in grammar, whose duty it shall be to instruct in the rudiments of grammar the said indigent scholars, and all others whatsoever who may come together from any part of our kingdom of England to the said College, gratuitously, and without the exaction of money or any other thing."

It will be seen from this charter that the provision of education for the boys of other than indigent persons was provided for by the Founder simultaneously from his first intention. Edward Hall, the chronicler, says that Henry VI. "founded a solempne school at Eton, a towne next unto Wyndesore, in the which he hath established a college of sad priestes, with a greet nombre of children, whiche bee there of his coste frankely and freely taught the eruditaments and rules of grammer."

Henry VI. lost no time in making nominations to his new foundation, for in the Papal Bull, which immediately ensued, the following names are given:—

Provost—Henry Sever.

Vice-Provost—John Kette, late Rector of Eton.

Priest-Fellows—William Haston and William Dene.

Clerks—Gilbert Grese and John Mondjoy (?).

Choristers—Roger Flecknowe, William Kent, John Halywyn alias Grey, Henry Cokkes.

Scholars—William Stokke, Richard Cokkes.

Bedesmen—John Burdon and John de Evesham.

As no name is mentioned of a Magister or Informator, it may be assumed that the appointment had not been made. Subsequently, as stated before, the Founder remodelled his body corporate on the lines of that at Winchester, acting no doubt under the advice of Thomas of Bekynton, an old Wykehamist, and of William of Waynflete, who left the Head-mastership of Winchester to take up that of Eton, and brought with him Fellows and Scholars to form the nucleus of the new foundation. The statutes first drawn up in 1443, and added to from time to time during the ensuing years, were obviously based, both as regards Eton College and King's College, Cambridge, on the statutes of William of Wykeham for Winchester College and New College, Oxford. They provide for a Provost, ten Priest-Fellows (from whom a Vice-Provost, precentor, sacristan, and two bursars were to be chosen), ten chaplains, ten clerks, sixteen choristers, a Head-master (*magister* or *informator*), an Usher (*ostiarius*), seventy poor scholars, twenty commensales, and thirteen bedesmen. The scholars were to be boys of good character and decent life—poor and needy, with a competent knowledge of reading *Donatus* (the Latin grammar of the period)—and plain song, and to be not less than eight years old, or more than twelve, except specially well-read boys, who might be received up to the age of seventeen. They were to be chosen, in the first place, from natives of the parishes in which either Eton College or King's College held property, and then from natives of the counties of Buckingham and Cambridge, failing all of which they might be chosen from all English-born subjects. The choristers of both Eton and Kings's had a preferential claim to election. The scholars were all destined for the service of the Church, but special care was taken to prevent the College from falling under any monastic influence. They received yearly a gown and hood, intended to last three years, and also clothing and bedding up to a charge of a hundred marks a year for all of them, including the choristers. In addition to other regulations, each scholar had to swear that he did not possess more than five marks a year.

In conformity with the arrangements at Winchester and Oxford, the Founder re-modelled his college at Cambridge to admit of a regular progression of scholars from Eton to King's College. In order to cement the fusion of the two foundations, two Fellows of King's College—William Hatcliffe (afterwards Secretary to Edward IV.) and William Towne—were brought to Eton, incorporated as Fellows of Eton College by Waynflete, and then proceeded immediately by election to King's College, Cambridge, thus inaugurating a procession of scholars from Eton to King's, which has continued with but slight intermissions up to the present day. The number of scholars, seventy, remains the same; and the boys were known as King's Scholars as early as 1621, although it is generally stated that they were so styled at the wish of King George III. The next three scholars elected to King's were part of the Wykehamist contingent which accompanied Waynflete to Eton.

In his provision for the admission of *Commensales*, or Commoners, the Founder was unconsciously taking a step fraught with the greatest importance for English history. The idea was again borrowed from Winchester. Henry had been brought up as a boy with the sons of the nobility, who were of his own age. He was not likely to neglect their interest. When performing the pious duties of charity, religion, and education, he added a provision for those who did not require the former, but were in no less need of assistance in the other matters. Twenty sons of nobles, or of special friends of the College, were to be allowed to sleep and board in the College, and be free from any charges beyond their instruction in grammar. That these were boys of the highest rank and station is evident from the statement of John Blakeman, one of the earliest Fellows of Eton, that Henry, though he not unfrequently met and exhorted the Eton scholars in Windsor Castle, still disapproved of their coming to Court on account of the vicious tone of morals which then prevailed. An inferior class of commoners were also to be admitted, who were to dine in hall with the scholars and choristers, and to receive their instruction gratuitously. Beyond this, according to the statutes of 1440, instruction was to be given to any other scholar who might resort thither from any part of England. Provision was thus made from the outset for the instruction of students of independent means, who, under the name of *oppidani* or town boys, have now increased in such numbers as to form the real body of the school, and at the present day have annexed and absorbed a large portion of the College revenues for their own use.

Mention has already been made of the Head-masterships of William of Waynflete and his successor, William Westbury, of their successions to the Provostship, and of the debt owed to them by the college and the school.

At the time of the installation of Waynflete as Provost, in December 21, 1443, before Bishop Bekynton and the Earl of Suffolk, as Commissaries to the King, the following names appear on the foundation, in addition to the Provost:—

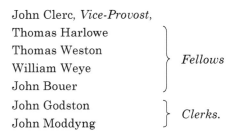

John Clerc, *Vice-Provost,*
Thomas Harlowe
Thomas Weston
William Weye   } *Fellows*
John Bouer
John Godston   } *Clerks.*
John Moddyng

46

Thomas Constantine	
John Payne	
Thomas Saye	
Thomas Siggefeld	
John Goldsmith	
Edward Hancock	*Scholars.*
Richard Fawley	
William Stok	
William Walker	
John Plente	
John Browne	

Six of these scholars were elected to King's College, Cambridge, in the following year.

Two of the scholars elected to King's in 1445—Edmund Hampden (afterwards D.D.) and Roger Flecknowe—appear to have been choristers on the foundation at Eton, and therefore eligible for scholarships at either college.

One of the above-mentioned Fellows, William Weye, desiring to make a pilgrimage to Jerusalem, obtained a special license from the Founder to be absent from the college, and at the same time to enjoy all the fruits and benefits of his position. The King's original license to Weye for this 'Peregrinage' and "blessed Purpos and Entent," "given under oure Signet at oure Castell of Kenelworth," is still preserved at Eton College. An interesting record was kept by Weye of his pilgrimage.

By the statutes of 1443 the Head-master (*magister informator, ludimagister*) was to be appointed by the Provost and Fellows, to be a man of good character, skilled in grammar and teaching, unmarried,

47

and, if possible, a Master of Arts. He was to instruct the scholars, choristers, and other boys coming to the school, and to have leave to punish them in moderation. Under him was the Usher (*ostiarius*), later to be known as the Lower Master, who was to be a layman, unmarried, and, if possible, a Bachelor of Arts. Both received a salary, their commons, and cloth for their gowns, but they were not allowed to make any charge for instruction. The Head-master and Usher both resided in the school buildings on the northern side of the schoolyard. The scholars, and apparently the choristers also, all slept in one long dormitory on the upper floor, with the rooms of the Master and the Usher at either end, the former at the western end, the latter at the eastern, and one schoolroom on the ground floor was sufficient for working purposes.

Of Westbury's immediate successors in the Headmastership little is known beyond their names. Clement Smyth, however, who was Head-master of Eton from 1453 to 1457, when he became a Fellow, became Headmaster of Winchester, apparently a more profitable post at the time, in 1462. During, however, the crisis in the history of the College in the days of Edward IV. he returned to Eton in 1464, and for six years supported Provost Westbury in his efforts to save the College from destruction. His successor, John Peyntour, elected to King's in 1467, was the first Head-master of Eton educated at the school itself. The next Head-master of interest was William Horman, a Wykehamist, who was Head-master of Eton from 1484 to 1495. Horman was a prolific writer of school-books, one of which was printed by the celebrated printer R. Pynson, under the title of *Vulgaria Puerorum*, and was doubtless a textbook in use in school at Eton. Several allusions are made in this work to the study of Greek. A controversial work by Horman, entitled *Antibossicon*, played some part in the religious literary quarrels of his day. Horman exchanged his post at Eton for a similar one at Winchester, but became Fellow of Eton in 1502, and from 1525 to 1534 was Vice-Provost, dying in 1535, almost a century old. His successor, Edward Powell, only held the post a few months, leaving it for a Fellowship at Oriel College, Oxford. Subsequently he made himself too conspicuous in his support of Cardinal Fisher and others in resisting the King's will, and found his way to the most elevated position perhaps ever held by a Head-master of Eton, by being hanged, drawn, and quartered on the scaffold at Smithfield.

For several years to come the Head-masters at Eton left but little mark on the history of the College. Some were Wykehamists, one of whom, Thomas Erlysman, in 1515, left Eton for Winchester. His successor, however, Robert Aldrich, raised the post to some distinction. Aldrich had known Erasmus at Cambridge, and kept up a correspondence with him in after years. It was, however, as Provost that Aldrich looms largest in the history of Eton, to which fact allusion has already been made. Under Richard Coxe, who was appointed Head-master in 1528, Eton College seems to have first reached high repute as a school. Old Fuller, in his *Worthies of England*, says that the school "was happy, with many flourishing wits under his endeavours." Coxe was a zealous Lutheran and Reformer. In later days he became tutor to

Edward VI. and Dean of Christ Church. Elizabeth made him Bishop of Ely, and throughout his life he played a conspicuous part in Church history.

His successor, Nicholas Udall, another Wykehamist, had a very curious career and very varied reputation. He became Head-master at the age of twenty-eight, having published an edition of Terence, a stock subject in school. In the preface to Roger Ascham's *Scholemaster*, a former scholar of Eton describes Udall as "the best scholemaster and the greatest beater of our time." He published a selection from the plays of Terence, which was long used as a school-book at Eton. A curious chance connected with Udall's Head-mastership has gained him a niche in the history of English literature.

The Eton scholars from a very early date were accustomed to give theatrical performances usually at Christmas. They were superintended by the Head-master, and Udall, who had a literary gift, appears to have written small pieces to be acted by his scholars. One of these, a short comedy called *Ralph Roister Doister*, has accidentally been preserved, the only copy known being in the College Library, and is the earliest English comedy at present known, although such comedies had been in existence for many years. Udall, however, got involved, much to his discredit, in a scandal connected with a robbery of silver plate and other misdemeanours committed in 1541 by two Eton boys of good family. The Head-master of Eton and father of English comedy found himself in the Marshalsea Prison, where he spent a short but miserable time. As might be expected he was removed from his post. After his release Udall took to translating the works of Erasmus, besides pleading his innocence and repentance, gained the patronage of Edward VI. and the Protector Somerset, and *mirabile dictu* he managed to end his life as Head-master of Westminster School. His successors had short careers until the appointment in 1546 of William Barker, who successfully defied the Founder's statutes by marrying. This scandalised many good folk, who attributed to the Head-master several cognate vices, such as riotous living and gaming. The only fault, however, which seems to have been discoverable against Barker was, that " he is sumwhat to gentle, and gyvethe his scholears more licence, thane they have byn usid too before tyme"; and what Eton boy is there who would think of imputing this to a Head-master as a crime? Barker was Head-master during the 'purification' of the College under Edward VI., and managed to continue his post as Master during the 'revival' under Mary. He resigned in the summer of 1555. It is uncertain who actually succeeded him, but in 1561 the post was held by an Etonian and Fellow of King's, William Malim.

In the Founder's original statutes it was laid down that the scholars were to have a competent knowledge of reading, Donatus, and plain-song. Music had formed part of the *curriculum* in all or most educational establishments in the Middle Ages. There is, however, a special interest in noting the elaborate arrangements made by the Founder for the study of music and the use of music at the services in the Collegiate Church. The choristers were to be sixteen in number and under twelve years of age, to sing in church and serve the priests at the daily masses. Of the four clerks, one was to be organist and instructor of the choristers. There was also to be a parish clerk, chosen, if possible, from among the scholars of the school, who was to be skilled in Sarum use and in singing. The choristers, as stated before, had a preferential right to vacant scholarships. The provisions for musical education are noteworthy, because at this date the English school of Music, of which John of Dunstable was the leading exponent, was the most important in Europe, and had a lasting and widespread influence on the ensuing and better-known schools of music in Italy and Germany. In the college library there is preserved an interesting volume of manuscript music, evidently used at singing-schools in the church. The compositions are all by English musicians, and some of the composers were Scholars or Fellows of Eton itself. One piece is signed by Robert Hacombleyn, afterwards a well-known Provost of King's. The volume can be dated by internal evidence to the time of Provost Bost, 1477-1503, and is a most interesting relic of musical history at this date.

Latin seems to have been the subject principally taught in school, both translation and composition. The earliest mention of the life and work of an Eton boy is not, as might have been expected, that of a scholar on the foundation, but that of an oppidan, William Paston. Young Paston writes to his brother from Eton two letters on November 7, 1478, and February 23, 147$^8/_9$, concerning money to be paid for his board, and to his 'creanser,' Thomas Stevenson, who seems to have been his tutor, and to be identical with the Thomas Stevenson who was elected a Fellow in the following July. His letter is mainly concerned with his desire to marry a young lady of Eton, to whom he was deeply attached, and of whose beauty he was assured, although he had some doubt about the thickness of her hands. William Paston was more precocious in lovemaking than in writing Latin verses, for he laments the little progress he makes in them, and sends his brother a specimen, which bears out his statement. Latin verses, therefore, seem to have been a staple of education at Eton from the earliest days. Boys who groan at the end of the nineteenth century at the tyranny of Latin verses can comfort their minds that for four hundred years most Eton boys have done the same.

These boys were, as stated before, oppidans or *commensales*, of whom we learn from a biographer of Henry VI. that "when King Henry met some of the students in Windsor Castle, whither they sometimes used to go to visit the King's servants, whom they knew, on ascertaining who they were he admonished them to follow the path of virtue, and besides his words would give them money to win over their good-will, saying to them, 'Be good boys, be gentle and docile, and servants of the Lord.'"

It is not, however, until the beginning of the reign of Elizabeth that any light is thrown on the internal life and economy of the scholars on the foundation at Eton. It will be remembered that upon the death of Provost Bill in 1561, the Fellows proceeded to ignore the right of nomination held by the Crown, and to elect Richard Bruerne to be Provost on their own account. This roused the anger of both the Court and the Church, and brought upon the College a visitation under Matthew Parker, Archbishop of Canterbury, in person. Among the manuscripts bequeathed by Archbishop Parker to Corpus College, Cambridge, is one which was probably drawn up in view of the intended visitation.

In many of the medieval monastic institutions a daily rule, or Consuetudinarium, was drawn up, to regulate the daily life and work of the members of the community throughout the year. Such a *Consuetudinarium* was drawn up in 1561, either by William Malim, the Head-master, in view of the Archbishop's visitation, or possibly for him, as a guide to him on entering upon his new duties. The whole forms a most interesting insight into the life of a schoolboy at that date. It is divided into two sections, the first containing the customs to be observed at different seasons of the year, detailed month by month, the second describing the daily routine of school life.

Taking the *Consuetudinarium* as it comes, and beginning with a calendar of the months, the boys are found at school on the first day of January, but not at regular work. On New Year's day the boys play for the interchange of small gifts (*strenuis*), and compose verses of a complimentary nature, which they send either to the Provost or Master, or other masters, or bandy to and fro among themselves. Work began again on the day after the Epiphany, *strenue vel invitis animis*. On the 13th William of Waynflete was commemorated, and each boy received twopence. On or about the Conversion of St. Paul the annual procession, *ad montem*, took place, a festival which will be specially noticed elsewhere. In February took place the commemoration of Provost Bost on the 7th. On the Monday (*die Lunæ Carnisprivii*) before Lent the boys composed verses in praise of Bacchus or the contrary, and in any metre; the compositions of the boys in the three upper forms were fixed to the lower shutter of the college. Bacchus was regarded as the patron of all poets, and in this custom there may have lingered some traces of the old Dionysiac festival to celebrate the approach of spring. On Shrove Tuesday a curious custom prevailed: the cook came and tied a pancake to a crow at the door of the school, according to the saying, *Pullis corvorum invocantibus eum.* It was the custom in England on Shrove Tuesday to indulge in many sports and pranks corresponding in some way to the Carnival of the Catholic Church. Cock-fighting was indulged in in many places. Football also was played and tolerated in the streets. The connection between the pancake, the well-known attribute of Shrove Tuesday, and the crow is an obvious allusion to the approaching fast, as indicated by the quotation from the 147th Psalm, "Who giveth fodder to the cattle, and feedeth the young ravens that call upon him." On Ash Wednesday the boys all went, collegers and oppidans alike, to church at ten o'clock and selected priests, to whom they made confession of their sins, the next four days being spent in penitence. This ordinance was, however, erased either by the Head-master, Malim, himself, or by order of the Commissioners. On February 27 Provost Lupton was commemorated, and the boys received one penny each. In March the only event was the Feast of the Annunciation, when the Head-master might give a holiday if he chose. In April the chief ordinances are for Holy Week and Easter. On Wednesday in Holy Week ordinary work was set aside, and lessons in writing given. This must have been in the finer and more elaborate forms of writing, and leading to a kind of freehand drawing. Those boys learnt to write who could not yet paint cleverly; but those who could do anything elegantly with the hand, drew figures and offered them as models to their comrades. On the Thursday in Holy Week, in addition to certain services in church, certain boys who had been selected to communicate in church were allowed to roam about the country out of bounds, provided that they did not enter any wine or beer shop. On Good Friday, after a writing lesson and morning prayer in the church, the boys assembled for an oration, given by the principal monitor of the school, and addressed chiefly to the elder boys, upon the Holy Eucharist. On the Saturday writing lessons and prayers were the order of the day, but the boys went to bed early, in order that they might get up at daybreak on Easter day. It had been the custom for four of the older scholars to watch the Holy Sepulchre throughout the night with tapers and torches lest the Jews should steal the Lord's body, or (as it is more rationally and quaintly put) rather that no accident should happen through neglect of the burning lights. This custom seems, however, to have fallen into neglect.

On May Day (the Feast of St. Philip and St. James), if the Headmaster gave permission, and if the day was moist, they might rise early and collect boughs of May blossom, and decorate with them the windows of the dormitory. The boys were not, however, to get their feet wet. They were also encouraged to extol the spring in rhymed or English verse, as well as in selections from the Latin poets. On the Feast of St. John, *ante Portam Latinam*, the boys had a holiday, and a 'long lie' or sleep after dinner in school, until they were summoned to hall, *ad merendam*. Football, also, was probably indulged in, as a current saying ran as follows:—

Porta Latina pilum, pulvinar, pocula præstat.

This day seems to have inaugurated a similar relaxation of the daily routine of work throughout the summer. On May 21 the Founder was solemnly commemorated, and each boy received twopence.

On Ascension Day holidays began, and any boy who was carried away with the desire of visiting (*studio efferuntur visendi*) his parents or guardians, was allowed to be absent until the day before the Feast of Corpus Christi, when if he did not turn up in the evening, he was liable to be flogged. If he was away longer, he might be deprived of his scholarship. These three weeks seem to have been the only holidays during which the boys, at least the scholars on the foundation, were away from Eton. Probably there were many boys who, in those days of difficult travelling, were unable to avail themselves even of this privilege.

On Midsummer's Day (St. John the Baptist) it had been the custom for the boys to erect a bonfire at the eastern end of the church and sing anthems, before going into hall for their drink. On the evening before they used to paint pictures and compose verses on the life and deeds of St. John the Baptist and fix them to the foot of their bedsteads. These customs had, however, already ceased. The bonfire was similarly lit on the Feasts of St. Peter and of St. Thomas, but the latter festivity had

57

also been abandoned. In July took place the annual election of scholars to King's College, Cambridge, and that of scholars into college at Eton. In August the boys had a whole holiday on the Feast of the Assumption of the Virgin Mary, the patroness of the College. The Feast of the Decollation of St. John the Baptist marked the close of the summer regime. A holiday was usually begged for by the College stewards (*promus*). In September the boys on some suitable day went out nutting (*itur collectum Avelanas*), a kind of minor form of *Montem*, and on their return offered some of their spoils to the Head-master and other Masters. Before they started, however, they had to compose verses describing autumn and winter. Nutting was a regular custom in English village life. At Eton, however, a play was intended upon the words *nuces* and *nugæ* and the surrender of the gathered nuts typified the resignation of the boys to the severer and less genial life and work of the winter months. In October, on the Feast of St. Edward, commenced a rule that the boys should arise at 4 a.m. on the morning of every saint's day for special instruction in religion and the Bible; this lasted till Easter. In November the boys had a whole holiday on All Saints' Day, and on All Souls' Day they went to church in surplices to pray for the dead, and hear lessons from the Head-master on death and the hopes of immortality. On the Feast of St. Hugh it had been the custom to elect a Boy-Bishop, a Bishop of Nothing, but this had been abandoned. It is stated that the ceremony at Eton had been well known. In December, on St. Andrew's Day, the Head-master, here called *ludimagister*, superintended theatrical performances in Latin, but sometimes in English, to be performed during Christmas in public by the boys. The object of this was to teach both the speech and action of an orator, and a proper and graceful deportment of the body. Udall's comedy of *Ralph Roister Doister* has been alluded to before. After December 20 regular lessons were suspended, the days were spent in writing-lessons, verse-making, games, and theatricals.

The *Consuetudinarium* then goes on to describe the daily routine of an Eton scholar's life. The boys all slept in one dormitory—the long room, known as 'Long Chamber.' There were four praepostors in the dormitory. In the morning (except when it was a saint's day) at five o'clock the praepostor for the week shouted *Surgite*. All boys arose, and said prayers during dressing, each in turn, with the rest replying. When prayers were finished beds were made, and each boy swept out the dust from under his bed into the middle of the room, which was afterwards swept into a heap and removed by four boys, selected by the praepostor. They all descended in line to wash their hands, and on their return went into the schoolroom and took their allotted seats. At six o'clock the Lower-master (*hypodidascalus*) entered and read prayers. After this he came to each of the lower forms—first, second, and third—and examined them in the work which had been set to them the day before. To the other forms, from the fourth (which then sat at his end of the room) to the seventh, he only gave attention if any difficulty arose. Meanwhile one praepostor was engaged in taking down the names of the boys absent from prayers, and another in examining the hands and faces of the boys to see that they were clean. At seven o'clock the Head-master (*ludimagister*) entered. The boys with dirty hands or faces were brought to him, and the names of boys absent that morning, or from school the evening before, were handed in by the praepostors. The fourth form changed ends of the room, and the forms then repeated their lessons, beginning with the *custos* or lag of each form. At eight o'clock the Head-master gave sentences to be translated, varied, or put into verse, according to the divisions of the school, and the Lowermaster similar sentences, even a very short one, to the first or lowest form of all. A proverb or useful sentence was written up to be copied out and recited by memory the next day. At nine o'clock or thereabouts, probably after a short interval for breakfast, the *custos* of each of the upper forms recited and explained the lesson for the day, after which the two masters lectured thereon to the boys. Themes and verses were done by the upper forms after the -boys left school. At ten o'clock they returned to the schoolroom, and repeated prayers under the direction of a praepostor. At eleven the boys filed out in two lines and went to the dining-hall for dinner, returning to school in the same order. At twelve o'clock the Lowermaster came in and went through the lessons of the day with the four lower forms, the praepostor checking the names of absent boys as before. From one to three the Head-master and Lower-master presided over the work of the divisions. At three o'clock they both left school, returning at four o'clock, when further lessons were said to them. At five o'clock the boys left school and returned in procession as before, probably for supper (*cœna*). At six o'clock work was carried on under supervision of the praepostors or moderators, chosen by the Head-master from among the boys themselves. At seven o'clock the boys were dispersed for a meal of drink, and on their return resumed their work, unless they were let off by the Head-master. At eight o'clock the boys went to bed, intoning prayers. On Friday the work was somewhat varied; but this day was a black day for the boys, as all complaints and punishments were meted out upon this day. On Saturday the work set on Friday was gone through, and as no translation exercises are mentioned, it must be presumed that the boys had a half-holiday. The daily routine mapped out above may be assumed to apply only to the scholars on the foundation. The schoolwork would apply to both, but the regulations for the dormitory would naturally only apply to the scholars, and those for hall to the scholars and such oppidans as might have the privilege of dining at one or other of the tables in hall. Probably part of the work done by the oppidans was under a private tutor, such as Thomas Stevenson, mentioned in William Paston's letter. These tutors are perhaps the *magistri* mentioned more than once, though the Fellows may have been meant. The school was governed to a great extent by the monitorial system. There were four praepostors in school, and certain moderators or controllers in other places, namely, one in hall, two in church, four in the playing fields, four in the dormitory, two to look after the oppidans, and one to supervise the cleanliness and tidiness of the boys. From other sources it appears that at first both collegers and oppidans alike wore a gown of black frieze. Similar duties are still performed by praepostors in school and chapel, and the old name has been preserved.

The boys rose early, and were kept close at work all day, except on the not unfrequent saints' days and other commemorative festivals. Three meals only are mentioned—dinner (*prandium*) at eleven o'clock, supper (*cœna*) at five o'clock, and a draught (*potus*) at seven o'clock. The boys must have had something in the way of breakfast before eleven in the morning, but no provision is made for it in the timetable, and it does not appear to have been a recognised meal. The necessary opportunities, however, of leaving the room were given to the boys after seven o'clock in the morning, but not to more than three at a time. There were seven forms, three in the upper school and three in the lower school. The fourth form occupied an intermediate position, and corresponds to the Remove at the present day; in fact, it spent part of its day in removing from one end of the schoolroom to the other. The work consisted of Latin themes or verses and translation from Latin authors, with lectures from the masters thereon. On Mondays and Tuesdays, in the sixth and seventh forms, Caesar's Commentaries and Cicero are mentioned as being read; in the fifth, Justinus; in the fourth, third, and second, Terence; and in the first or lowest form, Vives. On Wednesdays and Thursdays the sixth and seventh forms read Virgil, the fourth and fifth Ovid, the third Cicero's Letters, the second Lucian, and the first Vives as before. In the afternoons of these days the sixth and seventh forms did Greek grammar if the Head-master allowed, the fifth read Valerius Maximus, Lucius Florus, or Cicero's Letters, or Susembrotus. On Fridays the sixth and seventh forms read Lucan or some other poet, the fifth Horace, the fourth Epigrams and Apophthegms of Martial,

Catullus or Sir Thomas More. They also were set themes and verses to be shown up on Saturday, and the lower school read Æsop's Fables and Cato.

Some of the annual customs mentioned in the above *Consuctudinarium* remained in force until quite recent years. The *Calendœ*, or New Year's copy of Latin verses, continued to be composed by the captain of the school until about 1870. Some of the later compositions were of considerable merit, and were printed in the *Musod Etonenses*. The *Bacchus* verses continued to be written until the nineteenth century, and have gained a curious notoriety from having been noticed by Samuel Pepys during a flying visit to Eton in 1666. The long rolls on which the verses were written were hung up in the college hall. Porson, the great scholar, wrote one, which is still preserved in the college library. Saints' days are still observed as holidays for the boys, except for an increased length in the chapel service. The Christmas theatricals were continued for many years, and are now represented by the Speeches delivered by the sixth form in each school time.

Though instruction was given at first gratuitously in accordance with the Founder's statutes, the number of *commensales* or oppidans increased so rapidly, that the cost of their commons and other expenses had continually to be raised. It may be said that the cost has gone on steadily increasing, and has not reached a *maximum* at the present day. From a bill sent in about 1555 by William Grene, the usher, to Sir Gilbert Dethick, Garter King-at-Arms, for the board of his son Nicholas, it would appear that the usher was allowed to make a charge for acting as tutor to an oppidan. Two young 'swells,' the sons of Sir William Cavendish and the famous 'Bess of Hardwick,' who came to Eton in 1560, boarded in the town, but had dinner and supper in the college hall. In 1608 about thirty oppidans are mentioned as 'in commons' in hall, in three classes of noblemen, *generosi commensales* and *commensales*. Such was the state of the school at Eton College in the year that William Malim became Head-master. His tenure of office was marked first by an outbreak of the plague and the first use of a sanatorium removed from the College, and next by the arrival of Queen Elizabeth at Windsor in 1563. On this occasion, under Malim's directions, the Eton boys greeted her in copies of Latin verses, no less than seventy-two compositions being contained in the manuscript volume still preserved in the King's Library at the British Museum. In a preface written in Latin prose, obviously by Malim himself, the boys are made to solicit her gracious Majesty for the promotion of their Master to some higher dignity. During the Queen's residence at Windsor some excitement was caused by some boys running away from Eton to avoid flogging. This event formed the subject of discussion at dinner in Windsor Castle, there being present Sir William Cecil (afterwards Lord Burghley); Sir Richard Sackville, who had himself some fifty years before been driven "with feare of beating from all love of learning, probably at Eton; Walter Haddon, the well-known Eton scholar; Roger Ascham, the Queen's tutor; and John Astley, Master of the Jewel House, Ascham's friend. The discussion on school discipline led to Ascham's famous treatise on *The Scholemaster*, Thus Nicholas

Udall's accidental propensity to theatricals led to Eton being the birthplace of English Comedy, and the 'plagosity' of William Malim led to the composition of one of the masterpieces of English prose.

Of Malim's successors in the Head-mastership not much is known. Reuben Sherwood, appointed in 1571, took to medicine, and became a physician at Bath. Thomas Ridley, appointed in 1579, took to law, became a Master in Chancery, and a knight. John Hammond, appointed in 1582, abandoned medicine for Eton. His successor, Richard Langley, appointed in 1594, held two rich benefices "farr distant from his schoole, an act of pluralism described by the Bishop of Lincoln, as Visitor to the College, as 'an apostemated ulcer.' After a prolonged controversy with Provost Savile the Bishop succeeded in procuring Dr. Langley's dismissal. Savile promoted the usher, Richard Wright, to the post, which was the source of great controversy between the Bishop and the Provost. Wright only, however, held the post two months, and was succeeded by a King's man, Matthew Bust, with whom the Bishop was satisfied.

The only lists by which the names of boys in the school can be traced for the earlier years are the names of the scholars proceeding from Eton by election to King's College, Cambridge. The first batch of scholars proceeding from Eton to King's in 1443 contains three names of men who rose to importance in their day— *William Hatcliffe, John Chedworth*, and *Thomas Scot* alias *Rotherham*. John Chedworth became second Provost of King's, and was in 1452 made by Henry VI. Bishop of Lincoln. In that capacity he acted as Visitor of the College, and with Waynflete revised the statutes of the College. He was conspicuous in the persecution of the Lollards, and seems to have found no difficulty in transferring his support from the House of Lancaster to that of York.

William Hatcliffe, one of the two original Fellows of King's, who came to Eton to inaugurate the scholars of the two colleges, afterwards became a doctor of physic and secretary to King Edward IV., a circumstance which may help to account for that King's subsequent moderation in his treatment of the College. *William Towne*, Hatcliffe's companion, became a doctor of divinity, and was buried in King's College Chapel. The other most distinguished scholar of the year of foundation besides Bishop Chedworth was *Thomas Scot*, alias *Rotherham*, who became the leading prelate of his day, enjoying the confidence of Elizabeth Widvile when Lady Grey, and through her of Edward IV. After succeeding Chedworth as Bishop of Lincoln, he became in 1474 Chancellor of England, and in 1480 Archbishop of York. During the troubled years of Richard III.'s reign he maintained his position with some difficulty, although he played a prominent and important part in the history of England at this date. He was a great benefactor to both Universities, and in emulation of Winchester and Eton he founded a 'fair College' at his birthplace, Rotherham, in Yorkshire.

John Marshall, elected a Fellow at Eton College about 1460, was also a Fellow of Merton College, Oxford, of which he was a benefactor, and in 1478 became Bishop of Llandaff. Other prelates of distinction occur among the scholars of Eton and King's at this period. *Oliver King* (1449) became in succession Bishop of Exeter (1492), and Bath and Wells (1495); he was principal secretary to three successive kings, and was buried in St. George's Chapel, Windsor, being truly said *principibus placuisse viris.*

William Atwater, Fellow in 1482, became Dean of Salisbury in 1509, and Bishop of Lincoln in 1519.

Nicholas West (1483) is a consoling instance to Etonians how youthful escapades can be condoned by subsequent rectitude and virtue. His biography states that he "was born at Putney, in Surrey, being factious and turbulent while he was Scholar, set the whole College together by the Ears about the Rectorship, and when he could not obtain his Desire, he set the Provost's Lodge on Fire, and stealing away certain Silver Spoons departed from the Coll: but shortly after he became a new man, repaired to the Univ:, and afterwards commenced D.D. He had a great Faculty in opening the Dark places of Scripture, was likewise well experienced in the Canon and Civil Laws was often sent Ambassador by King Henry 7 to Foreign Princes, was made Dean of Windsor and Register of the Garter. Afterwards Bp. of Ely, 1515. In Lieu of the Wrong he had done to the Coll: he gave it many rich gifts and Plate, and built part of the Provost's Lodge. Q. Catherine chose him and Fisher her Advocates in the Cause of Divorce, wherein he incurred the King's Displeasure. He kept daily in his house 100 Servants . . . relieved Daily 200 poor Folks at his gates with warm Meat and Drink . . . and lyeth buried at Ely under a Tomb built by him before his Death."

West was to have been succeeded at Ely by another Eton scholar, *Nicholas Hawkins* (1514), archdeacon of the diocese, who was at the time of Bishop Wesfs death "beyond seas in embassage." Hawkins died, however, before his consecration, not without suspicions of poison. It is recorded of him that "he sold in time of Famine all the Plate and Goods he had to relieve the poor People of the Isle of Ely, and was served himself in wooden dishes and earthen pots."

Jeffery Blyth (1483), after being Master of King's Hall at Cambridge, became Bishop of Lichfield, and in 1512 Lord President of Wales, "at which time, being attacked of treason, he cleared himself most worthily." *Thomas Lane* (1488) rose from being Usher at Eton to the Bishopric of Norwich in 1499. *Richard Coxe*, who has already been mentioned as a successful Head-master, became Bishop of Ely in 1560. In this year, too, *William Alley* (1528), a prominent Reformer, became Bishop of Exeter. *Edmund Gheast* (1536) "tarried in England" in Queen Mary's reign, "but often changed his Lurking-Place for his Preservation." On the accession of Queen Elizabeth he became her Almoner, and was appointed Bishop of Rochester. Somewhat later *John Long* (1564), "a profound scholar," became Archbishop of Armagh and Primate of Ireland; and *Thomas Ramme* (1588) Bishop of Ferns and Clogher. *Richard Mountague* (1594) became successively Fellow of Eton, Dean of Hereford, chaplain to James I. and Charles I., Bishop of Chichester, and eventually Bishop of Norwich, leaving a name honoured in the annals of the Church of England. Among other divines educated at Eton about this date may be noted *John Dogget, John Argentine,*

Richard Hatton, Robert Hacombleyn, and Edward Foxe, successive Provosts of King's. The last-named, Foxe, was secretary to Cardinal Wolsey, and a clever and successful diplomatist. He is credited with the origin of the phrase, so often quoted at the present day, that "the surest way to peace is a constant preparedness for war." Foxe eventually became Bishop of Hereford in 1585. *Thomas Wilson* (1541) became Dean of Durham, and afterwards, in the reign of Queen Elizabeth, was, as principal Secretary of State, one of the most influential statesmen of his time. Noteworthy, also, are *John Hodgkyns* (1450), D.D., a learned mathematician, often consulted by Henry VII.; *John Kyte* (1480), Archbishop of Armagh, and titular Archbishop of Thebes; *Thomas Franklyn* (1496), Dean of Windsor; *John Watson* (1483), the friend of Erasmus; *James Denton* (1485), Dean of Lichfield, and (like Bishop Blyth) Lord President of Wales. *Roger Goad* (1555), Master of Guildford Grammar School, became Provost of King's in 1569, and reigned there for forty-one years, which were some of the most exciting and eventful in the history of his College. *Thomas Ashley* (1501) held the chair formerly occupied by Erasmus as Lady Margaret Professor of Divinity at Cambridge, and was succeeded by *William Skete* (1524). *Jeffery King* (1583), chaplain to Archbishop Bancroft, was a learned scholar, and became Regius Professor of Hebrew at Cambridge, while *Samuel Collins* (1591), afterwards Provost of King's, was Regius Professor of Divinity, and refused the bishopric of Bristol. *Walter Haddon* (1533) bears one of the names most honoured in the annals of Eton, both for his eminence as a Latin scholar, and as a reformer of the ecclesiastical law. He became President of Magdalen College, Oxford, and was one of the most trusted and confidential advisers of Queen Elizabeth. He was Regius Professor of Civil Law at Cambridge. The reformed religion found its adherents among Etonians. *John Fryer* (1517) was one of the first to adopt Luther's doctrines in this country. *Thomas Whitehead* (1524), pantler at King's, is said to have hidden away all the Lutheran books in the College, when they were ordered to be destroyed. *John Fuller* (1527), *Robert Glover* (1533), and *Laurence Saunders* and *John Hullier*, both of whom proceeded from Eton to King's in 1538, died at the stake for their faith, Glover and Saunders at Coventry, Fuller and Hullier at Cambridge, on Jesus Green. *Richard Maister* (or *Master*) (1502), Rector of Aldington, Kent, became involved in the foolish conspiracy of the 'Nun of Kent,' and suffered death at Tyburn in 1534. *James Calfhill* (1545), Lady Margaret Professor of Divinity at Cambridge, was a zealous Protestant, and was Bishop-elect of Worcester, where he died. William Gouge (1595) was an eminent Puritan divine, and Prolocutor of the Presbyterian Assembly in London, and his example was followed by his son, *Thomas Gouge* (1625), who remained a Nonconformist after the Restoration, and was especially distinguished for his evangelical work in Wales. Among laymen, or scholars engaged in more secular pursuits, may be noted *William Coningsby* (1497), Justice of the King's Bench in 1541; *Richard Croke* (1506), the renowned Greek scholar, whose fame resounded throughout Europe; *John Bryan* (1510), another Greek scholar, and friend of Erasmus, who lectured on Aristotle in the original text, as a Greek writer, rather than as a philosopher; *Edward Hall* (1514), the chronicler of the Wars of the Roses; *Thomas Sutton*, founder of the hospital and school of the Charterhouse in London; *Sir Thomas Pope*, the founder of Trinity College, Oxford; *Nicholas Tubman* (1533), Rouge Croix Pursuivant-at-Arms and Lancaster Herald; *Richard Pallady* (1533) who became the architect of old Somerset House in the Strand; *William Buckley* (1537), who reduced the rules of arithmetic to Latin verse, which must have been a double horror to the boys; John Pace (1539), jester to the Duke of Norfolk and Queen Elizabeth, the "bitter fool," of whom it was said "that it was better for the common weal for wise men to go in fools' coats than for fools to go in wise men's gowns"; *Sir Richard Morysine* (or *Morrison*), not only Secretary for some time to Thomas Cromwell, but a noted scholar and able diplomatist; and *Sir John Osborne* (1568), an eminent lawyer in London.

Many Etonians and King's men at Cambridge at this date adopted the profession of physic and medicine, of whom *John Blyth* (1520), *William Ward* (1550), *William Burton* (1578), and *Ralph Winterton* (1616), held in their turn the post of Regius Professor of Physic. *Thomas Hatcher* (1555), M.D., son of another Regius Professor of Physic, was the first to collect the notices of Eton scholars and the history of the Colleges, upon which all subsequent works have been based.

Among Haddon's successors as Regius Professor of Civil Law at Cambridge were *John Cowell* (1570), Vicar-General to Archbishop Bancroft, and compiler of a still-quoted dictionary of law; *Thomas Morison* (1586), and *Thomas Goad* (1635). *Richard Jugge* (1531) became an eminent printer and publisher in London, a profession adopted by two Eton scholars of the same year (1571)— *Richard Day*, son of the famous publisher John Day, in London, and Thomas Thomas, who set up a printing-press in the University of Cambridge. *William Oughtred* (1592), the famous mathematician, was both born and bred at Eton, his father being writing-master to the school. Oughtred himself was almost as much renowned for his beautiful handwriting as for his learning. Eton produced also several other literary celebrities of some renown in their day. *Thomas Anton* (1561), a lawyer in Ireland; *John Hatcher* (1584), son of Thomas Hatcher, the antiquary; *Albertus Morton* (1602), step-nephew to Sir Henry Wotton, secretary to Elizabeth of Bohemia, and in 1625 Secretary of State; and *Dudley Carleton* (1615), clerk of the Privy Council, and nephew of the diplomatist, all served their country well enough to obtain the honour of knighthood.

Giles Fletcher (1565) was not only scholar and poet, but a diplomatist and lawyer besides. He was sent by Elizabeth on an embassy to Russia, and became afterwards Master of the Court of Request. He was the father also of another distinguished Etonian, *Phineas Fletcher* (1600), poet and author of *The Purple Island*.

Thomas Tusser (1543), who appears to have been originally a chorister before coming to Eton, and perhaps there also, was the author of the famous *Hundreth Poinies of Husbandries* the Georgics of Eton, in which he alludes to the severe use of the birch by Head-master Udall.

Abraham Hartwell and *John Forsett* (1559) are recorded as poets, and *John Taylour* (1552) gained some repute for his translation of

72

Valerius Maximus. William Temple (1573) was secretary to Sir Philip Sidney at the time of his death, and afterwards to the ill-fated Earl of Essex. He was subsequently Provost of Trinity College, Dublin, and was knighted.

William Lisle (1584), of Wilbraham, Cambridgeshire, was noted in his day as a "rare antiquary"; and *Thomas Mowthwe* (1571) enjoyed the distinction of being the first member of Parliament for the town of Cambridge.

It is more difficult to recover the names of boys in the early days who were educated at Eton, as *commensales* or oppidans. Traces are found of such well-known names as *Lytton, Wriothesley, Willoughby, Dormer, Stanhope, Arundel, Cavendish, Fitzwilliam, Grey, Cornwallis, Bertie, Throckmorton,* and others, pointing to the high social status of the boys in the school. *Sir John Harrington,* the author of *Nugæ Antiquæ,* and the translator of Ariosto, was at Eton in 1575; he was a godson of Queen Elizabeth, who, when he was still at Eton in that year, sent him a copy of her speech in Parliament to peruse and ponder over.

After so long a list of churchmen and civilians, it is perhaps surprising to learn that the first scholar of Eton College, mentioned in the Papal Bull of 1441, *William Stokke,* became a soldier. Michael Palmer, scholar of King's in 1458, "in defence of his founder was slain at the battle of St. Albans, and thus became the first of a long line of Eton heroes, ready to lay down their lives for their sovereign and their country in Europe, Asia, Africa, America, wherever the summons may come to them. Of such a type was *Sir Humphrey Gilbert,* renowned in the history of the Elizabethan navy, who is stated on good grounds to have been originally an Eton boy.

One collier, *John Greenhall* (1576), gained a distinction, as unenviable as it was fortunately unique, for he took to highway robbery, and won, it is true, an elevated position for himself, but on the gallows. Another colleger, *Richard Juxon* (1628), perhaps related to the Archbishop, "died A.B. suddenly at a cock-fighting at the Blue Boar in Cambridge, where he was laughing extremely."

The school, however, continued to gain in repute, not only for its aristocratic students, but also for the high level of its scholarship. This was especially the case under Sir Henry Savile, the fact being well illustrated by the action of the great scholar, Isaac Casaubon, who was so much impressed by the advantages of an Eton education that he got his only son, *Meric Casaubon*, placed upon the foundation.

Baldwin Collins (1561) deserves a special notice among the Fellows of Eton. He became Vice-Provost in 1595, a post of more active influence in the school even perhaps than that of the Provost himself. During his tenure of office "he preserved many poor but good scholars," and was "A man of great Learning and Humility, so far from ambition that he often refused Preferments offered to him; so far from Avarice that he treasured up his goods in the Bowels of the Poor; so far from Idleness in his ministerial Function that almost every Sabbath Day, as long as Health of Body and Strength of Nature permitted, he did voluntarily and gratis preach the Word at one Town or another neighbouring upon

Eton. He died Fellow of Eton 1616, and was buried in the Chappel at the Entrance into the Choir, a little above the Brazen Desk."

IV

ETON IN THE SEVENTEENTH CENTURY

Sir Henry Wotton was Provost of Eton for fifteen years. Though it might have been to him little more than a haven after an industrious and fatiguing life, he threw himself with great success into the duties of his post. Savile had been something of a martinet. To him the plodding student was more pleasing than the elegant wit or brilliant scholar. Wotton found the boys more interesting than their work, and was the first pedagogue, if indeed he can be ranked as such, who taught boys to look upon a master as a friend, instead of only a teacher and inflicter of punishment. "He was a constant cherisher," says Walton, "of all those youths in that school, in whom he found either a constant diligence or a genius that prompted them to learning." "One or more hopeful youths," as Walton has it, "were taken and boarded in his own house." "Even in the schoolroom the Provost was a familiar figure, and he was ahead of his age in seeing that learning can be taught through the eye as well as through the ear, "for he caused to be choicely drawn the pictures of divers of the most famous Greek and Latin historians, poets, and orators," which he fixed to the wooden pillars in the schoolroom (Lower School), that seem to have been erected about this time. "He could never leave the school," adds Walton, "without dropping some choyce Greek or Latin apophthegme or sentence such as were worthy of a room in the memory of a growing scholar." *Phihsophemur* is the inscription on the portrait of Wotton preserved in the Provost's Lodge. Wotton was a friend and correspondent of John Milton, the poet, when the latter lived a few miles off at Horton. *Robert Boyle*, the famous philosopher, who was sent to Eton at the age of eight in 1635, together with his elder brother, describes Wotton, under whose special protection they were placed, as "a person that was not only a fine gentleman himself, but well skilled in the art of making others so." John Harrison, who succeeded Bust as Head-master in 1630, seems to have been very easy-going, and, judging from Boyle's account, inclined to make favourites among the boys. He gave Boyle, who was, perhaps, an exceptionally 'hopeful' boy, private instruction, instead of the ordinary school-work, which was all very well, but he also would 'cloy him with fruit and sweetmeats,' and let him off school, and what was perhaps worse, "bestow upon him such balls and tops and other implements as he had taken away from others that had unduly used them." Probably little Boyle's tenure of the latter gifts was a stormy one. It is not astonishing, therefore, that Boyle found Harrison's successor, *William Norris* (1623), 'a rigid fellow.' The school at this time was "very much thronged with young nobility," and many well-known surnames occur in the Eton Audit Books. Brothers were described as Compton A, Compton 1, Compton Minor, and so on. Scholarships were also eagerly sought after, and each election a cause of much distraction to the Provost. Wotton speaks of the trouble caused by the correspondence concerning the elections, and how one boy nominated by his dear patroness, the Queen

77

of Bohemia, had to be rejected, because he had been foolish enough to have been born at Delft in Holland. This is the more surprising, because a dispute arose at this time between Eton and King's concerning the appointments to Eton Fellowships and the reduction of their number to seven, instead of the ten appointed in the Founder's statutes. The Fellows of King's claimed a vested interest in the Fellowships at Eton, and among various charges brought by them against the Eton authorities for breach of the statutes, they alleged that the scholars "had been deprived of breakfasts, clothing, bedding, and all other necessaries, which the statute amply allows them, and forced to be content with a bare scanty diet and a coarse short gown, whilst the College revenues are shared amongst a few." The large increase in the number of commensales or oppidans had no doubt increased the standard of comfort in the school, both in College and outside, far beyond that contemplated by the pious Founder. Probably long before this time the oppidans had discarded the black gown, which became the distinctive mark of a King's scholar, who was hence styled 'togatus,' shortened in ordinary conversation to 'tug.' The dispute between Eton and King's was heard before Archbishop Laud in 1636, who decided in a way calculated to satisfy both parties. Wotton died in 1639, and was buried in the chapel. His dislike of religious squabbles was set forth by his own request on his tomb in the sentence, *'Disputanti pruritus est ecclesiarum scabies."* He was succeeded by Richard Steward, Dean of Chichester, Clerk of the Closet to Charles I., a safe, worthy, and pious man, of no particular importance. Norris was succeeded as Head -

master by Nicholas Gray, a Westminster scholar, who had already been Head-master of Charterhouse and Merchant Taylors' School.

Wotton was by no means the only interesting figure at Eton College in the early part of the seventeenth century. Among the special protégés of Sir Henry Savile at Merton College, Oxford, had been John Hales, a scholar of much repute. Savile made Hales a Fellow of Eton, the appointment being one of those, no doubt, which caused umbrage to the Provost and Fellows of King's. Hales, however, spent some years as chaplain to the English ambassador, Sir Dudley Carleton, in Holland. He settled at Eton in 1619, and was on excellent terms with Sir Henry Wotton, who called him a '*bibliotheca ambulans*,' Hales is more remarkable for his recognised position in the world of letters in London than for his plunge into schismatic controversy, which afterwards cost him dear. His friends styled him 'the ever-memorable John Hales.' He was as great a favourite at Court as among writers and scholars. Ben Jonson, Sir William Davenant, Falkland, Sir John Suckling, are known to have been his friends. Suckling describes his quiet, retiring nature in the following lines:—

> Hales set by himself most gravely did smile
> To see them about nothing keep such a coil.
> Apollo had spied him but, knowing his mind,
> Past by, and called Falkland that set just behind.

No writer on Eton can afford to omit a quotation from the account given by Charles Gildon to Dryden in 1694 how John Hales upheld the supremacy of Shakespeare in literature:—

"Mr. Hales of Eaton affirmed that he wou'd shew all the Poets of Antiquity outdone by Shakespear, in all the Topics, and Common Places made use of in Poetry. The Enemies of Shakespear wou'd by no means yield him so much Excellence: so that it came to a Resolution of a trial of skill upon that Subject; the place agreed on for the Dispute was Mr. Hales's Chamber at Eaton; a great many Books were sent down by the Enemies of this Poet, and on the appointed day my Lord Falkland, Sir John Suckling, and all the Persons of Quality that had Wit and Learning, and interested themselves in the Quarrel, met there, and upon a thorough Disquisition of the point, the Judges chosen by agreement out of this Learned and Ingenious Assembly unanimously gave the Preference to Shakespear. And the Greek and Roman Poets were adjudged to Vail at least their Glory in that of the English Hero."

Thus did Eton place the laurel crown on Shakespeare's brow.

The good reputation of John Hales was preserved after his death by one of the most famous Eton scholars, *John Pearson* (1632), Bishop of Chester, and author of the famous *Exposition of the Creed*. In his famous defence of the *Letters of St. Ignatius*, Pearson alludes to Eton as the place to which he owed his grounding in literature. He is said to have spent all his money at Eton in buying books. Pearson collected and published the *Golden Remains* of John Hales, with an affectionate preface in praise of his old friend.

Eton was at a considerable height of prosperity when the Civil Wars burst upon England. Pious and worthy Provost Steward, less pliable and prudent, if more loyal and true than his predecessors on similar occasions, followed his sovereign's fortunes to Oxford. He was removed from his Provostship by the Parliament, and the income of the post for a time sequestrated. By order of the King all elections of scholars from Eton to King's were suspended in 1643, and though some scholars were allowed to proceed without election, the regular course of election was not resumed until October 1645. The *commensales* ceased to come or were withdrawn. As these boys were for the most part likely to belong to Cavalier families, this was not very surprising. Many of the older boys no doubt found pistol and sword more interesting weapons than the Latin grammar. The revenues, however, of Eton College again escaped during the general confiscation of church property, which was commenced by the Parliamentary Government. It is true that the iconoclastic hand of the infuriated Colonel Venn was extended to the "scandalous monuments and pictures" at Eton. Perhaps it was due to the wise moderation of Cromwell's nominee to the Provostship, that the hand of the destroyer was stayed at Eton.

Traces of the Civil Wars occur in the lists of Eton scholars, chronicling how *John Younge* (1625) "lost his leg by a cannon shot in the king's service"; *Sampson Brigges* (1630) "died at the siege of Gloucester, slain in the king's army"; *James Eyre* (1638) "was slain in the service of the king at Berkeley Castle"; *Charles Howard* (1646), young and gallant like his namesake at Waterloo, was "killed at Newark, captain in the king's service"; and how *Arthur Swayne* (1639), holding a Lieutenant-Colonel's commission, "in 1644, teaching his boy to use his arms, bid him aim at himself and fire, not imagining the gun to be charged, which the servant performed too well." *Robert Devereux, third Earl of Essex,* the gloomy parliamentary general, was for a few months in 1610 a boy at Eton.

Francis Rous, the new Provost, was a prominent member of the Long Parliament, and noted for his extreme Puritan views. He continued to sit in Parliament after his election to the Provostship, and in the 'little' Parliament of 1653 he was elected to the Speaker's chair. Cromwell raised him to the peerage in 1657, little more than a year before his death, though the title was not, of course, recognised at the Restoration. Provost Rous proved an unexpected benefactor to Eton College, which, cavalier as it always has been in sentiment, had little reason to regret his usurpation. He saved the College from taxation, and renewed the elections from Eton to King's. As might have been expected, the Puritan service was introduced in the chapel, and the royalist Fellows were ejected in favour of Puritans. The Fellows, however, were now allowed the liberty of receiving their commons in money instead of in kind, and to have their meals in their own houses. Among the Fellows who refused to take the oath of allegiance to the Commonwealth was John Hales, who was ejected from his Fellowship, but allowed to live in lodgings at Eton until his death in 1656, when he was buried in the churchyard. Nicholas Gray, the Royalist Head-master, was deprived of his post, and was succeeded for a few months by *George Goad* (1620), a member of an Etonian family, many of whom were Scholars or Fellows of Eton or King's. His successor, *Thomas Horne,* in 1648 was chiefly known as the writer of some much-used school-books.

The Protector in person showed that he regarded Eton College as of importance in the cause of education, and no doubt looked on it as a promising nursery for the sons of Reformers. Cromwell had a ward, a boy named Dutton, whom he entrusted to the tutorship of Andrew Marvell, the famous Puritan poet. Marvell accompanied the boy to Eton, and they were boarded in the house of one of the new Puritan Fellows, by name John Oxenbridge, a man almost as remarkable in his way as John Hales himself. Oxenbridge and his wife, having been treated as schismatics by Archbishop Laud, had left the country and led a roving life, preaching the gospel across the seas. For some time he and his wife had pursued their evangelical career in the islands of the Bermudas, Shakespeare's 'vexed Bermoothes,' thus anticipating by about a century Dean Berkeley's spirited attempt to propagate Christianity in America. During the Commonwealth they returned to England, and both became noted for their powers of preaching. Oxenbridge was in 1652 rewarded with a Fellowship at Eton, and he and his wife settled there. Marvell wrote to Cromwell from Eton describing his pupil's progress, and thanking him for placing him in so godly a family. Mrs. Oxenbridge died and was buried at Eton, where a tablet was placed to her memory with an inscription composed by Marvell. This was defaced at the Restoration, a piece of petty spite. Oxenbridge, on being ejected from his Fellowship, married again and resumed his missionary efforts in Surinam, Barbadoes, and other places, and eventually found his way to the new settlement at Boston, Massachusetts, of which he became the first pastor, thus forging a curious link between Eton and the New

World. Marvell at Eton knew and admired John Hales, saying that he had "one of the clearest heads and best prepared hearts in Christendom."

The affectionate interest taken by Provost Rous in the College was shown by his instructions to be buried at Eton, "a place which hath my deare affections and prayers, that it may be a flourishing nursery of pietie and learning to the end of the world.*" He died in January 165$^8/_9$. All royal and ecclesiastical patronage having been appropriated by the Parliament, the office of Visitor of Eton College had shared this fate. On the death, therefore, of Provost Rous, the Vice-Provost (John Oxenbridge) and the five Puritan Fellows (Bachiler, Goad, Lockyer, Penwame, and Boncle) addressed themselves to "Richard, Protector of England, Scotland, and Ireland," as Visitor, informing him that they had selected as Provost Nicholas Lockyer, lately chaplain to the now deceased Lord Protector. Lockyer, however, had not held the post long before a fresh turn of Fortune's wheel brought the royal house of Stuart back to the throne, and the sons of the cavaliers back to Eton. A new 'purging' of the College ensued, and besides the Provost, most of the Puritan Fellows resigned or were ejected, including Oxenbridge and John Boncle, who had been for a short time Head-master. One Puritan Fellow, however, Nathaniel Ingelo, a member of a family long connected with Eton, managed to get readmitted to his place, and, becoming later on Vice-Provost, made himself a thorn in the flesh of all cavalier boys and scholars, trusting, no doubt, to another fresh turn of the wheel in favour of his party. When the spoils of war came to be divided, Eton

College was not overlooked, and the rich prize of the Provostship of Eton was bestowed not unnaturally on Nicholas Monck, younger brother of the famous General Monck. Monck was shortly after created Bishop of Hereford, but only held his two posts for a few months, as he died in December 1661, and was buried in Westminster Abbey. Charles II. wrote to the Vice-Provost and Fellows recommending Thomas Browne, "late chaplaine to our deare and Royall sister, the Princess of Orange, deceased," adding a royal dispensation, since Dr. Browne was not a member of the Foundation, and was therefore disqualified by the statutes. Subsequently, however, probably in answer to a protest from the College, Charles II. substituted the name of Dr. John Meredith, one of the royalist Fellows, who had been reinstated on the Foundation. Nicholas Gray, the ejected Head-master, was elected a Fellow, together with General Monck's chaplain, John Price, and Isaac Barrow, who was afterwards to be Bishop of Sodor and Man, and must not be confused with the famous Cambridge mathematician. Singleton, the Headmaster, was dismissed, and the Usher, or lower-master, *Thomas Mountague* (1632), who had managed, though a royalist, to continue in his post, was made Head-master. Stringent reforms were introduced into the regulations in force both in the College and in the school under Provost Meredith, until his appointment to be Warden of All Souls' College, Oxford, in 1665. Charles II., not a great respecter of men or statutes, then offered the Provostship to Robert Boyle, the distinguished scholar, and the most prominent Etonian of his day. Boyle, however, had conscientious scruples, first against violating the statutes by

85

holding the post as a layman, and next against following the example of Sir Henry Wotton, in taking holy orders for the purpose. He therefore refused this very creditable offer on the part of the king. Charles therefore offered the post to another distinguished Etonian, *Edmund Waller*, the poet. Waller was not burdened with the same scruples as Boyle, and would have accepted the post gladly, but was thwarted by the unexpected attitude of Lord Chancellor Clarendon, who declined to sanction any such breach of the statutes. The post, therefore, went a-begging for the moment, until Charles bethought himself of the debt owed by him to Richard Allestree, Canon of Christ Church, Oxford, who had been a useful servant to the royal cause, and is said to have fought at Edgehill with a musket in one hand and a book of learning in the other. Allestree is reputed to have been noted for his ugliness, and to have owed his advancement to being thus accidentally recalled to the notice of the king. Though there is little to support this tradition, it would be in keeping with the character of Charles II., first to let a deserving retainer slip from his memory, and then to reward him handsomely for some humorous reason such as the above. Ugly or not, Allestree proved one of the best Provosts that Eton College ever had. He restored equilibrium in its finances, and took a personal share in introducing harmony and comfort into the life in College. On the school he conferred an inestimable benefit at the time. Up to this date the boys had all attended school in the old room under Long Chamber, now known as 'Lower School,' or the small rooms adjoining. After the Restoration the number of oppidans increased so rapidly at Eton that this room became quite inadequate for its purpose. Provost Allestree built at his own expense a building connecting the ante-chapel with the tower at the end of 'Long Chamber,' and consisting of a long schoolroom on the upper floor, and a colonnade with smaller rooms below. This building was in use for twenty years or more, when it was found to be insecure, and was taken down. Provost Allestree may, however, be regarded as the founder of Upper School.

There had up to this date been but little alteration in the daily routine of school life as described in Malim's *Consuetudinarium*. Discipline, however, seems to have been very lax during the continual changing and 'purging' of Provost, Fellows, and Masters in the earlier part of the seventeenth century. From the reforms reintroduced by Provost Meredith, it appears that there was only one half-holiday in the week, and that only when there was no saint's day, or other whole holiday; also that the King's scholars and choristers shared the 'Long Chamber,' with the Head-master and Usher sleeping at either end. The 'writing times' were still kept up, for the Master and Usher were to pay special attention to the scholars during that period. The 'election week' seems to have been a time for much disorder and misbehaviour among the boys. The scholars were now to be kept severely in bounds, and the doors of the school and Long Chamber were to have new locks put to them. Discipline seems to have been very lax in this respect, for "It was ordred alsoe that if any Schollar doe presume to ly out of the Coll. one night without Leave of the Provost or Vice-Provost he shalbe whipt and Registred for the first fault, and for the second he shalbe expelled, and also "that Clark, Stone, Curwin, and Whittaker, whoe lately accompanied Garaway and Langston at the Christopher and Thos. Woodward's, shall have a forme of Repentance drawne for them which they shall read in the School before the Vice-Provost and Fellowes in English, and that their fault of being out of their bounds shalbe Registred *pro prima vice*." The 'forbidden fruit' seems, however, to have been too tempting for Curwin, since it is recorded that very shortly after "Curwin and Baker were admonished and whipt and Registred for goeing out of their bounds to the Datchet ale houses and beating the fishermen in their way home, to the great scandal of the College. Curwin for the second time, and Baker for the first." That they should have gone to Datchet for beer was another treasonable offence, for the College beer was famous at this date, and was patronised by royalty. A curious rule, marking the date 1662, was the order for the boys to smoke tobacco in school daily, as a preventative against the plague; boys were even whipped for not smoking. It could not have been pleasant for the Headmaster and Usher, although they were probably provided with a pipe of tobacco themselves; and the scene in school must have been very curious. It was in Mountague's time that Samuel Pepys, the diarist, paid his immortal visit to Eton in February 166$^5/_6$ in the company of Dr. Child, the organist of St. George's Chapel, where he found "all mighty fine," especially the College beer, and "the School good." In 1671 Thomas Mountague was succeeded as Head-master by John Rosewell, under whom the school continued to increase in numbers and repute. A list of the school in 1678—the earliest complete list extant—gives the names of 207 boys, 78 of whom were in College. The seventh form had long been abolished, the sixth being the highest. In each form, except the sixth, the names of Collegers and oppidans are given separately. In this list also, brothers were distinguished by the style of major, minor, and minimus, and so forth, as at the present day. Rosewell resigned his post in 1680, through distress, it is said, from having caused a boy's death through flogging. *Charles Roderick* (1667), his successor, was more notorious from the circumstances connected with his promotion to be Provost of King's than for his work as Head-master of Eton. He was succeeded by his Usher, *John Newborough* (1673), who has been highly extolled for his management of the school. In his time Upper School was rebuilt, and a porter attached to the gateway under it, to prevent the scholars from going out at night, which they seem to have done in Roderick's time with the help of false keys. Newborough was succeeded by *Andrew Snape* (1689), chaplain to Queen Anne. Dr. Snape made himself famous by his controversy with Dr. Hoadly, Bishop of Bangor, and the 'Bangorian Controversy' on orthodoxy carried confusion and dispute even into the staff of Masters at Eton. When Dr. Snape was promoted to be Provost of King's in 1720, the numbers of the school had risen to 399. In 1718 the numbers had been 353, the forms being divided into Sixth, Fifth, Remove, Fourth, Third, Lower Greek, Second, Lower Remove, First Form, and Bible Seat. After 1720 the numbers rose to 425, but fell again after the crash of the South Sea Bubble. Assistant-masters were now employed directly in the school. The oppidans, who were lodged and boarded in Eton, were usually entrusted to private tutors, who took part in the school teaching without being on the regular staff. In a Lower boy's bill for 1719 charges are made: 'To Mr. Burchet halfe a year's Tuition' and 'to Mr. Good [the Usher] halfe a year's Teaching.' Dr. Snape was succeeded by *Henry Bland* (1695), an assiduous courtier and adherent of the Whig party, who was rewarded in 1728 by promotion to the rich deanery of Durham, when he was succeeded by *William George* (1715), an accomplished scholar, more remarkable for the quality of the boys who came to Eton under his regime than conspicuous for his merits or his success as a Head-master.

The laxity at court and the flagrant abuse of patronage led to some competition for the Fellowships at Eton. During the dispute between King's and Eton, mentioned before. Archbishop Laud had decreed that out of the seven Fellowships at Eton—that being the number given instead of the ten appointed by the Founder—at least five should be reserved for King's-men, and one annexed to the vicarage of Windsor. Charles II. was not a man to be troubled with such small worries as statutes, and in the case of patronage the chief importuner usually carried the day. The powerful Grenville family, who had with Monck been some of the king's trustiest champions, had obtained the promise of a Fellowship for one of their relatives. When the vacancy came the king appointed Denys Grenville; but having forgotten that this vacancy had been 'ear-marked' for the vicarage of Windsor, he was forced to cancel the appointment and to appoint Dr. Heaver, the Vicar of Windsor, which was right and appropriate. He promised the next to

Grenville, who exchanged his reversion with one Timothy Thriscrosse, perhaps the Mr. 'Thruscross' who baptized one of Izaak Walton's children in London. When the next vacancy occurred Thriscrosse claimed his right, but the Earl of Arlington induced the king to appoint Henry Bold of Christ Church, whose election was completed before Thriscrosse had time, as he did, to get the complaisant monarch to revoke it. Thriscrosse, therefore, had to wait a year. Provost Allestree petitioned the king to confirm Laud's decree. The king willingly acceded in 1670, and the very next year violated it by appointing Zachary Cradock of Queen's College, Cambridge, and six years later *Henry Godolphin,* an Etonian scholar, but not a King's-man, Canon of St. Paulas and Fellow of All Souls', Oxford. This was too much for the King's-men, who this time got Archbishop Sancroft to remonstrate with the king, and obtain his signature to a stronger decree than before. From this time there was no further dispute.

Provost Allestree terminated his honourable life in January 168⁰/₁. Edmund Waller, now that Clarendon was out of the way, applied again, "tug'd hard" (as Antony à Wood says), for the coveted post. Charles referred the matter to the Privy Council, who decided in favour of the statutes. The king therefore appointed Dr. Cradock, who, although not an Etonian, had been very active in the management of the school. Antony à Wood says, however, that Cradock was appointed "by Virtue of the Election thereunto of the Fellows." Upon his death, in 1695, the College submitted meekly to the appointment of Dr. Godolphin, who had been a Fellow for eighteen years.

Henry Godolphin was a man likely to be useful to the school. His brother Sidney, Earl of Godolphin, was the most influential Minister of the day, and the College could hardly fail to prosper under the beneficent sun of such a high connection. Godolphin proved a kind and munificent ruler. He died in 1732, and left in his will a large sum of money to improve the scholars' Commons. The well-known statue of Henry VI. in the school-yard was set up at his expense. Considerable alterations were made at this time in the internal decoration of the chapel. In accordance with the taste of the time, and a style of decoration introduced by Sir Christopher Wren and other leading architects of the day, the whole interior was encased in panelling, reaching up to the base of the windows. A new wooden roof was constructed, plastered and painted over. A high organ-screen was constructed under the choir arch, entirely blocking out the west window and the ante-chapel. The work cost a great deal of money, which was defrayed by a subscription among present and old Etonians, the Provost contributing one thousand pounds out of his own pocket.

The names of distinguished Etonians during the earlier part of the seventeenth century are difficult to recover owing to the unsettled state of public affairs, which prevented some from going there and interrupted the careers of others. In addition to Robert Boyle, Edmund Waller, and Bishop Pearson, who have been already mentioned, the names should be recorded of *Henry More*, the 'Platonist,' who went to Eton in 1628, and, in spite of a Calvinistic education, became one of the most liberal-minded philosophical writers of his day; and of Dr. *Henry*

Hammond, afterwards of Magdalen College, Oxford, the royalist rector of Penshurst, who was so closely connected with the final scenes in the tragedy of Charles I. A friend and contemporary of Hammond at Eton, *Sir Philip Warwick*, also an eminent royalist, became after the Restoration Clerk of the Signet and Secretary to the Treasury; moreover it is from Warwick's *Memoirs of Charles I.* that much of the history of the period is derived. Another royalist Etonian, *Henry Bard* (1632), after losing an arm in the king's service, and fighting at Naseby and in other battles, was rewarded for his services to the king first with a baronetcy and then with the viscounty of Bellamont; he followed his sovereign into exile at the Hague, and was despatched by Charles II. on an embassy to Persia, during which he was overwhelmed by a sandstorm in Arabia, truly the most curious fate of any Etonian. Two boys, who proceeded together from Eton to King's in 1634, had also curious careers; one, *Anthony Ascham* (1634), espoused the cause of the parliament, went to Spain, and became resident Minister at Madrid, where he was murdered by some of his own countrymen; and the other, Samuel Collins (1634), went on a farther journey for a similar purpose, and resided at Moscow, as Minister to the Emperor of Muscovy, for nine years. In 1622, among the scholars elected to King's appears the name of *Edward Hawtrey*, the precursor of a family whose name has ever been treated with honoured respect at Eton, and who in after years were to exercise a powerful and undying influence on the school. *Thomas Page* (1628), became Provost of King's in 1675. He was succeeded in this post in 1681 by another Etonian, *John Coplestone*

93

(1641), a third Etonian, *Stephen Upman* (1661), a Fellow of Eton, being an unsuccessful candidate on the latter occasion, and again in 1689, although he gained the support of Archbishop Sancroft, on applying for the necessary degree of Doctor of Divinity.

After the Restoration, dating from Dr. Rosewell's appointment, the number of distinguished Etonians increases rapidly, and among the King's scholars alone there are many names well known in after life. In 1675 there was elected to King's *William Fleetwood*,afterwards Fellow and Bishop of St. Asaph; in 1677, *George Stanhope*, afterwards Dean of Canterbury; in 1682, *Stephen Weston*, afterwards Fellow and Bishop of Exeter, whose name is preserved for ever at Eton in 'Weston's Yard'; in 1687, *Edward Waddington*, afterwards Bishop of Winchester; in the following year, *Francis Hare*, who became a Fellow, and was celebrated afterwards as Chaplain-General to the Army, and Bishop successively of St. Asaph and Chichester; in 1689 occurs the name of *Andrew Snape*, afterwards Head-master and Provost of King's; and in 1691 that of *Barnham Goode*, who was ill-advised enough to measure literary swords with Alexander Pope, and was immortalised by the poet in *The Dunciad* as

> Sneering Goode, half malice and half whim
> A fiend in glee, ridiculously grim.

His younger brother, Francis Goode (1695) was Usher at Eton.

Two King's scholars, *Thomas Johnson* (1683) and *William Willymott* (1692), returned to Eton as Assistant-masters, and were associated in

94

the composition of some of the school-books which remained in use at Eton for more than a hundred years. Willymott was afterwards Vice-Provost of King's, and translator of the works of Thomas k Kempis. In 1695 Dr. Bland was accompanied to King's by a boy, destined, perhaps, to be the most distinguished 'tug' ever bred at Eton. *Robert Walpole* was at Eton under Dr. Newborough, and was distinguished there for his classical scholarship and oratory. His subsequent career as Prime Minister belongs to the history of his country. It is sufficient to note that he was the first of a long list of Prime Ministers of England who were educated at Eton. His younger brother, *Horace Walpole* the diplomatist, afterwards created Baron Walpole, was a few years junior to Sir Robert Walpole at Eton, and was elected to King's in 1698. At the same time with the Walpoles at Eton there were other budding statesmen in *Henry St. John, Lord Bolingbroke*, the brilliant genius, whose political vagaries are more than counterbalanced by his scholarship and his unrivalled contributions to English prose; and *Charles, Lord Townshend*, afterwards Chief Secretary of State, a member of a family which sent several brilliant youths to be prepared at Eton for distinguished careers in after-life; and *Sir William Wyndham*, one of the most admired statesmen of his day, of whom it was said by a contemporary that 'Everything about him seemed great. There was no inconsistency in his composition; all the parts of his character suited and helped one another.' Among other oppidans there may be noted the different careers of *James, first Earl Stanhope*, the eminent general; *Thomas Sherlock*, who was so well known for his

95

athletic prowess that in after years, having become in succession Master of the Temple, Bishop of Bangor, and eventually of Salisbury, he was still known as 'the plunging prelate'; *Charles Talbot*, who rose to be Lord Chancellor of England; and *William Broome*, a minor light of poetry, who was called in to assist the exhausted muse of Alexander Pope in completing the translation of Homer's *Odyssey*. *Sir Thomas Vesey* was created a baronet, besides being made Bishop of Killaloe and later of Ossory; he was the father of the famous "Bluestocking," Mrs. Elizabeth Vesey. *Stephen Poyntz*, captain of the school in 1702, in later life became governor to the Duke of Cumberland, and attained a comfortable position in the social world, insomuch that he eventually became grandfather of the Harrovian Premier, Viscount Althorp. *Thomas Thackeray*, who returned to Eton as Assistant-master, quarrelled with Dr. Snape during the Bangorian controversy, in which he took the part of Bishop Hoadly, and, resigning his post, became eventually Head-master of Harrow School, an example followed by more than one distinguished Etonian in later days. *Edward Littleton*, a pupil of Dr. Snape, who was elected to King's in 1716, also returned to Eton as a tutor and Assistant-master, and eventually became a Fellow, holding the valuable Eton living of Mapledurham. In 1718 a distinguished lawyer was elected to King's in the person of *Nicholas Hardinge*, reputed the best scholar of his day, afterwards Chief Clerk of the House of Commons and Secretary to the Treasury. Contemporary with him was a future Under-Secretary of State and Privy Councillor, *Edward Weston*, son of the Bishop of Exeter, mentioned before.

V

ETON IN THE EIGHTEENTH CENTURY

Under Dr. Bland, a typical Head-master of the old school, Eton attained still greater prosperity, and there is hardly a year in which the name of some Eton boy, Colleger, or oppidan, does not occur who was to be highly distinguished in later life. The most distinguished Etonian of this date is *William Pitt*, afterwards the great Minister and Earl of Chatham, and the real founder of England's empire in the world. Pitt was at Eton for several years, from 1719 to 1726, with his elder brother *Thomas Pitt*, afterwards Lord Camelford. Some letters and school bills, preserved in his family, show that the two Pitts were entrusted to a tutor named William Burchett, and that the fee to him was distinct from that paid to the Usher or the Head-master. Burchett writes to their father from Eton in February 1722, and says of the younger boy that he "has made a great Progress since his coming hither, indeed I never was concern'd with a young gentleman of so good abilities, and at the same time of so good a Disposition, and there is no question to be made but he will answer all your hopes." And Pitt did not disappoint Burchett's forecast, for his life forms part of the history of his country. Round Pitt also circled a group of Etonians, whose names in their families, their school, and their place in the history of their country, will ever be associated together. Pitt's future brother-in-law, *Richard*

Grenville, afterwards Earl Temple, who declined the Premiership, and *George Grenville*, who accepted it, are indissolubly connected with the political history of their time. To this band of Etonians belonged also their cousins *George Lyttelto*n, the poet-statesman, afterwards to be known as the 'good Lord Lyttelton,' and his brother, *Charles Lyttelton*, afterwards Bishop of Carlisle, the worthy forerunners of a notable branch of the family a century or so later. George Lyttelton at Eton wrote English poetry as easily as Latin verse, possibly too fluently. His writings, however, are not altogether forgotten in the history of English literature, a more fortunate fate than that which has befallen the pious dithyrambs of his future brother-in-law, *Gilbert West,* and those of the gentle *Sneyd Davies*, contemporaries at Eton. Eton also sent forth at this time another future Premier, notorious rather than distinguished, in *John Stuart, Earl of Bute*, and a statesman of another type, both distinguished and notorious, in *Henry Fox*, afterwards Lord Holland. *Henry Fielding*, the famous novelist, was at Eton with the Pitts, Grenvilles, and Lytteltons, and ever cherished a tender affection for the school. In *Tom Jones*, during an impassioned address to Learning, he says, "Thee in thy favourite fields, where the limpid gently rolling Thames washes thy Etonian banks, I have worshipped. To thee at thy birchen altar with true Spartan devotion I have sacrificed." *Sir Charles Hanbury Williams,* a good classical scholar, was a noted figure in society as a diplomatist and a satirical poet. *Evelyn Pierrepont, Duke of Kingston*, also a prominent figure in social life, owes notoriety to his disreputable wife, or pseudo-wife, the bigamous Miss Chudleigh.

Frederick Cornwallis, whose family was for generations educated at Eton, rose from being an oppidan to be Archbishop of Canterbury. He had a twin brother at Eton, *Edward Cornwallis*, afterwards a general in the army, and they were so alike that it was difficult to know them asunder. A curious figure at Eton must have been *Thomas Augustine Arne*, the future musician and composer of 'Rule Britannia.' His musical tendencies, like those of another great English musician to be mentioned hereafter, were irrepressible and strongly developed at Eton. Dr. Burney records that "with a miserable, cracked common flute he used to torment them night and day, when not obliged to attend the school."

Dr. Bland succeeded Dr. Godolphin as Provost in February 1732, but the prosperity of the school, and the budding distinctions of Etonians, continued to grow and multiply under the auspices of Bland's successor as Head-master, William George. Dr. George was a great contrast to the amiable Dr. Bland. He was pedantic and queer-tempered, and nicknamed 'Dionysius the Tyrant.' Eton, however, did not suffer under his rule. During his fourteen years' rule up to his translation in 1742 to the Provostship of King's, in which he succeeded his predecessor at Eton, Dr. Snape, the lists of Eton school show a continuity of distinguished names, both among Collegers and oppidans. Taking the Collegers alone who were elected to King's, the names occur in 1721 of *Thomas Morell,* a learned divine and antiquary; *William Battie*, one of Eton's most distinguished scholars, son of an Assistant-master, and afterwards married to the aforesaid Bamham Goode's daughter. Dr.

Battie seems to have been able to combine the respectable and venerable character of a scholar and physician with the most undignified tomfoolery. In 1723 four of the six scholars elected to King's became distinguished: *Stephen Sleech*, as Fellow and Provost of Eton; *John Sumner*, as Head-master and Provost of King's; *John Ewer*, as Bishop of Llandaff and Bangor; and John Chapman, as Archdeacon of Sudbury, a disappointed and vigorous theological controversialist. *Thomas Reynolds* (1724), afterwards Fellow of Eton, is best known as the uncle of the famous painter. Sir Joshua Reynolds, who painted a magnificent portrait of him, now in the Provost's Lodge. *Richard Mounteney*, elected to King's in 1725, was the well-known editor of *Demosthenes*, and afterwards Baron of the Exchequer in Ireland. *Ralph Thicknesse*, elected in 1726, afterwards Assistant-master at Eton and editor of *Phœdrus*, serves to illustrate the extent to which music was cultivated at Eton. When on a visit to his brother, Philip Thicknesse, at Bath, he died suddenly at a morning concert, while playing the first violin at the performance of one of his own compositions. In 1731 one of the most celebrated Etonians was elected to King's. *Charles Pratt*, the son of a Chief-Justice of the King's Bench, was destined to attain even higher rank in the same profession as his father, and through his own abilities and his friendship with William Pitt and George Grenville he became not only Chief-Justice, but also Lord Chancellor, being created after retirement. Earl Camden. Etonians will cherish the memory of "an orator so accomplished, a judge so firm a friend to liberty, a statesman so far-sighted and pure-minded," as Charles Pratt, Earl Camden. The name of *Jacob Bryant* (1736) connects the scholars in College with a famous and interesting group of oppidans. The centre of this group was *Horace Walpole*, the sprightly art-amateur and writer. Walpole went to Eton in 1727, and though a delicate boy, unable to play games, he loved to dwell on Eton when corresponding with his former comrades, *Thomas Gray*, the poet, *Richard West*, deprived by an early death of possible literary distinction, and *Thomas Ashton* (1733), afterwards Fellow of Eton and an eminent London preacher. The four friends formed a 'Quadruple Alliance' under the names of Tydeus, Orosmades, Almanzor, and Plato. True also was Walpole's friendship for George and *Charles Montagu*, with whom he formed another coterie known as 'the Triumvirate.' In the last few months of his life Walpole described himself as a "superannuated old Etonian."

Jacob Bryant enjoyed an immense reputation in his day for learning and scholarship. After a long life, as 'the sage of Cypenham,' he is best known by his most inglorious achievement, his championship of Chatterton's 'Rowley' poems. *Thomas Gray* was the nephew of Mr. Antrobus, one of the Assistant-masters. He not only stereotyped, so to speak, his literary rank with his famous *Elegy*, but he also enshrined Eton in the temple of poetry by his 'Ode on a Distant Prospect of Eton College.' Great as the famous Ode is as a specimen of literary craft, there may be some Etonians who will feel less moved by Gray's somewhat artificial lines:—

> Ah happy Hills' ah pleasing Shade,
> Ah Fields beloved in vain,

Where once my careless Childhood stray'd

A stranger yet to Pain.

I feel the gales that from ye blow

A momentary Bliss bestow

As waving fresh their gladsome Wing,

My weary Soul they seemed to soothe,

And redolent of Joy and Youth

To breathe a second Spring—

than by the simple, tender stanzas of his friend Richard West:—

Oh! how I long again with those,

Whom first my boyish heart had chose

Together through the friendly shade

To stray as once I stray'd!

Their presence would the scene endear,

Like Paradise would all appear;

More sweet around the flowers would blow,

More soft the waters flow.

William Cole, one of Walpole's correspondents, missed his election to King's, but eventually became a gentleman-commoner of the College together with Walpole. Afterwards he resided at Milton, near Cambridge, where he compiled the voluminous manuscript collections of history, gossip, and archaeology, which he bequeathed to the British Museum, as a treasure-house for students, including those of the history of Eton College. A brother antiquary was *Jeremiah Milles*, afterwards Dean of Exeter and President of the Society of Antiquaries, who shared Bryant's unfortunate belief in the genuineness of Chatterton's poems. The two brothers, *Thomas* and *Richard Rawlinson*, were famous for their antiquarian and book-loving tastes, commenced at an early age at Eton; the latter bequeathed to the Bodleian Library at Oxford the famous collection of manuscripts which bears his name. *Richard Owen Cambridge* is famous as the author of *The Scribleriad*, a satirical poem, much quoted but little read. Like Bryant, he was highly esteemed and venerated by his contemporaries as a scholar and man of letters. *William Coxe* (1737) became Archdeacon of Wiltshire, and as historian of Charles V. and Marlborough, has maintained his reputation to the present day. *Christopher Anstey* (1742) brightened literature with one famous satirical poem. *The New Bath Guide. Robert Glynn*, afterwards Glynn-Clobeny (1787), and *George Baker* (1741), are well-known names in the medical profession, Sir George Baker becoming private medical attendant to the king. Two other King's scholars, *George Lewis Jones* (1741) and *Edward Young* (1742), attained distinction in the Church of Ireland, as Bishops respectively of Kilmore and Dromore. By no means the least attractive figure among the oppidans at this date was *George Augustus Selwyn*, the famous wit, the playmate of politics and society, the master of that

> Social wit, which, never kindling strife,
> Blazed in the small, sweet courtesies of life.

Two Etonians were conspicuous in after-life for their share in the government of the country. *John Montagu, fourth Earl of Sandwich*, was one of the most remarkable men of his generation. For many years he practically controlled the Admiralty, and much of the blame attaching to the mismanagement of the navy during the American war was laid somewhat unreasonably to his charge. He was the most trusted friend of his sovereign, George III., and his assiduity in office was such that he is stated to have invented the well-known sandwich as a means of snatching a hasty meal without leaving his work. Of all sports and athletics Sandwich was an ardent votary—cricket, fencing, racing—whatever came in his way. Music, too, and the drama, found in him a warm and liberal patron. Unfortunately for Sandwich his brazen-faced profligacy and indecorous profanity left a stigma on his name. This and his association with Wilkes, and subsequent behaviour to Wilkes, raised him a cloud of enemies, whose vituperation remains to this day triumphant. Another able statesman was *Charles Montagu, Marquis of Halifax*, who filled many offices in the State, and was especially distinguished as Lord-Lieutenant of Ireland. *Sir John Cust, Bart.*, a member of a family that has now for seven generations sent its sons to Eton, rose to be Speaker of the House of Commons at a critical period in its history, and died a victim to the strain on his constitution imposed on him by his office. From Eton, too, at this date came two soldier heroes, the famous *Marquess of Granby* and *Henry Seymour Conway*, Horace Walpole's cousin and friend, the two most popular generals of their day. *Earl Howe*, the victor of the glorious 'First of

104

June,' was a short time at Eton, but his brother William, afterwards Viscount Howe, remained longer, and was destined to play one of the most honourable parts in the war with the American Colonies. *Sir William Draper* (1740) distinguished himself as the conqueror of Manila in the Philippine Islands, and also in the unexpected role of an actor in the correspondence of the mysterious 'Junius.'

William George, the Head-master, was elected Provost of King's in 1742, and was succeeded by one of the Assistant-masters, *William Cooke* (1730), a former scholar and King's-man. Cooke was not a great success as an administrator, although he was a good scholar. After three years he resigned, ostensibly owing to ill-health, and eventually became a Fellow of the College, and later Provost of King's College, Cambridge, in which post, oddly enough, he succeeded his successor in the Headmastership of Eton. William Cole, the antiquary, a man of strong prejudices, described Cooke as "a formal, impotent Pedant, who will be a schoolmaster in whatever station of life his fortune may advance him to." The school, however, continued to prosper and multiply.

Dr. Cooke was succeeded as Head-master by the Lowermaster, *John Sumner* (1723), an Eton and King's scholar from the west country, who was the first member of a family destined to confer great lustre on the scholastic annals of Eton College. Both Cooke and Sumner illustrate the prevailing advantages at Eton due to a family connection with members of the Foundation. In the list of Eton and King's scholars several names occur frequently, generation by generation, showing in how small a circle the world of Eton moved at this date. Earliest of these, and perhaps the most honoured, is the familiar name of Hawtrey, already mentioned in these pages. The family of Goad has also been alluded to before. About 1690 the organist at Eton was named Sleech, whose widow re-married Dr. Newborough, the Headmaster. His son, *Richard Sleech* (1693), became a Fellow of Eton in 1715, and Canon of Windsor, and his daughter married Bishop Weston of 'Weston's Yard.' Canon Sleech himself married a daughter of Stephen Upman, Fellow of Eton, and was the father of *Stephen Sleech* (1723), who became Fellow of Eton in 1729, and succeeded Dr. Bland as Provost in 1746, holding that post for nineteen years. Of Provost Sleech's sisters, one married *Charles Hawtrey* (1706), another married George Harris, Fellow of Eton, in 1731, and a third was the wife of Dr. Cooke, the Head-master. *Henry Sleech* (1741), a Master at Eton, and another member of the family, married Dr. Cooke's sister, and their daughter married Thomas Dampier, the younger, afterwards Bishop of Ely. The members of the Sumner family will be alluded to hereafter. By such family combinations was Eton College governed, and it is not surprising that the tone of its administration was essentially conservative.

John Sumner does not appear to have made any great mark as a Head-master, and during the nine years of his Head-mastership the most important external event seems to have been a visit from George II., in August 1747, when he was received with Latin orations from two of the Collegers, Sclater and Marsham. Among the boys, however, educated at Eton under Dr. Sumner, there were some who became distinguished in many divers ways in their subsequent careers. Few names were more conspicuous in the history of England during the second half of the eighteenth century than that of *Frederick, Lord North,* who left Eton in 1749, leaving a reputation for Latin verses, and became the clumsy, obstinate Prime Minister of George III., but nevertheless the most conspicuous statesman who bridged the interval between the two William Pitts. His ill-starred colonial policy, which resulted in the loss of the American colonies, connects his name with that of his contemporary at Eton, *Charles, Marquess Cornwallis,* the hero of the American war, and afterwards to be most highly distinguished, as Governor-General of India and Viceroy of Ireland. While at Eton Cornwallis had one of his eyes accidentally injured by another boy, the *Hon. Shute Barrington,* who proceeded to rise through high positions in the Church to be Bishop of Salisbury, and eventually to be Prime-Bishop of Durham. Another hero of the American War was *Hugh, Earl Percy,* afterwards second Duke of Northumberland. Of very different build to these Etonians were *Sir James Mansfield* (originally Manfield) (1750), afterwards Chief-Justice of the Common Pleas; *George Steevens,* the eccentric, cross-grained editor of Shakespeare's works; *John Horne*, a Colleger, afterwards *Horne-Tooke,* the notorious Radical; and *William Smith,* the 'gentleman' actor, whom Churchill, in the Rosciad speaks of as "Smith, the genteel, the airy, and the smart." It is noteworthy that Home-Tooke was the son of a poulterer in London, although perhaps related to the Vice-Provost of the same name, and Smith of a wholesale grocer and tea-dealer in the City. *Joseph Pote,* also the well-known Eton bookseller, not only kept a boarding-house in Eton, but several members of his family were educated on the Foundation.

When Dr. Sumner resigned in 1754 the post of Headmaster, there seemed every probability that the Usher, *Thomas Dampier*, would follow in his footsteps and succeed to his post. Dampier was a man highly popular in society, a well-known figure in social and literary centres in London, a *bon vivant*, and in every way a *persona grata* to his aristocratic pupils and their parents. After a severe contest the post of Head-master was conferred on *Edward Barnard*, a former King's scholar, who from superannuation had proceeded to St. John's College instead of to King's College at Cambridge. Barnard was supported by the Townshend family, to one of whom he was resident tutor at Eton two years before his election. Dampier, who was greatly disappointed, was subsequently rewarded with the rich deanery of Durham. The appointment of Barnard, however, proved in every way successful. He was a competent and elegant scholar, and an able administrator. Under him the school grew and flourished in a way which was at the time unprecedented, and during the eleven years of his rule the number of boys rose from 300 or so to over 500. Under Dr. Barnard the school lists contained many names from the flower of the British aristocracy, some of whom obtained distinction in public life, the oppidans being particularly remarkable for their abilities and accomplishments. *Charles James Fox*, the brilliant and wayward genius, whose very faults seemed to add lustre to his political eminence; *William Windham*, the handsome and polished orator; and *William Wyndham, Lord Grenville*, distinguished as a Latin scholar at Eton, afterwards Prime Minister, and not the least distinguished of a remarkable family, have left names written upon the history of their country. His cousin, *James Grenville,* afterwards created Baron Glastonbury, maintained the family tradition. *James Hare,* wit and politician, grandson of Bishop Francis Hare, an Etonian of a former generation, was a member of a coterie in London, principally composed of Etonian contemporaries, conspicuous among whom were *Frederick, fifth Earl of Carlisle,* an aristocratic poet and patron of the fine arts, *William, second Earl Fitzwilliam, Henry, third Duke of Bucchuch, Henry Thomas, second Earl of Ilchester, and Anthony Morris Storer,* the last of whom left a valuable collection of books and prints to the College Library.

Two Etonians obtained conspicuous honours in the domain of Science. Charles, third Earl Stanhope, the eccentric Radical peer, has obtained more notoriety for his sympathy with the French revolutionists than for his numerous contributions of undoubted value to mechanics and experimental physics. One summer evening an Eton boy was returning alone from bathing, when he was struck by the beauty of the flowers in the hedgerows by the lane. He determined to study botany, though there was no one to teach him but the old wives of the neighbourhood. During the holidays he found in his home at Revesby Abbey, in Lincolnshire, an old book, Gerard's *Herball,* which he carried back in triumph to Eton. That boy was *Sir Joseph Banks,* afterwards to be the companion of Captain Cook in the voyage of the

Endeavour to Australia, the discoverer of Tahiti and Botany Bay, and for thirty-two years President of the Royal Society.

Among literary celebrities, if of the second rank, may be named *George Hardinge*, lawyer, author, antiquary, and poet, son of Nicholas Hardinge, the Etonian scholar, nephew of Earl Camden, and uncle to one of Eton's *raræ aves*, a sailor hero, *George Nicholas Hardinge*, killed in action off Ceylon; and *Thomas James Mathias*, author of a satirical poem, *The Pursuits of Literature*, which created some stir in his day, and also editor of the works of the Etonian poet, Gray.

Joah Bates (1759), afterwards Fellow of King's, was a well-known musician, and not only promoted, but actually conducted the Handel Commemoration Festival at Westminster Abbey in 1784.

Horace Walpole, writing to Sir Horace Mann in October 1762, says, "Your nephew Foote has made a charming figure; the King and Queen went from Windsor to see Eton; he is captain of the oppidans, and made a speech to them with great applause. It was in English, which is right. Why should we talk Latin to our kings rather than Russ or Iroquois? Is this a season for being ashamed of our country? Dr. Barnard, the Master, is the Pitt of masters, and has raised the school to the most flourishing state it ever knew."

Provost Sleech died in 1765, and Dr. Barnard was elected to fill his place, continuing to exercise in that most dignified post the same accomplished and humane talents which had so much adorned his career as Headmaster. The high position which Provost Barnard held in intellectual society is shown by the anecdote told by Bennet Langton of a party at Mrs. Vesey's, where "the company consisted chiefly of ladies, among whom were the Duchess Dowager of Portland, the Duchess of Beaufort, whom I suppose from her rank I must name before her mother, Mrs. Boscawen, and her eldest sister, Mrs. Lewson, who was likewise there; Lady Lucan, Lady Clermont, and others of note both for their station and understandings. Among the gentlemen were Lord Althorp, . . . Lord Macartney, Sir Joshua Reynolds, Lord Lucan, Mr. Wraxall, . . . Dr. Warren, Mr. Pepys, the Master in Chancery, . . . and Dr. Barnard, the Provost of Eton. As soon as Dr. Johnson was come in and had taken a chair, the company began to collect round him, till they became not less than four, if not five deep; those behind standing and listening over the heads of those that were sitting near him. The conversation for some time was chiefly between Dr. Johnson and the Provost of Eton, while the others contributed occasionally their remarks."

When Dr. Barnard died in December 1781, Dr. Johnson is said to have remarked that "he was the only man that did justice to my good breeding, and you may observe that I am well-bred to a needless degree of scrupulosity." Such a compliment from the Great Cham of literature was a feather in the cap even of so high a dignitary as the Provost of Eton. As Provost Dr. Barnard was a genial host, delighting especially in the society of men of worthy genius, like Foote the actor. On his tomb in the chapel it is stated that at Eton he *disciplinam et famam auxit et stabilitavit.*

When Dr. Barnard vacated the Head-mastership there seemed little doubt about his successor. *John Foster* (1748), one of the Assistant-masters, was so much esteemed for his high character and sound scholarship, that he seemed marked out for the post. The best scholars and the most upright and high-minded disciplinarians are not always the most successful administrators in any profession. Dr. Foster was a conspicuous example. He failed to win the confidence or affection of the boys, and numerous exhibitions of tactlessness and temper on his part led to a serious rebellion in the school. This was not a mere outbreak of mutinous or high-spirited youth, but a deliberate and organised resistance of the head boys of the school to the petty tyrannies of the Head-master. Failing any redress, no less than one hundred and sixty boys left the school, and marched in good order to Maidenhead, where they remained for the night. The next day they returned to Eton, but as the Head-master still remained obdurate, the boys, with but few exceptions, returned home to their surprised and indignant parents. Dr. Foster's misdirected system of discipline had after this event a depressing effect upon the school, for during the eight years of his rule the number of the boys steadily decreased. In 1772 Dr. Foster, broken in health and spirits, gave up the Head-mastership, and retired to the congenial haven of a canonry at Windsor, where he died some two years later. He was succeeded as Head-master by *Jonathan Davies* (1755), a pupil and protégé of Dr. Barnard, and one of the leading Assistant-masters in the school. Dr. Davies ruled the school for eighteen years, but as far as his personal influence was concerned, the progress of the school was slow and uneventful. The number of boys continued to sink, reaching its lowest point in 1775, when there were only 246 boys in the school. If the number of the boys was diminished, their calibre was, if anything, increased, and their achievements in after life are among the brightest treasures of Eton's fame and renown.

The most conspicuous of Etonians at this date may be said to have been *George Canning*, who, as an Eton boy, enjoyed a reputation perhaps unprecedented since his time. In after life, as Canning mounted step by step the ladder of his great parliamentary career, he remained an Etonian at heart, constantly revisited the school, and at the zenith of his life declared that no one is ever so great a man as when he was a sixth-form boy at Eton.

Hardly second to Canning in parliamentary renown was *Charles, second Earl Grey*, the future Prime Minister, although he was at heart less of an Etonian than Canning. Earl Grey was, however, at Eton and Cambridge one of those elegant scholar-statesmen whose classical and literary exercises his contemporaries were proud to record. Among the names most treasured in the annals of Eton is that of another scholar-statesman, *Richard Colley Wellesley, Marquess of Wellesley*, scholar, poet, orator, in after life destined to fill such important posts as Governor-General of India (in succession to another Etonian, Marquess Cornwallis), Commander-in-Chief in India, Ambassador to Spain, Secretary of State for Foreign Affairs, Lord Lieutenant of Ireland, and Lord Chamberlain. After all these high distinctions and at the close of his long life and eventful career, the Marquess Wellesley had only one desire remaining to him, that his body should be buried in the chapel of his beloved Eton. His epitaph he composed himself. It has become almost proverbial, both for the depth of its sentiment and the beauty of its Latinity. For both these reasons it cannot be too often quoted, and every Eton boy should know it by heart:—

> Fortunæ rerumque vagis exercitus undis,
>
>> In gremium redeo serus, Etona, tuum.
>
> Magna sequi, et summæ mirari culmina famae,
>
>> Et purum antiquæ lucis adire jubar,
>
> Auspice te didici puer, atque in limine vitæ
>
>> Ingenuas verse laudis amare vias.
>
> Si qua meum vitæ decursu gloria nomen
>
>> Auxerit, aut si quis nobilitarit honos,
>
> Muneris, Alma, tui est. Altrix da terra sepulchrum,
>
>> Supremam lachrymam da memoremque mei.

With Wellesley at Eton (Wesley was their surname then) was his world-renowned younger brother, *Arthur Wellesley*, the future *Duke of Wellington*. At Eton the future victor of Waterloo and Prime Minister of England made but little mark. The facts of his having cut his name on the kitchen door at his Dame's and of his having vanquished Robert Percy (Bobus) Smith in a mill, seem to compose the 'short and simple annals' of his career as an Eton boy. His tribute, however, in later life to Eton and its playing-fields is a household word in English history. Moreover, in the whole history of Eton, there can hardly have been a more moving incident than when the great Duke, on revisiting Eton in

114

the days of his glory, was seized by a sudden impulse to climb upon the wall and run along it, oblivious of his age and his dignity, but for once again feeling himself an Eton boy.

Among noted Eton parliamentary figures, educated under Dr. Davies, were *George Tienriey*, one of the most conspicuous and successful debaters in the House of Commons, and *Samuel Whitbread*, the earliest representative of the mingling of piety and brewing, which has since become a conspicuous feature in English society. *Henry Richard Fox*, afterwards third *Lord Holland*, nephew of Charles James Fox, became afterwards one of the most conspicuous members of the Whig party in Parliament. During his lifetime and that of his wife, Holland House, his residence at Kensington, became the centre of political and literary society in London. The following lines, written by himself shortly before his death in 1840, may be commended to the mind of any Etonian:—

> Nephew of Fox and friend of Grey,
> Enough my meed of fame
> If those who deigned to observe me say
> I injured neither name.

The political fame of *Edward Smith Stanley, thirteenth Earl of Derby*, one of the supporters of the Whig party under Earl Grey, has been overshadowed by that of his more famous son. The thirteenth earl is better known for his great interest in zoology, and as president for many years of the Linnean Society and the Zoological Society. *John Hookham Frere* was one of Canning's principal friends at Eton and in after life. He joined with Canning at Eton in producing the Microcosm, and in after life in a similar enterprise with the Anti-Jacobin. After a short but distinguished career in politics and diplomacy, Frere devoted himself to literature, producing among other works his unrivalled translations of Aristophanes. More interesting perhaps to Etonians was his *Ode on Æthelstans Victory*, written in early English verse, while still a boy at Eton, like an Eton Chatterton, of which Sir Walter Scott said that it was the only poem he had met with, which, if it had been produced as ancient, could not have been detected on internal evidence. To the poet Coleridge, John Hookham Frere appeared the man, who most eminently deserved the epithets of 'ὁ καλοκἀγαθός ὁ φιλόκαλος.'

The classical reputation of Eton at this date was adorned and for ever increased by the presence in the school of *Richard Parson*, the great Greek scholar. Porson became a Colleger in August 1774, his education being supported by a wealthy friend. At Eton he showed little signs of his future eminence as a scholar. Handicapped by his humble birth, he was backward in his studies when he came to Eton, and did not display any abilities above the average until he went to Cambridge, where he was placed at Trinity College owing to his not being of standing enough to get an Eton scholarship at King's. At Eton, however, his natural abilities were so strongly marked, that, when his benefactor died in 1777, and his future career was in peril, both past and present Etonians contributed to a fund to provide for his maintenance at the University. To Eton, therefore, the 'great Grecian' owed a debt, which he readily recognised in after life.

116

One of the great names in English literature is that of *Henry Hallam*. His father, *John Hallam* (1747), was a scholar of Eton and King's, highly respected among his contemporaries as Canon of Windsor and Dean of Bristol. Hallam's mother was sister of Dr. Roberts, afterwards Provost of Eton, so that the historian may be said to have been an Etonian in his cradle. It is sufficient to mention Hallam's histories of *The Middle Ages* and *The Literature of Europe* to denote his position in the hierarchy of English men of letters. *Robert Percy Smith,* Wellington's boyish foe, who was always known affectionately in after life by his Eton nickname of 'Bobus Smith,' was one of the brilliant friends at Eton of Canning, Hookham Frere, and Lord Holland. Had he not had Sydney Smith for a younger brother he could have ranked among the wittiest, most original, and most correct of English writers. Another man of letters, well known in his day, if somewhat forgotten now, was produced by Eton in the person of *William Smyth*, poet and historian, the son of a Liverpool banker, tutor to Sheridan's son, and afterwards Regius Professor of Modern History at Cambridge, where his lectures on Modern History and on the French Revolution were much esteemed.

Politics and literature were not by any means the only fields in which an Etonian could gain distinction. *Charles Simeon* (1778), the famous evangelical preacher at Cambridge, is almost as remarkable a product of Eton as his contemporary, Richard Porson. It is curious to find that at Eton Simeon was noted for athletics and a love of dress. In 1776 a day of fasting and penitence was observed at Eton on account of the disasters to the British forces in America. Such an event could weigh but lightly on the mind of an ordinary Eton boy. It has, however, been recorded by Simeon himself that this event was the first to divert his mind towards religion. When he went from Eton to King's he was destined to exercise an influence throughout both University and town, unparalleled, it may be said, in either University, even at Oxford in the days of Keble and Newman, for Simeon's work was of a missionary nature to rich and poor, to learned and unlearned alike, and his influence is abiding even to the present day. *Thomas Dampier* (1766), eldest son of the jovial Lower-master, climbed higher on the ladder of the church than his father, becoming Dean and Bishop of Rochester, and later of Ely, and also known as a bibliophile of importance. His half-brother, *Sir Henry Dampier* (1776), pursued the fortunes of the family further as a Baron of the Exchequer, and a distinguished authority on ecclesiastical law. Another Eton Colleger, *John Luxmoore* (1775), a west-country boy, whose name has been continued by other honoured representatives to the present day, became bishop successively of Bristol, Hereford, and St. Asaph. Preferment in the cases of Dampier and Luxmoore, well deserved as it was and proved to be, may, however, be credited to the fact of their good fortune in being selected as tutors to the sons of important and influential noblemen. As a matter of fact at the date in question, preferment in any profession of life was most easily obtained by the favour and patronage of royalty or nobility, the days for the recognition of individual merit having hardly as yet dawned.

It was during the Head-mastership of Dr. Davies that the king, George III., began to evince that interest in Eton which was shown in so many ways, until the unfortunate event of the king's insanity. It is a curious coincidence, that the two kings of England, to whom Eton was cherished, and who are commemorated by Etonians as it were among the patron saints of the College, Henry VI. and George III., should both have shared the same sad fate at the close of their lives. The king and queen had visited Eton in 1762 shortly after their marriage and been much gratified by their reception. In 1778 they attended speeches in Upper School, when Lord Wellesley drew tears from the royal eyes by his recital of Strafford's last speech.

Provost Barnard died in 1781. He was succeeded by a former Assistant-master and Fellow, *William Hayward Roberts* (1752), one of the fat and gouty divines whose fondness for port and cheerful company were so mercilessly caricatured by Gillray and Rowlandson. A Gloucestershire man, he was nicknamed 'Double Gloucester' from his resemblance in shape to the cheese of that name. Provost Roberts in more ways than one filled the post genially and urbanely for ten years. Cole, the antiquary, says that he was "a portly man and of much pride and state, and was used to have routs, as they were called, in the College apartments for card-playing, which filled the College court with carriages and tumults, not much to the edification of a place of education." Perhaps this is the reason for the severe discouragement in after days of the innocent whist-parties, which the Eton boy must now enjoy under a sword of Damocles, and certainly without carriages or tumults, like this revered Provost.

Provost Roberts terminated his cheery regime in 1791, and was succeeded by the Head-master, Dr. Davies, who did his best to maintain the reputation of the Provost's table. Provost Davies was a not unfamiliar figure in the *salons* of the Prince of Wales. His loud voice and love of London brought him under the lash of the Etonian satirist, Mathias, together with the Lowermaster, *Dr. William Langford* (1762), who combined this post with that of Canon of Windsor and chaplain to the king, although both the latter posts at times involved duties and residence in Windsor Castle.

Dr. Davies was succeeded as Head-master in 1792 by *George Heath* (1768), one of the Assistant-masters, who held the post for nine years. Dr. Heath was a man of little importance, and the school under his management failed to recover the position, in point of numbers, to which it had attained under Dr. Barnard. The quality, however, of the boys at the school remained as high, and the alumni during the last decade of the eighteenth century were in many cases destined to play a large part in the history of their country. Otherwise the period of Dr. Heath's administration calls for but little comment. Under him were trained a future Prime Minister in *William Lamb, second Viscount Melbourne,* a future Speaker of the House of Commons in *Charles Manners Sutton,* a future Archbishop of Canterbury in *John Bird Sumner* (1798), a future Governor-General of India in *George Eden, Earl of Auckland,* and of Canada in *Charles, Lord Metcalfe.* Three of the most noted diplomatists were also at Eton under Dr. Heath, *Stratford Canning* (1805), afterwards Lord Stratford de Redcliffe, a scholar on the Foundation, renowned afterwards as 'the great Elchi' at Constantinople, *Charles Stuart*, Lord Stuart de Rothesay, and *William A'Court*, Lord Heytesbury. In the profession of the law were *Thomas, Lord Denman*, the famous judge. *Sir Christopher Puller, Sir Lancelot Shadwell, Stephen Lushington, William Frere*, younger brother of John Hookham Frere, Master of Downing College, Cambridge, and *William Selwyn*, the first of a race of Eton heroes. With the army are connected the names of *Sir Patrick Stuart, Sir Horatio Townshend*, a member of another Eton clan, *Lord George Beresford*, and *Sir John Fox Burgoyne*, Even in the navy we find the names of *Sir George Mundy* and of *Edward Hawke Locker*, afterwards Commissioner of Greenwich Hospital. To literature belongs *William Stewart Rose*, the translator of Ariosto.

It was the age of dandies and wits, and it may be considered one of the feathers in the cap of Dr. Heath that he bred up no less a personage than *George Brummell,* the famous 'Beau,' and not only him, but *Thomas Raikes* as well, a City merchant as well as dandy, dubbed 'Apollo,' by his friends, since 'he rose in the east and set in the west,' the forerunner of the dandies of the present day, who are understood to be 'something in the City.' Three Etonians gained some notoriety from their friendship with Lord Byron, two of them oddly enough Collegers, *Francis Hodgson* (1799), to be mentioned later as Provost, and *Scrope Berdmore Davies* (1801), scholar and Fellow of King's and one of the cleverest men of his time, but more notorious as a dandy and a gambler in after life, than as a scholar. *Charles Skinner Matthews,* Matthews *major*, scholar of Trinity College, Cambridge, and ninth wrangler in 1805, was one of Byron's principal friends at Cambridge, and a partner in the famous frolic at Newstead Abbey, when the party dressed up as monks and quaffed burgundy from a human skull; he was drowned in the Cam in 1811. His younger brother, *Henry Matthews* (1807), Matthews *minor*, was afterwards better known as the author of a *Diary of an Invalid in Portugal, Italy, Switzerland, and France*, and for his work as judge in the Supreme Court of Ceylon. *Henry Warburton* was one of the best-known figures in Parliament during his day. *Sir Thomas Charles Morgan* became a fashionable lady's doctor, and the husband of Sydney Owenson, 'the wild Irish girl.' *Richmond Makepeace Thackeray*, one of a family much connected with Eton, gained renown from his famous son, William Makepeace Thackeray, the novelist. *Joseph Planta*, son of the principal librarian of the British Museum, became a diplomatist and privy councillor. Coming events in the educational history of Eton cast their shadows beforehand in the presence as boys in the school of *John Keate* (1791), *Thomas Carter* (1794), *George Bethell* (1797), *John Francis Plumptre* (1799), *Henry Joseph Thomas Drury* (1796), and *Edward Craven Hawtrey* (1807).

In reality Eton made but little progress under the rule of Dr. Heath as Head-master, and Dr. Davies as Provost. The numbers of the school rose but slowly, and the average of scholarship fell below that of a score or so of years before. The taint of a corrupt and debauched aristocracy hung over the fashionable world, and it speaks well for Eton and its administrators that, on the whole, they came so well through a time, when both private and public life presented an evil example, which was only too likely to be contagious.

VI

BUILDINGS, SCHOOL-WORK, ETC.

In a previous chapter it has been recorded how Provost Allestree about 1670 built a new schoolroom on the west side of the outward court of the College at his own expense. This school occupied the site of the present Upper School. Previous to this a wall of red brick had extended from Long Chamber to the chapel with a gate in the middle. This wall is shown in the small view of the College, depicted on the monument of Sir Henry Savile at Merton College, Oxford. Allestree's new school consisted of a one-storeyed building, with a double row of windows on the western or outer side, in addition to an archway through the centre. On the eastern side towards the schoolyard there was an ambulatory below the eastern half of the buildings, the upper storey being supported by slender columns. A view of this side is shown in a view of the College, engraved by Wenceslaus Hollar in 1672, while the outer side towards the street is shown in the bird's-eye view of the College, engraved by David Loggan in 1688. The construction of this building proved, however, defective, and the whole building had to be taken down and rebuilt in 1689. The present 'Upper School' was then erected and finished in January 1691, the upper storey being supported upon massive piers, instead of the slender columns in the previous building. It has been recorded that the payments for the restoration passed through the hands of *John Hawtrey* (1661), then a Fellow of Eton, and great-grandfather of the future Headmaster and Provost. David Loggan was an engraver, who excelled especially in his bird's-eye view of college buildings, a style of topographical engraving which he brought from the Netherlands. To him we owe much knowledge of the appearance of the colleges at the two Universities in the seventeenth century. It is interesting to see in his view of Eton College, what the buildings were which existed about 1688. In front of Allestree's new school ran what was for long known as 'The Long Walk,' planted with trees, and bounded towards the road by the familiar low wall, with its white coping. On the left of this wall towards the north, there was at one time a low building used as the Provost's stables, which remained there until 1722, when they were removed to a more suitable spot adjoining the Provost's garden. The wall was then completed up to the arch, which led from the Slough road into the playing-fields. The present coping seems to date from 1753, and the lime trees appear to be of the same age.

Taking Loggan's view as a guide, there are seen abutting upon the Slough road the range of low picturesque houses, which were erected in 1603-4 under Sir Henry Savile. This range of buildings was used for various purposes. Some of the Commensales were lodged here, and also some of the under officials of the College. Savile's printing-press was also set up here, and from the building accounts it would appear that some portion was used as a granary. Behind this building was the stable-yard, known in later days as Weston's Yard, from Dr. Stephen Weston, first Usher and then Fellow of Eton, and afterwards Bishop of

Exeter. It is not quite clear why his name was given to the yard. Passing into the school-yard, it appears in Loggan's view to have been covered with turf with intersecting paths, like a quadrangle at one of the Universities. It remained so until 1706, when it was paved. Provost Godolphin in 1719 presented the bronze statue of the Founder, King Henry VI., by Francis Bird, which is so conspicuous a feature at the present day. In Loggan's view Lupton's Tower appears without the wooden turrets, and without the clock. The great clock was for many years placed against the easternmost bay of the chapel, and it was not until 1765 that it was removed to its present situation in Lupton's Tower, when a pair of wooden turrets were added to receive its bells.

Loggan shows in the inner quadrangle the buildings much as they were left when completed at the end of the fifteenth century. He shows the one-storeyed building with the gallery running round the north-east and south sides, the southern side abutting on the hall, and with an arched cloister underneath the gallery. The iron railings enclosing the central court were erected in 1724-5. In 1759, chiefly owing to the want of accommodation for the Fellows and other persons lodged in the College, and partly owing to an opportunity afforded by the need of extensive repairs to the roof, it was decided to erect an attic storey over the north and east sides of the cloister. The towers at the angles of the quadrangle were raised, and the general proportions observed with great care. The appearance of the buildings was considerably enhanced by this elevation, especially when seen from the river side. The introduction of sash windows, however, took something off the architectural effect.

In 1720 the Provost and Fellows determined to build a new library. The books belonging to the College had at first been placed in the vestry on the north side of the Collegiate Church, a very common position for Church libraries at that date. When Lupton's building was completed, the books were removed to one of the rooms, probably Election Hall. Under Sir Henry Savile they were removed to a small room on the ground floor, under Long Chamber, at the eastern end near the Usher's apartment, afterwards known as Lower master's Chamber. They were again removed in 1675-6 to a room made for the purpose in the southern side of the gallery.

When the question of a new library was mooted in 1720, the first intention was to build an octagonal building at the east end of the chapel, with a dome something like the Radcliffe 'Camera' at Oxford, to be entered from a cloister uniting the chapel with the Fellows' building at its south-western angle. This idea was however abandoned, and in 1725 the present College library was built on the southern side of the cloister, parallel to and abutting on the Hall. For some unexplained reason no attempt was made to preserve the symmetry of the external style to that of the buildings connected with it. Internally the College library is a fine and dignified room. The collection of books was probably in early days rich in missals and books of devotion, but it was thoroughly purged of all such heresy under the pious ordinances of Edward VI. and the Duke of Somerset. Sir Henry Savile found it in a sadly neglected condition, set it up and rearranged it, and had very considerable additions made to it. When the library was removed to its present situation, many contributions and additions of books poured in. In 1730, upon the death of Richard Topham, a well-known antiquary, his library and a valuable collection of archaeological drawings were presented by his executors to the College.

In 1799 Anthony Morris Storer, who had been at Eton with Charles James Fox, the fifth Earl of Carlisle, and others, and who had succumbed to a craze, then popular, for collecting rare books and prints, died and left to the library of Eton College his books and collection of prints. The books included three from the press of Caxton, besides other rarities, while among the prints were a valuable series of mezzotint engravings after Sir Joshua Reynolds, and a copy of Granger's *Biographical History of England*, interleaved and illustrated in many large volumes. Bishop Waddington bestowed a large mass of theological literature to fill the shelves. Among other rarities and objects of interest to be seen in the College, in addition to the charters and other books and documents relating to the history of the College and its valuable manuscripts, are a 'Mazarin' Bible, the first book printed by Gutenberg & Fust at Mayence about 1455; Erasmus's edition of the Greek Testament (the first published); Archbishop Parker's History of the British Church; a first folio Shakespeare, and the only known copy of Udall's *Ralph Roister Doister*.

The library has been frequently visited by eminent strangers from all parts of the world. In 1842 it was visited by the King of Prussia, who presented to it one of the only two copies of the *Nibelungen-Lied*, printed on vellum, which had been specially issued in honour of the fourth centenary of the invention of printing. King Louis Philippe of France visited the library in 1844, on which occasion he was accompanied by Queen Victoria and the Prince Consort. The Emperor of Germany was a visitor in the summer of 1891.

The College Hall remained much in the same condition from the middle of the sixteenth century to the middle of the nineteenth. It had been panelled along the north and south sides in 1547, by which the fine old original fire-places were entirely concealed. The screen and gallery was of earlier erection still. The most conspicuous alteration lay in the erection of the flight of stone steps leading into the ambulatory of the cloister, which were completed in 1690.

Little or no alteration was made in the accommodation for the masters and scholars in College. As late as 1661 the old statute is recapitulated that "all the King's Schollers and Choristers shall ly in the Long Chamber, that the Scholemaster and Usher shall lodge in their Chambers at the ends of the Long Chamber to prevent disorders which may otherwise happen in the said Chamber."

The chapel, however, underwent various alterations and so-called embellishments from time to time. *Thomas Weaver*, Fellow of Eton from 1612 to 1650, and Vice-Provost, carried out at his own expense a number of additions and alterations to the internal fittings of the chapel. In a contemporary note of the work done (1625), it is stated that, among other gifts, "He sett up Seates for ye oppidalls, and the great Pew under ye Pulpitt for the use of ye Fellowes, Scholm^r and their Families; He gave fowre strong formes to stand in ye lies of ye Church for the Townemen to sitt on; He gave two deskes graven wth ye Coll. armes for ye Fellowes to read Prayers; He adorned the deskes for ye Clerks; He translated ye Vestrie, built ye Portall; He repayred ye seat in Dr Lupton's Chappell and sett up a presse ther to laye up ye Songe books; He repared ye Seates and pewes on ye North and South sides of ye Church; besides diverse other things; The Colledg alowed him towards ye work six Loads of rough Tymber." All Weaver's wood-work has, however, now disappeared and been reformed away into dust and oblivion by his presumably more intelligent successors. One item, however, remains in the 'translated' vestry and the portal on the north side. From this portal steps led down to the schoolyard. These steps were rebuilt in 1694-5, and proved, as will be recounted in a later chapter, an important and indispensable factor in the history of one of the principal Eton games.

In 1698 and 1699 the exterior of the chapel was repaired, and the inside entirely rearranged. A 'new, strong, and very handsome roof' was provided, of wood, for there does not seem to have been any design at any time of making the perpendicular buttresses support a stone roof, as in the chapel of King's College, Cambridge. The Provost and Fellows issued an appeal to old Etonians and others to help in the 'Enlarging and Beautyfying' the choir of the College chapel. They state that, considering "that it conduceth highly to the Honour of God and the benefit of Religion, that the Publick worship of God should be performed with as much decency as possible where so great a number of Children, both of the Nobility and Gentry, have their Education," they intended to proceed to the 'Beautyfying and Enlarging the Choir,' "that so all the Children of the Schole may appear under one View; and likewise that they, and all the people of the Parish, may be so conveniently seated, as to hear with ease all the publick offices of the Church, which at present, by reason of their number, and the ill disposition of the place, they cannot possibly do." The money was raised by subscription among the Fellows, Masters, and old Etonians, the Provost, Godolphin, subscribing himself one thousand pounds.

In restorations of this kind posterity has often reason to regret that the plans of a restorer should involve the complete effacement of previous work. In Eton Chapel everything was swept away, even Weaver's gifts of woodwork, in order to make way for a complete design in the classical panelling, which had then come into fashion. The side walls were panelled right up to the east end, even the entrance to Lupton's chapel being sacrificed and concealed in order not to interfere with the design. A lofty baldacchino was erected over the altar, and an organ loft in the same classical style was erected across the chapel towards the west end, though not immediately under the chancel arch. The roof was divided off into panels, and painted to look like stone. The general effect, judging from the drawing of F. Mackenzie, reproduced in Ackermann's Eton, must have been handsome and dignified. A similar style of internal decoration can still be seen in the chapel of Trinity College, Cambridge, which was carried out a few years later than the

131

work in Eton Chapel under the mastership of the great Dr. Bentley. The tradition that the designs of Sir Christopher Wren were used in Eton Chapel, though not established by any record, becomes not incredible, supposing that the Mr. Banks, under whom the internal decorations of Wren's great library at Trinity College, Cambridge, were carried out in 1686-87, is the same as the 'Mr. Banks, surveyor,' who designed the internal decoration of Eton Chapel some twelve years later, and probably identical with the 'Matthew Bankes, master carpenter,' who was so largely concerned in the decoration of Sir Christopher Wren's work at Kensington Palace, Hampton Court, and other places.

The ante-chapel was 'repaired and beautified' in 1769, chiefly with stucco-work. The full-length marble statue of the founder, executed by John Bacon, R.A., was presented in 1799 by the Rev. Edward Betham, Fellow of the College.

The internal arrangement of the chapel remained in the same condition for more than a hundred years. As it still remained the parish church of Eton, seats had to be provided for many of the parishioners. Large pews were also set apart for the servants of the College. The sons of noblemen, according to old College fashions, and the Sixth Form occupied special seats, raised above the others.

In spite of the ingrained conservatism of Eton College, the daily work and discipline of the school had undergone several gradual changes, inevitable with the march of time, since the days of William Malim. One of the most important of these changes was the introduction on to the staff of permanent Assistant-masters, and the gradual development of the tutorial system, which before long became one of the principal features of the educational system at Eton. In 1718, under Dr. Snape, the names of nine Assistant-masters are given in a manuscript list or bill of the school, but the name of 'Mr. Antrobus' occurs three times in the list. Under Dr. George, there were in addition to the Lowermaster six Assistant masters, three in the Upper School, and three in the Lower School. This number remained the same under Dr. Cooke, but was increased by two in 1755, and again by two in 1760. The boarding-houses seem to have been still kept by Dames or Dominies, some of the latter being employed as private tutors or extra-masters in the school. The working-days in the week were divided as they are now, there being three regular working-days. Instead, however, of Tuesday, Thursday, and Saturday being half-holidays as at the present day, Tuesday was a whole holiday; on Thursday a half-holiday was granted by the Provost, provided that some boy had done a copy of verses good enough to be copied out on gilt-edged paper and presented to the Provost by noon on that day, when that boy was said to have been 'sent up for play.' On Saturday (and on Thursday, if no boy was sent up for play), there was a 'play-at-four,' when the first afternoon lesson was followed by chapel or prayers in school, and the boys were then free for the rest of the day. The actual work of tuition now began to be shared by the Assistant-masters in their tutorial capacity out of school, resulting in a considerable relaxation of the actual number of hours spent during the week in the schoolroom. The increase in the number of

133

the boys must have made it difficult even at that date to convey instruction to so many boys *en masse* with the limited staff and accommodation of the existing schoolrooms.

Saints' days, or red-letter days, were observed as whole holidays, and their vigils as half-holidays, and, what with anniversaries and court festivities, in many of which Eton shared, the Provost and Head-master must have found it sometimes difficult to ensure a regular routine of work. There were now three regular vacations in the year, one month's holidays at Christmas, beginning the second Monday in December, a fortnight at Easter from the Monday before Easter Sunday, and one month beginning the first Monday in August, at what was then known as Bartlemetide.

Greek had now become an important item in the curriculum of the upper forms, and, if the selection from the great writers seems a limited one, it must be remembered that the editions of the Greek classics were few and far between, and that the selections used in school, were for the most part prepared for the purpose of actual use in teaching, rather than for the sake of their literary value or for the display of learned or ornate scholarship. Homer, Virgil, Horace, and Terence remained the classical authors who were chiefly read *in extenso*, Lucian and Ovid in selections. For most of the other great classical writers recourse was had to the selections in the *Poetæ Græci*, or *Scriptores Romani*. In 1758, on the publication of Dr. John Burton's *Pentalogia*, the Upper boys were introduced to a Greek play in its complete form. Of the seventeen school-hours which the Upper forms attended during the week, seven were devoted to repetition and ten to construing. The boys in fifth form had to compose three Latin exercises during the week, two in verse, elegiac and lyric, and one in prose. The sixth form varied the lyrics with Greek iambics. The curriculum for the Remove was on a slightly lower plane and included Greek grammar and geography, the latter involving the drawing of a map out of school in addition to their other exercises. The fourth form had longer school hours, if easier authors to construe, such as Æsop and Caesar, while in the Lower School the work was confined to easy and elementary instruction in grammar and in Latin. The writing lessons, which figure in Malim's *Consuetudinarium*, were still kept up on holidays and half-holidays, but in addition to writing lessons, which were mainly confined to the younger boys, part of these hours were spent in the study of mathematics. To become 'compleat scholars,' the elder boys were supposed to get through a considerable course of reading in history and literature during their leisure hours. 'Trials' were customary when boys were removed from one form to another, both as a test of industry and capacity, and as a means of stirring up a feeling of emulation among the boys. Dancing and fencing each had a representative on the staff.

This system of education, elastic rather than lax, for it could be rendered more strict at any time, remained in force with but little variation until some fifty years ago. Other regulations, such as those for the Praepostors, who checked the attendance of boys in school and chapel, fetched their excuses if 'staying out' from their Dames, or in

135

Sixth Form presided at the execution of the boys sentenced to be flogged, remain much the same to the present day. In the days of the huge divisions of boys in Upper or Lower School, it was necessary to have a Praepostor in school to walk about and keep the boys quiet. College had its own system of discipline and hours for meals, prayers, and lock-up. Of the life and discipline in the boarding-houses, it is difficult to say much, for the arrangements were of a private nature between the parents and the Dame or Dominie who kept the house, and the College authorities did not interfere, except in the case of some breach of the regular school discipline. 'Absence' was called on half-holidays at two in the afternoon, on whole holidays at nine o'clock in the morning. In the summer 'absence' was called at six in the evening, except on whole school-days. The oppidans were locked up in their boarding-houses at six in the winter, and the Collegers after prayers in Lower School at eight, though in their case 'lock-up' was practically an hour earlier, as they had to assemble in the College-hall at seven for study. On Sundays both oppidans and Collegers attended chapel at ten and at three, and submitted to a pious discourse in Upper School previous to the afternoon service.

Up to the end of the eighteenth century Eton may be said to have held, almost unchallenged, the supremacy among the great public schools of the country, although the time was rapidly drawing near, when this supremacy was likely to be put severely to the test by the rapid advance and development of other schools.

Winchester, the mother of all public schools, Eton included, has throughout its history maintained a steady and dignified reserve, resting for support almost entirely upon itself. Few schools can point to such a calm and even existence, the very uneventfulness of its history proving the stability of William of Wykeham's foundation, and the sagacity and prescience of its founder. Closely linked and deeply indebted as Eton College was to Winchester at the outset, the histories of the two royal colleges took different roads, and, until the revival of the ancient intimacy through the game of cricket, the two Colleges interfered seldom in each other's affairs.

This was not the case elsewhere. As other schools came into existence, Eton was looked to as the chief place of education, from which teachers could be supplied. The first public school of importance to be founded after Winchester and Eton was the school founded in 1512 by Dean Colet in St. Paul's Churchyard. The first head of 'high' master appointed by Colet was William Lily, the famous grammarian. In 1517 a second master (surmaster), corresponding to the 'usher' at Eton, was appointed in the person of *John Rightwise* (1508), a scholar of Eton and King's, who married Lily's daughter, and succeeded him in 1522 as high master of St. Paul's school. The connection, apart from the history of St. Paul's school, is not unimportant. The first Latin grammar printed in England was published by John Anwykyll, Head-master of Magdalen School, Oxford, and printed at Oxford about 1481. Another was published about 1497 by John Holte of Magdalen College, Oxford, under the title of *Lac Puerorum*. This was issued, together with some similar small works, by John Stanbridge, second Head-master of Magdalen School, and supplemented by Robert Whittinton. Dean Colet himself compiled a short work, *Rudimenta Grammatices*, in 1510, for the use of his school. To this work Lily contributed a short Latin syntax, with the rules in English, which was afterwards revised at Colet's request by Erasmus, and published with the rules in Latin. Rightwise added to Lily's Latin syntax a short supplement of his own. Both the Stanbridge-Whittington and the Colet-Lily-Erasmus grammars were largely used in schools, and what has been called a 'bellum grammaticale' raged for some time between Lily and Whittington, which found vent in the satire, called *Antibossicon*, published by William Horman, Vice-Provost of Eton, in 1521. Lily's grammar, however, won the day, and in 1540 his and Colet's works were combined into a single grammar, enjoined by royal authority for use by boys throughout England. In 1548 a further proclamation to the same effect, issued by Edward VI., caused the grammar to be known as 'King Edward the Sixth's Latin Grammar.' This Latin grammar went through several editions, and was certainly used by Shakespeare at school, since he quoted it more than once. Eventually, after various revisions, it was recast in 1758, and issued apart at Eton, after which it was known as *The Eton Latin Grammar*. Some of the most familiar and most often quoted rules were among those retained from the original grammar of Lily and Rightwise. Other Etonians followed Rightwise as Head-master of St. Paul's School, from which many men of eminence issued in the sixteenth and seventeenth centuries.

There were other grammar schools founded about the same date, all of which came to Eton for Head-masters. *Richard Martindale* (1546) was master of the Mercers' School; *Richard Mulcaster* (1548), first of Merchant Taylors' School and then of St. Paul's; *Rodolph Waddington* (1548), of the Grey Friars' School. The great school at Westminster, founded by Henry VIII. in connection with the College in the Abbey, passed under the sway of Nicholas Udall, the ex-Head-master of Eton, in 1554. It was reconstituted and refounded by Elizabeth, who sought to link it with Trinity College, Cambridge, on the same lines as Eton was with King's, and one of its earliest Head-masters after its reform was an Etonian, *Thomas Browne* (1550). When Cardinal Wolsey founded his great school at Ipswich, about 1524, he selected an Etonian, *William Goulding* (1515), as Head-master. Goulding (or Goldwyne) later on returned to Eton, and was for two or three years Head-master there, from 1526 to 1529, after which he became a Fellow and Vice-Provost. Elsewhere in the provinces Etonians were in demand during the second half of the sixteenth century, Bury St. Edmunds, Chelmsford, Durham, Guildford, and others, all coming to Eton and King's for their Head-masters.

The accession of Queen Elizabeth to the throne was the signal for an outburst of activity in the educational world. Edward VI. had busied himself with converting the schools which existed in several important towns into properly organised and constituted grammar schools, but these had little influence except locally.

The reconstitution of Westminster in 1560, and the foundation of Merchant Taylors' School in 1561, was quickly followed by the foundation of Rugby School in 1567, and the reconstitution of Harrow School by John Lyon in 1571, both of which were to openly challenge the supremacy of Eton in public estimation.

Rugby School maintained a somewhat precarious existence for the first two hundred years of its career. It cannot be said to have taken its rank until as late as 1778, and its elevation was due to the efforts of two Etonians, former King's scholars and Fellows of King's College, *Thomas James* (1767), who was appointed Headmaster of Rugby School in 1778, and *James Chartres* (1772), who was appointed Second-master at the same time. With the history of Rugby School it is unnecessary to deal here, as it has been already ably dealt with in a previous volume of the series, wherein the debt owed by Rugby to Eton, in the person of Dr. James, is fully acknowledged and described. Suffice it to say that James introduced the Eton system of teaching and discipline into Rugby School with complete success so far as concerned the prosperity of the school, and that when he died a memorial tablet was erected in Rugby Chapel to commemorate his Head-mastership. Even the latest historian of Rugby School is constrained to admit that Dr. James was the real creator of Rugby as it now is, even more than his once famous successor in later days, Dr. Thomas Arnold. James was succeeded at Rugby by an Eton and Cambridge contemporary, *Henry Ingles* (1768), who carried on the Eton traditions on the same lines as his predecessor, but did not attain to anything like the same distinction in the ranks of head-masters. It may, perhaps, reflect back upon Eton with some credit that the famous Dr. Samuel Butler, Head-master of Shrewsbury School, was James's most successful pupil.

Harrow School, like Rugby, was slow in pushing its way to the front, and it was not until the nineteenth century that it began to show itself as the formidable rival to Eton, which it is at the present day. Towards the middle of the seventeenth century Harrow fell under the sway of a series of Eton Head-masters, all Collegers and King's men, which lasted for about one hundred and fifty years. The first was *William Horne* (1656), son of the Head-master of Eton, and for a time Usher there himself. He was the first man of mark to be Headmaster of Harrow. His successor was followed by *Thomas Bryan* (1677), who was in his turn, after a short interlude, succeeded by *Thomas Thackeray* (1711), great grandfather of the novelist, and formerly Assistant-master at Eton, a post which he resigned in consequence of his share in the famous 'Bangorian Controversy' between Dr. Snape, Head-master of Eton, and Bishop Hoadly of Bangor. Thackeray was a candidate for the Provostship of King's College, Cambridge, on the death of Dr. Snape, when he was defeated, after a hard fight, by Dr. George, the Head-master of Eton. Thackeray was succeeded by another Etonian, *Robert Carey Sumner* (1747), and Sumner in his turn by *Benjamin Heath* (1758), who was successful against the popular candidate, Dr. Samuel Parr, whose cause was adopted by the anti-Etonian party at Harrow. Heath was succeeded by his brother-in-law, Joseph Drury, whose sons, *Henry Joseph Thomas Drury* (1796) and Benjamin Heath Drury (1800)

141

continued a traditional connection with both Harrow and Eton far into the nineteenth century.

The history of Harrow School will be recounted in another volume of this series. It will be sufficient to admit here that the long series of Etonian Head-masters does not seem to have been of any special benefit to Harrow in the long run, and that it was not until Harrow had established a record and regime of its own that it came into the front rank of public schools. Even in more recent days, when a distinguished Eton and King's scholar, *James Edward Cowell Welldon*, was appointed Head-master of Harrow, it may be said that the ten years of his Head-mastership did more to make him a Harrovian than to introduce any element of Etonianism into the strictly individual character of Harrow School itself.

Amid the scandals of the court, the political corruption of Parliament, and the general coarseness and recklessness of polite society during the last quarter of the eighteenth century, the one figure which stands out prominent in its homely simplicity is that of the king, George III. At Windsor George III. always showed special favour to the Eton boys, and would recognise boys and speak to them, when walking on the terrace, reviving thereby memories of the pious founder, whose sad fate was, alas, to be imitated in him. Many pleasing tales are told of the king's love for Eton and his familiarity and pleasantry with the boys. The King's scholars he evidently liked to fancy were so called out of compliment to him, and although they had been so styled long before, George III. very probably ended by believing that they owed their name to him. Miss Burney narrates in her diary how the king and queen again went to hear speeches on Election Monday in 1787, and how they heard George Canning and 'Bobus' Smith deliver orations.

So deeply did Eton venerate the person of their kindly king that his birthday, the 4th of June, was appointed to be observed as a whole holiday. It does not seem that it was intended to mark this day as a permanent festival, but a custom once established is not easily dropped, and the anniversary has now become immovably fixed in popular favour as the principal festival in the Eton calendar.

VII

DR. GOODALL AND DR. KEATE

Dr. Heath resigned the Head-mastership of Eton in 1801, and retired to the congenial obscurity of a Fellowship. He was succeeded by one of the Assistant -masters, *Joseph Goodall* (1778), who had had as brilliant a career at Cambridge as was then possible for King's men. Dr. Goodall has left the reputation of having been very successful as Head-master of Eton. He was indeed in all appearances an ideal Head-master. Handsome and dignified in mien, he was courteous, hospitable, and not without a fitting supply of wit and humour. His discipline was enforced as mildly as possible. He was a prime favourite with the king. Dr. Goodall was only Head-master for eight years or so, since he succeeded Dr. Davies as Provost in 1809, a post which he occupied in dignified state for about thirty years.

Dr. Goodall was the strongest of conservatives. His whole life and soul was bound up in Eton, and every stone or pinnacle of the College was dear to his heart. To him the Eton system of education and living was the best possible, apart from it having been handed down by a tradition which it would be heretical to question. No reform, therefore, took place in school or College during Dr. Goodall's regime. Though the said regime was far from being inglorious and unsuccessful, and Eton waxed fat and well-liking under the sympathetic guidance of Dr.

Goodall, it yet may be compared to that of the *Grand Monarque* in France, who raised his country to an exalted eminence, but who not only made the Revolution possible, but bequeathed it to his successors as a certainty.

That Dr. Goodall was appreciated as a Head-master, at all events by the boys who worked immediately under him, is well shown by the tribute paid to him by one who was a sixth-form boy under him, and was destined to succeed eventually to the post of Head-master—Edward Craven Hawtrey. Hawtrey said that Goodall "had a peculiar talent of finding out and stirring up latent powers—powers of which, from snubbing and neglect, the possessor himself was wholly ignorant, and ready to give up all exertion in despair. Goodall caught at the first symptom of merit, gave it more than its due praise, but not more than the broken spirit required; and if he found responsive diligence, he took the earliest opportunity of rewarding it, and thereby making a character which might, by less kind management, have soon sunk into absolute and inconceivable nothingness."

Dr. Goodall, too, was fortunate in the boys whom he sent out into the world from Eton. Taking the Church first, the profession which comprised for long most of the scholarship of England, there came from Eton during the few years of Dr. Goodall's rule, in addition to the deaneries and canonries which formed the appanages of a territorial aristocracy, such distinguished churchmen as *John Lonsdale* (1806), Fellow of Eton and Bishop of Lichfield; *Henry Hart Milman*, Dean of St. Paul's; *Charles Richard Sumner*, Bishop of Winchester; *Christopher*

Benson, Master of the Temple; *Robert Buttock-Marsham*, Warden of Merton College; *Hugh Percy*, Bishop of Carlisle; and *Charles Lloyd*, Bishop of Oxford. In the history of Great Britain and the expansion of England, Etonians have always played a great part. Few can be said to have served their country abroad with greater distinction besides *Stratford Canning*, mentioned before, than *Edmund Law*, afterwards famous as Earl of Ellenborough and Governor-General of India, and *John George Lambton*, who earned undying fame as Earl of Durham and Governor-General of Canada. With India, too, are connected the names of *Sir Thomas Metcalfe*, Commissioner at Delhi at the outbreak of the Sepoy mutiny; *Sir Edward John Gambier*, Chief-Justice of Madras; *Sir Charles Grey*, Chief-Justice of Bengal. Under the head of judges came *John Patteson* (1808), and *John Taylor Coleridge*, united by friendship in College at Eton, and by other links between two eminently Etonian families; and also *Richard Budden Crowder*. In Parliament and polite society the names were afterwards well known of the *Hon. George Lamb*; *Henry Gally Knight*, antiquary, amateur, and author; *John Nicholas Fazakerley*; Nassau William Senior, the political economist; *George Warde Norman*, the banker and founder of a prolific Etonian progeny; and *Sir Denis Le Marchant*. Two *Dukes of Northumberland* in succession, the *Duke of Marlborough*, the *Duke of Leinster*, and the *Duke of Buckingham* showed in after life that they had learnt at Eton to utilise their high rank in the service of their country. In diplomacy may be noted, besides Stratford Canning, the names of *Sir Edward Cromwell* Disbrowe, *Edward James Dawkins*, *Sir*

146

Thomas Cartwright. Scanty as was the mathematical education at Eton in Dr. Goodall's days, he yet produced a senior wrangler in *Sir John George Shaw-Lefevre,* and a second wrangler in *Thomas Shawe Brandreth.* Other Etonians were more singular in their fates. *Thomas Gordon* was one of the chief of the band of Englishmen who, with Lord Byron, Trelawny, and others, threw in their lot with the Greeks in their attempt to shake off the despotism of Turkey. *Sir George Cathcart's* name is linked with the Crimean War. *Sir John Herschel* was sent by his father at Slough to Eton, but only remained there a few months, so that his senior wranglership and subsequent fame can hardly be credited to Eton. It was during Dr. Goodall's reign that *Percy Bysshe Shelley,* the poet of poets, passed his wayward will-of-the-wisp career at Eton. Lovers of sports and athletics will be pleased to dwell upon the names of *George Osbaldeston,* the famous cricketer and huntsman; of *Francis Jack Needham, Earl of Kilmorcy,* who for a bet rowed from Oxford to London in one day; and perhaps of *Sir John Duncan Bligh,* afterwards Minister at Hanover, who was one of the few Eton boys who was both in the Eleven and the Eight, and captain of the oppidans besides. At the close of his long career as Provost, Dr. Goodall could therefore point with satisfaction to the distinguished Etonians whose paths he had first assisted in training. In 1809, upon the death of Provost Davies, the Provostship was bestowed, as had become almost regular and customary, upon Dr. Goodall, who exchanged the subordinate if dignified office of Head-master for the luxury and ease of

147

the Provost's lodge, and the still more pleasing prospect of being able to check and criticise his successor's career.

Among the Assistant-masters appointed by Dr. Davies had been *John Keate*, an Eton and King's scholar of course, who, like Dr. Goodall, had won as much distinction at Cambridge as a King's man at that day could. Keate returned to Eton as Assistant-master in 1795, and in 1802 succeeded the court favourite. Dr. Langford, as Lowermaster. This position marked him easily out for the part of Head-master, as successor to Dr. Goodall. No greater contrast could well be imagined between any two persons than that between Dr. Goodall and his successor. Dr. Goodall was tall, comely, well-proportioned in limb, courtly in demeanour, careful and elegant in his dress. Dr. Keate was short, thick-set, red-haired, loud-voiced, with a cast of features which lent themselves easily to caricature. And yet the fame of Dr. Keate has overshadowed that of Dr. Goodall, much in the same way as that of the *Grand Monarque* was to be cast in the shade by the subsequent fame of Napoleon.

It was not only in appearance that Keate was a contrast to Goodall. His manner was harsh and savoured of dictatorship, rather than a constitutional *régime*. His ideas of discipline were severe and extreme, and far from pleasing to the boys under him. As a boy wrote in 1810, "Keate will not bear being trifled with half so well as Goodall, and will deal his blows about with a heavy hand should they force him to extremities." Keate's indomitable pluck and spirit, however, enabled him to ride safely over the dangers which beset him during his Head-mastership.

Many are the tales, anecdotes, and legends which have grown up and become encrusted round the name of Dr. Keate. Many of them are well known, almost historical, and need not be repeated in a sketch of these abridged dimensions. The curious will find them for the most part recorded in Mr. Lucas Collins's *Etoniana*, or in Sir H. C. Maxwell-Lyte's *History of Eton College*. The days of Dr. Keate, moreover, are not so far removed from the present as to prevent even the living generations of Etonians from hearing good stores of anecdotes about Dr. Keate from their fathers or grandfathers. The greater number of these anecdotes relate to Keate's frequent and effective use of the birch-rod to enforce his discipline, and in this line he has become as historical as the 'plagosus Orbilius' who troubled the early years of Horace.

The use of the birch had been a powerful ingredient throughout the history of Eton as a means of imparting knowledge and preserving discipline. As early as 1500 John Stanbridge, the grammarian of Magdalen School, Oxford (mentioned in the previous chapter), is depicted in an old woodcut, as inculcating the Latin grammar with the help of the birch. Tusser the poet alludes to its frequent use in the often-quoted lines:—

> From Powles I went, to Aeton seat
> To learne straightwayes the Latin phraise,
> Where fiftie-three stripes given to mee
> At once I had

149

For faut but small or none at all,

It came to passe thus beat I was;

See Udall, see, the mercy of thee

To mee, poor lad.

Allusion has also been made to the frequency of floggings under Dr. Malim, and to the fact of some boys having run away from Eton to avoid it, having proved the theme of Roger Ascham's famous treatise, *The Scholemaster*. In this treatise Sir Richard Sackville, although first-cousin to Queen Anne Boleyn, regrets that "A fond schoolmaster, before he was fullie fourteene years olde, drove him with feare of beating from all love of learning."

A similar apprehension deprived Eton of the honour of educating John Evelyn, the celebrated antiquary and diarist, who says of himself that "My father would willingly have weaned me from my fondness of my too indulgent grandmother, intending to have placed me at Eaton; but I was so terrified at the report of the severe discipline there, that I was sent back to Lewes, which perverseness of mine I have since a thousand times deplored.", The resignation of Dr. Rosewell, the Headmaster in 1682, is reputed to have been due to his remorse at thinking that the death of one of the boys had been due to excessive flogging; but this has not been proved. After the famous rebellion of the boys and secession to Maidenhead under Dr. Foster, it is recorded that the parents of some of the leading boys in the greatest families compelled their sons to return for the inevitable flogging before they were allowed to leave the school. Dr.

Davies, when Head-master, seems to have used the birch plentifully, and when a kind of rebellion took place in his day, the first action of the boys was to wreak their vengeance upon the block upon which so many of them had knelt for execution.

It is obvious, therefore, that Dr. Keate, in governing by the birch, was creating no new precedent in the history of the school. It may, however, be alleged quite fairly that Dr. Keate carried the practice too far. Boys were flogged for the slightest offence in or out of school. It was even possible for a boy to be flogged three times in one day. Dr. Keate did not pause to listen to reason, and the birch rose and fell on more than one occasion before an innocent boy had time to plead his guiltlessness or prove or disprove his identity.

But if Dr. Keate is to be blamed for his frequent use of the birch, whereby all the same he has perhaps gained immortality, he was to a certain extent justified by the difficulties under which he laboured in making the school discipline effective. Although the numbers of the school showed a steady tendency to increase, the number of Assistant-masters and of classrooms remained practically stationary. Upper School, Lower School, and one or two poky little schoolrooms under Long Chamber or Upper School, were all the classrooms in which some six hundred boys had to be accommodated. The Head-master himself had upwards of one hundred and seventy boys in his division, separated only from the next division of equal dimensions by a curtain drawn across Upper School. It is small wonder that, with a division of this size, even so great a potentate as the Headmaster, though, as his pupil,

Kinglake the historian, has described, he had within his diminutive form the 'pluck of ten battalions,' should not unfrequently fail to keep order. Yet in spite of Dr. Keate's small failings in temper and dignity, in spite of his frequent and vigorous use of the birch, the reputation of Eton grew steadily under his rule. As the author of Etoniana has well said, Dr. Keate "was a great scholar, an elegant poet, a capital teacher; and we must not hold lightly the man who has flogged half the ministers, secretaries, bishops, generals, and dukes of the present century."

For twenty-five years Dr. Keate thundered and brandished his shaggy eyebrows at the farther desk in Upper School, or awaited his many victims in the neighbouring room. Those who judge of the success of a school by the amount of aristocratic pupils which it attracts, will be interested in the fact that Dr. Keate numbered among his pupils sixteen dukes, fifteen marquesses, more than fifty earls, with viscounts, barons, and baronets to be reckoned by the dozen. Among Etonian statesmen, who were at Eton under Dr. Keate, the most distinguished were *Edward, fourteenth Earl of Derby* and *William Ewart Gladstone*, both Prime Ministers, scholars, and lovers of the Homeric poems. Foreign affairs were administered for many years by Etonians in the persons of the *Earl of Malmesbury, Earl Granville*, and *Sir Stafford Northcote*, afterwards Earl of Iddesleigh, as they have been in these later days by the Marquess of Salisbury and the Earl of Rosebery. The Speaker's chair in the House of Commons was filled successively by Etonians, *John Evelyn Denison* (Viscount Ossington) in 1857, *Henry Brand*

(Viscount Hampden) in 1872, and *Arthur Wellesley Peel* (Viscount Peel) in 1884. The *Earl of Lincoln*, as Duke of Newcastle, became Chief Secretary for Ireland and Secretary of State for War at the outbreak of the Crimean War. *Sir George Cornewall Lewis*, Bart., who became Chancellor of the Exchequer, was accounted the soundest intellect and most learned man of his age. *Sir Charles Wood* (Viscount Halifax), *Sir John Pakington* (formerly Russell, and afterwards Lord Hampton), and *Sir John Young* (afterwards Lord Lisgar), were prominent politicians in their day; and of minor importance in politics were *Sir Thomas Fremantle* (Lord Cottesloe), *Colonel Beresford*, the *Earl of Carlisle*, *Spencer Walpole, Henry Tufnell, Sir Frederick Rogers* (afterwards Lord Blachford), *William Cowper* (Lord Mount-Temple), *Lord Redesdale*, and *Edward Ellice*, One Etonian, *Edmond Beales*, a well-known democratic agitator, gained unexpected notoriety at the time of the destruction of the railings round Hyde Park in July 1866.

The connection of Eton with India was kept up by *Charles, Earl Canning*, the first Viceroy, and his successor, *James Bruce, eighth Earl of Elgin*, while a large share in the government of India was contributed by *Sir John Peter Grant, Lord Elphinstone, Sir Henry Conyngham Montgomery, Lord Harris*, and *Sir John William Kaye*. The legal history of India comprised *Sir James W. Colvile, Sir Edward Shepherd Creasy* (1830), and *William Ritchie*, while one word is due to a Colleger, *Henry S. Polehampton*, who died while ministering to the religion of the unfortunate persons besieged in Lucknow. In the ranks of diplomacy were found *Sir Woodbine Parish, Lord Howard de Walden, Sir George Hamilton Seymour, Sir Ralph Abercromby, Earl Cowley, Lord Stuart de Decies, Sir Charles Murray, Sir Edward Harris, Sir John Crampton, Sir Henry Elliot,* and *Sir Henry G. Howard.* To the Church Eton sent Richard Durnford, Bishop of Chichester; *Walter Kerr Hamilton,* Bishop of Salisbury; *Edward Harold Browne,* Bishop of Winchester; *John Fielder Mackamess,* Bishop of Oxford; *John Charles Ryle,* Bishop of Liverpool. *Edward Bouverie* Pusey is one of the great names of the so-called Oxford movement. *Henry Michell Wagner* (1811) became the well-known clergyman at Brighton. The brothers *Richard William Jelf* and *William Edward Jelf* were well known in after life, the former as Principal of King's College, London, the latter as a Greek scholar and grammarian. *William Wigan Harvey* (1828), became famous as the hero of the Ewelme rectory appointment. Another family of brothers, *William Selwyn,* Lady Margaret Professor of Divinity at Cambridge; *George Augustus Selwyn,* Primate of New Zealand, and Bishop of Lichfield; and *Sir Charles Jasper Selwyn,* Lord Justice of Appeal, have left a name honoured in the annals of Eton. Another family of brothers, the Denisons, included not only the Speaker of the House of Commons, but *Edward Denison,* Bishop of Salisbury; *George Anthony Denison,* the well-known militant Archdeacon of Taunton; and *Sir William Thomas Denison,* Governor of Van Diemen's Land and New South Wales, and afterwards of Madras. Among lawyers educated under Dr. Keate, in addition to Charles J. Selwyn, were *Sir Anthony Cleasby,* who attained to the Bench, as did also *Sir George Mellish,* whose biographer says that "at school he was a good sculler, but neither an athlete nor a diligent scholar." *Sir John Wickens*, afterwards Vice-Chancellor, was of the highest repute as a lawyer, while *Sir Colin Blackburn* became one of the greatest lawyers of his time, and ended his days as a Lord of Appeal, with a peerage. *James Robert Hope-Scott* had so distinguished a career at the parliamentary bar, that a great future was predicted, and he was reputed even by so great an authority as Mr. Gladstone, to be "the most winning person of his day"; ill-health and domestic sorrow brought his life to a premature close. *Sir John Duke Coleridge* followed his father on to the Bench, and outstripped him by becoming Lord Chief-Justice of England. *Edmund Beckett-Denison*, lawyer and banker, still remains as Baron Grimthorpe, noted for a love of controversy and a weakness for the restoration of ancient buildings. *John Smith Mansfield* long presided with urbanity at the Marlbourgh Street Police Court.

Among the Etonians of Keate's day, who obtained fame in divers walks of life, the most familiar names are those of the poets *John Moultrie* and *Winthrop Mackworth Praed*, with such minor bards as *Frederick Tennyson* (brother of the Poet-Laureate, and as a poet overshadowed by his brother's fame), *Sir Francis Hastings Doyle*, and *William Sidney Walker*, the hero of bullying, akin to that which befell Shelley, but in spite of that a poet, scholar, and Etonian at heart; *Captain Gronow*, the chronicler of fashion, and *Edward Ball-Hughes*, the dandy; *Alexander William Kinglake*, the historian of the Crimean

155

War, and *Arthur Henry Hallam*, the much-lamented friend of Tennyson and Gladstone, like Lycidas "dead ere his prime"; *Sir George Kettilby Rickards,* the political economist, and *Charles Badham*, the greatest Greek scholar of his day, a worthy successor of Porson in the annals of Eton; *John Heneage Jesse*, the biographer; *Charles Duke Yonge* (1830), the historian, and *Matthew James Higgins* (Jacob Omnium), the journalist and pamphleteer; *Sir Arthur Helps*, Clerk of the Privy Council and essayist; *Capel Lofft* (1824), scholar and poet, whose father, Capel Lofil, a well-known miscellaneous writer, had also been at Eton; *George John Whyte-Melville*, the popular novelist and sportsman; *Sir Arthur Hodgson*, one of the makers of Queensland in Australia, and Guardian of Shakespeare's home at Stratford-on-Avon; *Robert Gordon Latham*, the learned ethnologist; *Thomas Gambier Parry*, the cultivated and ingenious artist; *Sir John Bennet Lawes*, the agriculturist; *Sir Thomas Myddelton Biddulph*, the trusted and confidential friend of Her Majesty, Queen Victoria. *Sir James Scarlett*, the leader of the heavy cavalry brigade at Balaclava; *General Anson*, commander of the troops in India at the outbreak of the Mutiny; and *Sir John Michel*, the hero of the Rajputana and China campaigns, were among the most distinguished of the many Etonians who entered the army, many of whom died for their country in the Crimea, in India, and elsewhere, wherever duty called them. A special bond of interest links together Mr. Gladstone with his two brothers, *Sir Thomas Gladstone*, Bart., and *Robertson Gladstone*, and his two future brothers-in-law. *Sir Stephen Glynne*, Bart., and *George, Lord Lyttelton*. The frequent occurrence of

156

the names of banking families—*Smith, Drummond, Goslings Lubbock, Scott, Cox, Hammersley, Farquhar, Barnett,* and others—denotes a firm financial basis for the prosperity of the school.

One of the most remarkable among Keate's pupils was *Charles Kean,* the famous actor. When his father, Edmund Kean, made his great success as 'Shylock' at Drury Lane, he hurried home to his wife, and said, "Mary, you shall ride in your carriage, and you, Charley, shall be an Eton boy." And an Eton boy Charles Kean became, so much so, that at the height of his success the school made him a presentation of a piece of silver plate.

The mere enumeration of these names is sufficient to show the high level in general estimation reached by the school under Keate, and yet there were crying abuses in teaching, discipline, food, comfort, &c., which Keate was unable or unwilling to combat, and which accounted probably for a considerable falling off in the numbers of the school during the last few years of his Headmastership. Such reforms as he wished to initiate were negatived by the all-powerful Provost, Dr. Goodall, who treated such suggestions in somewhat the same spirit as a Home Rule Bill might be treated in these days by the House of Lords. Truly it was Keate's indomitable pluck which maintained him successfully to the last, so that when he retired in 1834 he was more popular than when he entered on his post, and from the congenial seclusion of a country living he was able to observe and encourage the efforts of his successor to introduce some of the reforms for which his heart must have often yearned.

A side-light on Eton under Dr. Keate, not of the most favourable description, is thrown by Captain Gronow in his *Reminiscences*. Keate, after his retirement, paid a visit to the Continent, and was spied at Paris by some old Etonians, a smart set, including Gronow. They forthwith invited the Doctor to dinner and regaled him much to his satisfaction. Then, as Gronow relates, "after drinking his health, as the bottle passed gaily round, we took the opportunity of giving him a little innocent chaff, reminding him of his heavy hand and arbitrary manner of proceeding. We told him how two of his masters, Drury and Knapp, continued without his knowledge to go up to London every Saturday to dine with Arnold and Kean at Drury Lane. We spoke of Sumner's flirtation with the fair Martha at Spier's, of Mike Fitzgerald tripping up Plumtree the Master on his way to six o'clock school, of Cornwall's fight with the bargee, of Lumley's poaching in Windsor Park, of our constant suppers at the Christopher, of our getting out at night, of our tandem driving, and many other little episodes to show that his Argus eyes were not always open. The Doctor took our jokes in good part, and in his turn told us that, if he had a regret, it was that he had not flogged us a good deal more; but he felt certain that the discipline had done us a great deal of good."

Gronow's statements are not to be accepted without care, but the above may be taken generally as a fair description of Eton discipline. Although the Sumner mentioned above was *John Bird Sumner*, afterwards Archbishop of Canterbury, his supposed flirtation with the fair Martha at the sock-shop becomes more intelligible, when Gronow

158

narrates that the poet Shelley, with whom Gronow was intimate at Eton and afterwards, shortly before his death not only spoke of Eton with warmth and affection, but hankered for "some of the excellent brown bread and butter we used to get at Spier's," adding, "Gronow, do you remember the beautiful Martha, the Hebe of Spiers? She was the loveliest girl I ever saw, and I loved her to distraction." Truly a Hebe of the first quality must Martha have been to have been courted by such a poet and also by a future archbishop. *Henry Hartopp Knapp*, the Master referred to, was notoriously addicted to theatricals and a friend of the principal actors in London. A former pupil, defending him (in the Appendix to *Etoniana*) yet cannot refrain from recalling "the occasional rattle up to London with him—(the phaeton waiting in the Slough Road)— the Juliet—the Sir Giles—the Bedford—the broiled fowl and mushroom sauce—the Hounslow posters—and the return in time for six-o'clock lesson—*O nodes cœnœque Deûm.*" *Benjamin Heath Drury*, the bearer of a name honoured among the teachers at Eton and Harrow, sacrificed the brilliancy of his scholarship to a similar weakness. When there were but nine masters to 600 boys, and two of the staff indulged in such escapades, it is not surprising that Dr. Keate found discipline hard to maintain. The staff was a good one, but inadequate, although besides Sumner ('Crumpety' Sumner, as the boys called him), he was assisted by such well-known Eton figures as *Edward Craven Hawtrey, George Rowney Green, George John Dupnis, Richard Okes* (afterwards Lower-master and Provost of King's), *James Chapman* (afterwards Bishop of Colombo), *John Wilder*, and *Edward Coleridge*. Of these only

159

two, Hawtrey and Coleridge, were really alive to the necessity for reform.

Dr. Keate was succeeded as Head-master in 1834 by Edward Craven Hawtrey. Hawtrey was a member of a family that had been connected with Eton for more than two hundred years. His father was a Fellow of Eton and Vicar of Burnham, and two of his aunts had Dames' houses at Eton. His mother was sister of a former Head-master, Dr. Foster, whose memory Hawtrey always treated with the greatest respect. He entered Eton at the age of ten, and was distinguished for his scholarship at Eton and Cambridge. He was appointed an Assistant-master at Eton in 1814, and by degrees made his house the most fashionable and sought after in the school. During this period he lived in the old house in Weston's Yard, built and formerly occupied by Sir Henry Savile. Dr. Keate had resided in the large house at the farther end of the lane, which has ever since borne his name. Hawtrey, however, decided to remain where he was, and his house maintained for half a century or more the dignity of being the Head-master's residence.

VIII

DR. HODGSON AND DR. HAWTREY

The years immediately preceding the appointment of Dr. Hawtrey to the Head-mastership of Eton had been marked by a widespread and irrepressible desire throughout England for reform in every department of the state. The 'Condition of England' was made the subject of searching inquiry. The famous Reform Bill, finally passed in 1832 by the Etonian Prime Minister, Earl Grey, was only the outward and visible sign of the extreme pressure for reform that was felt by every class of society. Earl Grey's Bill for the reform of the franchise was but a moderate innovation compared to the more sweeping changes, to which the country agreed with complacency some fifty years later. The effect, however, was vast and ever-widening in its scope, like to the unbarring of a sluice-gate, and the gradual percolation of the dammed-up waters over a soil that showed signs of sterilisation. To put it shortly, the Reform Bill destroyed the monopoly of power held by the aristocratic and territorial classes, and admitted to an equal, if not a preponderating, share those classes which the rapid progress of trade and commerce had been gradually building up into a governing force in the land. The aristocracy, whose privileges were thus threatened, was fully justified in their resistance, tooth and nail, to the spirit of reform, although the wiser heads among them perceived that the impending changes were not a revolution brought about by tyranny, oppression, rapacity on one side and starvation and despair on the other, as in France, but by the gradual movement of the laws of nature, and the necessary expansion of a nation rapidly increasing in intelligence and prosperity. It is significant of the storm and stress of the time that the greatest reforms should have been brought about by aristocrats, who in these days might have been called Radicals, like Earl Grey and Lord John Russell, and representatives of the commercial middle class, like Sir Robert Peel and William Ewart Gladstone, who began their political careers as strong Conservatives.

It was not likely that while the spirit of reform was so strongly impregnating society, when neither Crown nor Church escaped criticism, that so strong a fortress of aristocratic Conservatism as Eton should remain unchallenged by the foe. The press was rapidly becoming a potent factor in social as well as political life, and its increasing cheapness and the improved facilities of circulation made it easy for the world at large to pry into the most sequestered nests of supposed abuses.

The defects in Eton teaching and discipline, not so much lamented as endured by the school, were sheltered behind the sacred and inviolable duties assumed by the Provost and Fellows of observing to the extreme letter the statutes drawn up by the founder four hundred years before. As early as 1818 a Royal Commission had been obtained by Lord Brougham, in his capacity as educational reformer and general iconoclast, nominally to inquire into the misuse of charities, into which an inquiry into Eton and Winchester had been introduced. The attack had been warded off by the general conservatism of Lord Chancellor Eldon and Sir Robert Peel some twenty years or more later. Another gun was fired by 'A Parent' in 'Some Remarks on the present Studies and Management of Eton School,' a pamphlet which quickly ran through several editions. Replies followed, and the *Quarterly Review* for August 1834 summed up the situation. Parents were alarmed, and the numbers in the school began to decline, falling in 1836 as low as 444. Dr. Keate, though inclined to reform, was not fresh or active enough to combat the inflexible attitude of the Provost. Dr. Hawtrey saw his opportunities, but had to wait for them, until the death of Provost Goodall on March 25, 1840.

No person could help admitting that the attitude taken up by Dr. Goodall was in many ways disadvantageous to the school. Yet it is not difficult to feel some sympathy with his view. To him and to his assistant-Fellows Eton College was a sacred institution, entrusted to their care, with which they had no right to interfere. The inner working or economy of the College was a mystery known only to the Provost and Fellows, as sacrosanct, it might be said, as the worship of Isis in ancient Egypt. Four hundred years had seen the College and the school advancing steadily in fame and prosperity. Most of the greatest names in English history had been connected with the school, and what was good enough for a Walpole or a Fox, a Wellesley or a Canning not unnaturally seemed likely to be good enough for their successors. Its defects were as privileged as those of the Crown, the Church, or the

163

Houses of Parliament. To allow the Head-master to initiate reforms in the school, would be to abnegate the duties laid upon the Provost by the statutes of the Founder. Secure, therefore, in the inviolable dignity of his post, Dr. Goodall returned an almost papal *Non Possumus* to the ever-increasing clamour for reform. No person ever loved Eton better than Dr. Goodall, or filled the Head-master's or Provost's chair with greater dignity. But, as has been said before, it was the dignity of the *Grand Monarque*, and if he foresaw, he was determined to do nothing to forestall the impending revolution.

Many old Etonians expected that Dr. Keate would be called from his retirement to fill the post of Provost, vacated by Dr. Goodall's death. He probably expected it himself. Lord Melbourne, an old Etonian, was then Prime Minister, and he at first seemed inclined to assert the accustomed privilege of the Crown and nominate a scholarly aristocrat, the *Hon. William Herbert* (afterwards Dean of Manchester), an old oppidan friend of his own. This being, however, directly contrary to the statutes, which enjoined that the Provost should have been educated on the Foundation at Eton or at King's Lord Melbourne, to the surprise of most people, nominated the Rev. Francis Hodgson, then Archdeacon of Derby, who had been a Fellow and tutor of King's, and for a few months in 1806 an Assistant-master at Eton. Dr. Hodgson was, however, not a Doctor of Divinity. This impediment afforded the Fellows an opportunity for exercising their constitutional right of election, and in defiance of the royal mandate, they proceeded themselves to elect one of their number, John Lonsdale, to be Provost. Queen Victoria, however, acting under the advice of Lord Melbourne, insisted upon the right of the Crown to nominate Dr. Hodgson, who had been quickly admitted to the requisite degree. Lonsdale therefore, rather than court the royal displeasure for the College, declined his nomination, and the Fellows submitted to the royal mandate.

Dr. Hodgson was chiefly known to the public as a writer of verse, and an intimate friend and correspondent of Lord Byron. This was perhaps sufficient to prejudice him in the eyes of many persons, whose estimate of Byron's genius had been warped by the greedy gossip which had battened on the scandals of Byron's private life. Dr. Hodgson, however, quite disappointed the best wishes of his enemies, and proved one of the best friends that Eton ever had. He came into his post with a mind trained and refined by contact with the outer world, without being steeped in the prejudices and traditions which not unnaturally encrusted the life of any one, whose sole progress in the world was that of Eton Colleger, scholar of King's, Assistant-master, Head-master, and Provost of Eton. His love for Eton was not less than that of Dr. Goodall, and it is well known, that he did not accept the post until he was assured that there was no chance of it being offered to his old tutor. Dr. Keate. The new Provost found at his hand a Head-master ready and yearning for reform. He was sagacious enough to see that much harm and little profit had accrued to the College and school by the assumption that the Headmaster was little more than an upper servant of the Provost and Fellows. It was quite clear that the College and the school were fast becoming distinct organisms and entities, and that,

165

without relinquishing any rights of government, it was easy for the Provost to confine his actual sphere of authority to the precincts of the College, and to delegate to the Head-master almost supreme authority in all matters relating to the discipline and teaching of the school. The condition of life endured by Collegers on the Foundation had become a crying scandal. Provost Hodgson therefore directed his whole attention to reform in this direction, and the Headmaster, Dr. Hawtrey, joyfully accepted the license to introduce the most pressing reforms necessary in the school outside.

One of the first and most salutary reforms introduced by Dr. Hawtrey was perhaps unconscious on his part. It lay in his treating the boys as gentlemen, and not driving or dragooning them as slaves, as Dr. Keate had done. It was his desire to encourage boys to work, and in view of this he added numbers of inducements and temptations to work by increasing the small list of possible distinctions that an Eton boy could gain. He at once abandoned the attempt, so heroically maintained by his predecessor, to teach alone about two hundred boys of the Fifth Form from the desk at the northern end of Upper School. He divided the Fifth Form into divisions, similar to those which already existed in the Remove and Lower School, and withdrew into the neighbouring library with the Sixth Form, and the first six Collegers and first six oppidans in the Fifth Form, the latter twelve being henceforth known as 'Liberty.' This room, which in the time of Dr. Keate was almost solely dedicated to the cult of the birch, Hawtrey decorated with some views of Athens, copies of the Parthenon frieze, and other archaeological objects, intended to afford pleasant mental recreation. Abandoning the attempt to teach in person to a third of the school the meaning of τύπτω in both its active and its passive senses, he devoted his attention to a real attempt to make good scholars of the first thirty-two boys in the school. Besides a better distribution of the Assistant-masters, he increased their numbers, and always did his best to be on friendly and confidential terms with his colleagues. He introduced new editions of the classics in place of the almost obsolete 'Poetœ Grœci' 'and 'Scriptores Romani,' which had been in use for centuries. He introduced a system of School Trials, which were a real test of a boy's industry and capacity, and enabled a promising boy to push his way to the front.

Dr. Hawtrey's most serious achievement was the introduction of the study of mathematics as part of the *curriculum* in the school. Previous to his time mathematics had been taught, or rather had been supposed to have been taught, in the school by one Major Hexter, who had inherited the monopoly of teaching writing and mathematics in the school. This monopoly Dr. Hawtrey was unable to disturb, except by buying out Hexter at a cost which was out of the question, so invulnerable was a time-vested interest at Eton in those days. He, however, was determined to amend matters, and after inviting *William Fuller Boteler,* a former oppidan at Eton, and thirteenth wrangler at Cambridge in 1833, who declined the post, he persuaded his cousin, the Rev. Stephen Hawtrey, to accept the post of mathematical master at Eton. Stephen Hawtrey erected at his own expense a circular building, containing a lecture-theatre, at the end of Keate's Lane. Neither

Hawtrey, however, was powerful enough to get mathematics introduced into the regular *curriculum*. It still remained an *extra*, occupying not more than three hours a week, with a little work thrown in to be done out of school time. Mr. Stephen Hawtrey's assistants were not placed on the regular staff, but only as assistants in his school, employed and paid by himself. Various other inducements were, however, offered to boys studying mathematics. In 1837 a prize was instituted by the Assistant-masters for proficiency in mathematics, and a second prize offered by the mathematical masters. The Tomline prize was founded in 1837, and nine years later was won by a boy, *Norman Macleod Ferrers*, who was senior wrangler at Cambridge, and is at the present day Master of Caius College. An attempt was made in 1849 to introduce the study of physical science, lectures being inaugurated in chemistry and astronomy by competent professors, and even on comparative anatomy. The same fate befell modern languages. French had been taught in the school for many years, but only as an extra out of play hours. A German master appears in the list of extra masters for 1831, but appears to have been as little employed as the drawing-master, the fencing-master, or the dancing-master, whose names remained on the list, some of them as late as 1860. In 1824 there is included in the list of extra masters a teacher of Italian and Spanish. A real incentive, however, to the study of modern languages was given by the foundation of three prizes for French, German, and Italian, given by H.R.H. the Prince Consort. French, German, and Italian were, however, even when the first language passed into the hands of the family of Tarver, treated for many years to come almost as *objets de luxe*. Eton scholarship had received a very great impetus from the foundation of the Newcastle Scholarship by the Duke of Newcastle in 1829. Previous to this the only prizes of this sort were those founded to assist superannuated Collegers, who were unable through age to proceed in the regular course to King's College, Cambridge. All other chances of distinction depended solely on a boy's skill in doing Greek and Latin verses. Dr. Hawtrey founded in addition an English Essay Prize, to encourage the study of English literature and history. Another drastic reform was carried out when the Head-master decided that all boys in future were to be entrusted to a tutor under the ordinary school regulations. Private tutors were thus abolished, except in the cases of a few sons of peers, who were allowed to have them in addition to their regulation tutor, the private tutor being responsible to the parents and not to the Head-master. It must be noted that in carrying out these reforms, certainly the earlier ones, Dr. Hawtrey consulted Dr. Keate, who informed him that he would not have had the courage to do them himself, but that he highly approved of them, and hoped that Dr. Hawtrey would get the fullest credit for them.

In most of them the Head-master obtained a free hand from the new Provost, Dr. Hodgson. On one point, however, the Provost was obdurate, which was when Hawtrey wished to abolish the necessity of filling up each vacant post among the Assistant-masters from Fellows or scholars of King's College, Cambridge. Only exhaustion of material had enabled Dr. Keate to appoint as Masters *Edward Coleridge* and *E. H. Pickering*, who had not been scholars of King's. Dr. Hawtrey wanted to appoint *Goldwin Smith,* one of the most famous Eton scholars at Oxford, and since the famous historian. The Provost, however, would not yield, and the opportunity was lost

Provost Hodgson was, however, at the same time engaged on important reforms in the internal life of the boys on the Foundation. The life of a Colleger, or 'tug'(*togatus*), had changed little for the better since the days of the pious Founder. Indeed it might be said to have changed for the worse, inasmuch as the arrangements made by Henry VI. were amply sufficient for the ideas and requirements of his age, but were singularly out of date, and it would have been thought unendurable, at the beginning of the nineteenth century. Up to the end of the eighteenth century Long Chamber was the dormitory for fifty-two of the King's scholars. Three small rooms were subsequently added, one known as Lower Chamber, on the ground floor, the other two known as Upper Carter's and Lower Carter's, being apparently part of the Lower-Master's rooms, surrendered or let for the purpose by the Lower-Master of that name. The beds, plain and wooden, were arranged in rows along the walls of the chamber. Each boy had a bureau, but chairs and tables were few and far between. Coverlets, with the arms of the founder and the queen, were given by Provost Bill and one of the Fellows, Matthew Page, in the reign of Elizabeth. In or about 1735, William, Duke of Cumberland, gave a set of handsome green rugs to the College, which were laid out on the beds on Election Saturday, on which occasion the floors received a temporary polish by the rough and ready process of rug-riding. The arrangements for ablution were of the scantiest, and almost wholly inaccessible to the smaller boys. The only washhand-stand for them was the pump in Weston's Yard. The sanitary arrangements would be a disgrace to a temporary barrack at the present day. Dinner and supper were the only meals provided by the College, mutton being the only meat, to which on Sundays plum-pudding was added, and thin beer the only drink. On certain occasions the Collegers were allowed refreshment in College hall at three o'clock, known as 'Bever.' Breakfast and tea were not provided, and most Collegers hired rooms "up town" in which they could wash, have their breakfast and tea, and obtain a little privacy for work. The only clothes supplied was a stuff gown apiece. The College gates were locked every night at eight o'clock throughout the year, but as the schoolyard gate was never shut, exercises and food for supper were handed in usually through the windows in Lower Chamber. Within College the Sixth Form reigned supreme, the Head-master and Lower Master having ceased to reside in College. It is not surprising that the smaller boys, when brought in close contact with those older and stronger than they, were subjected to a regular course of bullying, and fagging in College would perhaps have caused surprise even to a slave-driver in a West Indian plantation. The smaller boys had many of the discomforts and degradations of a charity school, which is sufficient to account for the position of inferiority which they occupied in the opinion of their more fortunate comrades, the oppidans. Reminiscences of the joys and discomforts of College life are to be found in various books by old

171

Etonians. In one of the most recent, *Eton in the Forties*, the author, Arthur Duke Coleridge, *togatorum togatissimus*, endeavours to make out that, rough as a small Colleger's life might be, he still managed "to snatch a fearful joy"; but allowance must be made for an enthusiast. The reminiscences of an 'Old Colleger' tell the same tale.

The election, too, of King's scholars, so elaborately sketched out by the founder, had become a mere farce. The old solemnities were observed. The Provost of King's drove up in his yellow coach, accompanied by two examiners or *posers*, and was met at the College gate by his brother of Eton in a fraternal embrace, while the captain of the school welcomed him with a Latin oration. They were lodged in the chambers between the Provost's lodge and the hall, where linen sheets, at first an extraordinary luxury, were provided for them. The munificent sum of five shillings was "distributed among them" for their trouble. It is evident that the posers derived some material benefit from this, for it is recorded that in 1562 Matthew Chalfont of King's, "because he might not be Poser, forsook the College and died miserably." The examination of candidates became a mere form, and the electors really nominated the candidates in the order of their seniority. Preference was naturally given to the sons of Fellows or Masters, or other persons nearly connected with the College, so that the whole Foundation became a private preserve. A curious custom prevailed in more recent days, whereby each poser adopted a Collier as his 'child' and gave him two guineas. Each 'child' in his turn adopted a small Colleger as 'grandchild,' and gave him five shillings. Posers, children,

172

and grandchildren then all partook of a hearty breakfast in the College hall, provided by the College gardener, the expense being defrayed by the 'children.' It may be supposed that the 'children' and 'grandchildren' were not without preferential claims, when the elections to King's were in progress.

With all these drawbacks and hardships it is not surprising that the numbers on the Foundation were seldom complete, sometimes barely half so, and the boys, *liberalis ingenii et egregiæ indolis*, who every year were publicly invited to compete, were often conspicuous by their absence.

The King's scholars, moreover, proceeded to King's College, Cambridge, by seniority in regular rotation, and not by competition. The number of vacancies was liable to vary from none to eight, and a Colleger might unexpectedly find himself superannuated, and obliged to find a home elsewhere in one or other of the Universities. The first step taken by Provost Hodgson was to increase the accommodation in College. A committee was appointed under the chairmanship of Lord Lyttelton to raise funds, and in June 1844 the foundation-stone of a new wing on the site of the College stable in Weston's Yard was laid by the Prince Consort. In this wing, completed in 1846, forty-nine Collegers could be accommodated with separate rooms, while the Long Chamber was partially divided off into cubicles to accommodate the rest. A proper staff of servants and a matron were engaged, a sickroom added, breakfast and tea provided in College, and, generally speaking, the arrangements were made similar to those of the boarding-houses for the oppidans. This reform was crowned by the appointment of a Master to reside in College in place of the Head-master and Lower-Master, who had ceased to reside there in open defiance of the founder's statutes. The boys on the Foundation had been thereby exposed to the taunt of being a race of young and not over-cleanly monks, without a particle of monastic discipline. The first man to undertake this duty was Dr. (afterwards Bishop) Abraham. As might have been expected, the number of candidates for College increased rapidly, and soon exceeded the number necessary to fill the vacancies.

Among the other reforms carried out by the Provost and Head-master were a completely new system of drainage, without however dispensing with the great sewer, built in accordance with the Founder's 'intention'; and the building of a sanatorium on the Eton Wick Road for cases of scarlet fever, the expenses of which were defrayed by an annual poll-tax on the oppidans. New houses were built for the Assistant-masters, and last, but not least, Dr. Hawtrey accomplished a successful crusade against what he called "the great evil of the Christopher Inn." The fact of the existence of a public hostelry and taproom in the heart of College was in itself a patent danger to school discipline. Its removal, however, was rendered easier, since the advent of the railway had made it possible for parents to come down to Eton to see their sons, and return the same day without any very great expenditure of time or need for accommodation.

The chapel also underwent extensive renovations. Gothic architecture was all the rage, and when the hand of the restorer was let

174

loose, the whole of the old panelling of the Wren period was removed, and the interior decorated with a series of Gothic wooden canopied stalls, with seats to match, of a very modern and commercial type. Altar, altar-rails, and pulpit were all erected in the same style. The pews for the servants and parishioners were done away with, and the Sixth Form and the young sprigs of nobility dethroned from the seat of the scornful.

A desire was felt to fill the great windows with stained glass in imitation of the great historic windows of the sister chapel at King's College, Cambridge. The great east window was first commenced, and a subscription levied among the boys, at first voluntary, afterwards compulsory, the window being completed piecemeal according to the amount of money in hand. The most eastern windows on the north side were filled with stained glass at the cost of the Assistant-masters and of the Rev. William Adolphus Carter (now Bursar). The remaining windows were completed a few years later by the Rev. John Wilder (Fellow, and afterwards Vice-Provost), in memory of his brother, Charles Wilder. Few greater opportunities have ever been offered to the exponents of glass-painting among the artists. Few opportunities have been worse used. Glass-painting was unfortunately at its worst, and there is scarcely a redeeming word to be said for the stained-glass windows in Eton Chapel. It is to be feared that they contain nothing dogmatical enough for any reformer, ritualistic or Protestant, to have an excuse for removing them.

The old organ screen was pulled down, and the organ at first erected half-way up the chapel on the south side. The west window of the choir was thereby uncovered and filled with stained glass at the expense of the Rev. Edward Coleridge. When the panelling was removed, there were discovered under the whitewash on the walls the old frescoes, which had been covered up by Provost Bill early in the reign of Queen Elizabeth. These frescoes were among some of the most important monuments of early English painting. Little attention, however, was paid to them, and the clerk of the works proceeded to obliterate them as ugly, superstitious, and very much in the way of his design. In spite of the protests of the Prince Consort and other lovers of the arts, they were ruined and covered up, and can only now be recalled by two or three sets of drawings made at the time.

The ante-chapel was also redecorated by private subscription, though mainly at the cost of Mr. Wilder. A font was added, given by the King's scholars to commemorate Bishop Abraham and his services to them. After Dr. Goodall's death, a life-size marble seated statue was erected to his memory in the ante-chapel.

It cannot be said that these 'improvements' were wholly worthy of their name, and the 'Grecian' panelling may have been something better than the cheap and pretentious Gothic introduced. The ponderous reredos may have been an eyesore, but it must have been more effective than the bare and feeble decorations, which were all that Provost Hodgson would permit at the east end. The old brasses, some of great historical interest, were torn up from their matrices on the pavement and fixed here and there on the walls, mended and repaired in careless haste. In one case certainly, that of the brass of Provost Bost, the arms were wrongly repaired, and the error transcribed and repeated in the ugly heraldic window erected in Lupton's Chapel. Would that the reformer's hand could have been stayed for some twenty years or more!

The servants and parishioners, then evicted from the College chapel, which it must be remembered was still the parish church of Eton, were accommodated in a chapel of ease built in the town of Eton.

Provost Hodgson also added greatly to the dignity and general appearance of Upper School by adding busts of eminent Etonians, some presented by themselves, others by friends or by subscription. The panelling of Upper School had by this time already been rendered historical through the names of Etonians which had been cut upon it. This practice of cutting the names of Etonians seems to have originated in the sixteenth century, when the names of the scholars elected for King's were carved in Lower School. Pepys in 1666 mentions "the custom pretty of boys cutting their names in the struts of the window when they go to Cambridge, by which many a one hath lived to see himself Provost or Fellow, that had his name in the window standing." The practice quickly spread to the new panelled walls of Upper School, a treasure-house of famous names, and is now regulated by the payment of a regular fee for the insurance of this kind of immortality.

The most remarkable, however, and the one which excited the most widespread attention, of the reforms carried out by Provost Hodgson and Dr. Hawtrey was the abolition of Montem, one of the most peculiar as well as the most time-honoured customs in the school. In Malim's *Consuetudinarium* drawn up in 1561, there occurs a passage describing how, on a certain day towards the end of January, near the Feast of the Conversion of St. Paul, the boys went out in procession at nine a.m. to Salt Hill, where "they dedicate the retreat to Apollo and the Muses, they celebrate it in song, call it Tempe, and extol it above Helicon." The novices were sprinkled with salt, and then addressed in witty verses, epigrams, &c., ending with a kind of initiation into good fellowship. The boys then returned at five o'clock and were allowed to play till eight.

This is the earliest account of this famous annual procession 'Ad Montem.' Its origin is lost in mystery. The idea of its connection with the rites of the Boy Bishop cannot be sustained. An examination of Malim's original Latin text shows that a number of Roman military terms were employed, and the whole festival would appear to be a survival, in a somewhat rudimentary form, of some Roman secular function. A somewhat similar function at Winchester, known as 'Hills,' is doubtless due to the same origin.

The history of 'Montem' is somewhat of a blank until early in the eighteenth century, by which time the real salt and epigrams of the old time had been reduced to a pinch of salt being offered to visitors in return for a donation of money. Later on the salt was changed into tickets inscribed "Mos pro Lege," "Pro More et Monte," or other suitable proverbs, though the name 'salt' was retained. The money collected as 'salt' was given to the captain of the school, in order to maintain him at

Cambridge. Two salt-bearers and twelve servitors in fancy dresses ran about the roads levying their 'salt' on every corner from king to cottager. The rest of the school marched in military uniforms, the smaller boys acting as 'pole-men.'

In 1758 the day for 'Montem' was transferred to the summer half on Whitsun-Tuesday, and the boys were allowed to wear their Montem dresses for the rest of the half. From 1778 onwards, Montem occurred every three years. Feasting and revelry characterised the rest of the proceedings. 'Montem' was an unique institution quite peculiar to Eton. As such it was beloved and cherished by past and present Etonians, as perhaps the greatest event of their youth. Kings and the royal family constantly attended, and were duly 'held up' for salt, from William III. to the late Prince Consort. Visitors came from all parts of England in chaises and chariots or on horseback, and all had to pay their salt. As much as £1250 was collected on one occasion, and the amount several times reached £1000. Even outsiders caught the enthusiasm for the "no-meaning of Montem." Charles Knight, in the Quarterly Magazine (i. 197-8), says that "I love the crush in the cloisters and the mob on the Mount. I love the clatter of carriages and the plunging of horsemen. I love the universal gaiety, from the peer, who smiles and sighs that he is no longer an Eton boy, to the country girl who marvels that such little gentlemen have cocked hats and real swords. Give me a Montem with all its tomfoolery—I had almost said before a coronation—and even without the aids of a Perigord pie and a bottle of claret at the Windmill."

But all good things must have their day. 'Montem' was a serious breach in the course of studies during the summer, and fairly demoralised the school. It was also a doubtful blessing for the captain of the school to have his pockets so well lined on first going up to the University. The festival had become the cause of extravagant and unnecessary expense. Last, but not least, the new railway brought down a large and promiscuous horde of sightseers, whose presence was anything but beneficial to the festival or to the school. Certain changes in the times and hours in 1844 proved of no efficacy. At last, in October 1846, Dr. Hawtrey, supported by Dr. Okes, intimated to the Provost his opinion as to the advisability of abolishing 'Montem.' The Provost was ready to meet them half-way, and, indeed, held stronger views on the subject than Dr. Hawtrey himself. As a man of the world and a courtier he did not take such a step without obtaining the consent of Her Majesty the Queen and Prince Albert, who, not liking to part with so old a custom in which they had taken much pleasure, referred the matter to the Prime Minister, Lord John Russell. He ascertained that the opinion of the outer world was in favour of the abolition of 'Montem.' One distinguished Etonian even went so far as to term it an "old and scandalous nuisance." The 'Montem' for 1847 in consequence did not take place. A few slight attempts at disturbance took place in the school, but it was evident that the loyalty was only skin-deep. Dr. Hawtrey's popularity was unshaken, and in a year or two the interesting old festival had become a matter of ancient history.

Let it not be forgotten, even in a sketch like this book in which so many details must be wanting, that the Head-master gave £200 out of his own pocket towards the expenses at Cambridge of the boy who would have, in the ordinary course of things, been captain of Montem. There are still many living who took part in the Montems of 1841 and 1844, if not at an earlier date. Some interesting pictures remain to preserve a record of the costumes and ceremonies. A procession of boys in 'Montem' dress, painted about 1793 by R. Livesay, was presented to the boys' library in 1891 by the Duke of Newcastle. Two interesting drawings of Montem were made by C. Turner for the Rev. John Wilder in 1820, when he was captain. Another pair of drawings, made in 1841 by William Evans for Mr. Smyth-Pigott, now belong to Viscount Braybrooke, and are familiar from engravings. In this year the captain was *Edward Thring*, afterwards so well known as Headmaster of Uppingham School, and for his share in the educational development of the country.

IX

REFORMS AT ETON

The abolition of 'Montem' may be considered to be the last of the reforms carried out at Eton by Dr. Hodgson, the Provost, and Dr. Hawtrey, the Head-master. Dr. Hawtrey's whole life as a Master at Eton was devoted to a policy of improving the education of the boys, encouraging and giving them inducements to learn, trying to gain their confidence by sympathy, generosity, and that combination of severity with consideration and reasoning, which is the most likely to carry weight with boys. He saw the dawn of a new era for education of all classes in England. Instead of closing his shutters upon the rays of the rising sun, he welcomed its warmth; and if the light somewhat cruelly revealed the dusty corners and cobwebs in the fabric of Eton, he did his best to clear up all the reproaches which were within his immediate reach. It is not surprising that after more than thirty years of work his energies somewhat relaxed, and the school suffered a little accordingly. This was, however, more a natural sign of exhausted vitality in the Head-master than of retarded progress in the school, and must always be liable to occur to any individual who has to maintain a post of an exceptionally trying nature for a number of years exceeding his strength. Apart from a few eccentricities of speech, costume, and demeanour, a few foibles of poetry and culture, there was nothing in the life and character of Dr. Hawtrey which does not command the gratitude and respect of every subsequent Etonian. In 1850 it seemed probable that Dr. Hawtrey would be elected to the vacant Provostship of King's, but other counsels prevailed at Cambridge, and it was perhaps a source of some mortification to him that the Lower-master of Eton, Dr. Richard Okes, was chosen over his head. Provost Hodgson, however, died in 1852, and *omnium consensu* Dr. Hawtrey was elected to the post. It is interesting to find that on this occasion also the Fellows did not omit to assert their right of election. Although they were in full agreement with the Crown as to the election of Dr. Hawtrey, they seized the opportunity, caused by an accidental delay in the delivery of the royal mandate, to assemble in the chapel and elect Dr. Hawtrey upon their own account.

Dr. Hawtrey was succeeded by one of the Assistant-masters, *Charles Old Goodford* (1830), a man of a good Somersetshire family, who had for long had one of the principal boarding-houses in Eton. Had he not come immediately after Dr. Hawtrey, Dr. Goodford would perhaps have been regarded as a considerable reformer, and gained some repute as a Head-master. He introduced several valuable and salutary changes into the management of the school, such as the admission of former oppidans to be Assistant-masters, the institution of an 'Army-class' to aid boys to proceed from Eton direct to commissions in the army, the introduction of a further form of religious instruction, in the shape of work to be done on Sundays, out of school, known as 'Sunday Questions,' and other similar innovations. He further subdivided the

183

work of the Fifth Form, and increased the opportunities of the upper boys to go ahead with their scholarships. Dr. Goodford was keenly interested in the development of athletic sports, though he abolished or discouraged several pernicious customs which had become traditional in connection with them. In most of the reforms introduced by Dr. Goodford, the Provost concurred gladly, but the corrupting atmosphere of the Provost's Lodge had already begun to influence his mind, and the reactionary Head-master of yore became almost as stiff and unbending an opponent of further reform, as Provost Goodall had been before.

Educational reform had, however, become a popular cry, and the attention of the public had been drawn to the great public schools. Dr. Thomas Arnold, the Headmaster of Rugby School, had found the quasi-Etonian system, inaugurated by Dr. James, in a very rusty condition. By exercising a very strong personal influence, he not only imparted fresh life to the teaching and discipline of Rugby, but he was able to stimulate and mould the minds of an exceptionally gifted circle of pupils. Chiefly through them, rather than through any actual or conspicuous success as a school administrator, Dr. Arnold came to be regarded as the great public school reformer of his day, and as such his name carried great weight with public opinion. Another great power among the public schools had been Dr. Samuel Butler, Head-master of Shrewsbury School from 1798 to 1836. Dr. Butler had created at Shrewsbury a school of the most perfect classical scholarship, in which he was most worthily succeeded by his pupil, Dr. Benjamin Hall Kennedy. Rugby for morals and Shrewsbury for scholarship were quoted by all those who were aggrieved or disappointed by Eton. With regard to Dr. Arnold, Eton was curiously free from any sort of influence derived from his reforms at Rugby. Most of them, which related to the boys themselves, were existent, if not strictly enforced at Eton. Eton scholarship perhaps had declined in comparison to the rise of Shrewsbury in this particular, but could still hold its own in the prize examinations at the Universities. The original impulse to reform in the Eton system of teaching came from an old Etonian, Sir John Taylor Coleridge, Justice of the King's Bench. Coleridge was one of a family closely connected with Eton. His brother, *Edward Coleridge*, was one of the Assistant-masters, afterwards Lower-master and Fellow, and always zealous in the cause of reform. Another brother, *Henry Nelson Coleridge* (1817), Fellow of King's, inherited a taste for poetry from his uncle, the famous Samuel Taylor Coleridge, whose daughter, Sara, he married. Their son, *Herbert Coleridge*, was Newcastle Scholar in 1848. *Henry James Coleridge*, a fine scholar, joined the Church of Rome. Another member of the family, Arthur Duke Coleridge, was author of a work on Eton already referred to. Sir John Taylor Coleridge's fame has been rather overshadowed by that of his more famous son, Sir John Duke Coleridge, lately Lord Chief-Justice of England, and created a peer. It may be doubted, however, whether the Justice of the King's Bench was not the equal in every point of the future Chief-Justice. Coleridge was an intimate friend of Dr. Arnold, and also of John Keble at Oxford, and was imbued by them with a deep desire for educational regeneration at Eton. In 1860 he delivered a lecture at the Athenaeum in Tiverton, in which he expressed his feelings somewhat strongly upon the defects of the Eton system. His words went further than he probably intended. In 1861 a less friendly critic, though also an Etonian, passed much more severe strictures in a series of articles, published in the *Cornhill Magazine*, under the name 'Pater Familias.' 'Pater Familias' turned out to be a well-known journalist and pamphleteer, Matthew James Higgins, a genial giant with a powerful if venomous pen, who had been himself, though for but a short time, a boy at Eton.

Public opinion was considerably excited upon the question. Unfavourable comments were freely made upon Eton as compared with Rugby and Shrewsbury, or with the more newly founded public schools, such as Marlborough and Cheltenham, where, as it was alleged, a much better education could be obtained at a much less cost. Henry Reeve, the editor of the *Edinburgh Review* was one of the leaders in the attack, and in April 1861 he wrote or promoted an article in his magazine, following the lead given by Higgins in the *Cornhill*. Writing to Lord Brougham, Eton's ancient enemy. Reeve speaks of having "in preparation a regular mine under Eton College.", and says "that the depredations of the Fellows go on with shameless audacity." Brougham replied that "the conduct at Eton is perfectly scandalous," and complained that his two boys never cost less than £200 a year while they were there. Eventually a Royal Commission was appointed in July 1861, ostensibly to inquire into the working of the nine chief public schools, but with the obvious intention of subjecting Eton to the most assiduous and searching criticism. The nine schools were Eton,

Winchester, Westminster, Charterhouse, St. Paul's, Merchant Taylor's, Harrow, Rugby, Shrewsbury. The Commissioners were the Earl of Clarendon (chairman), the Earl of Devon, Lord Lyttelton, the Hon. Edward Boyd Twisleton, Sir Stafford Northcote, Rev. William Hepworth Thompson, and Mr. Henry Halford Vaughan. These names were hardly encouraging for the prospect of Eton emerging intact from their examination. Only two of the Commissioners were Etonians. *George, fourth Baron Lyttelton* was one of the most distinguished of Etonians, and had just inaugurated a succession of eight sons, who were destined to exercise a more powerful influence upon the general character of the school than any Royal Commissions or Public Schools Act could achieve. Lord Lyttelton was, however, somewhat of a doctrinaire, and to some degree, especially in aspect, lacking in genial sympathy. Throughout life moreover he was guided by a high sense of moral and religious rectitude, which made it impossible for him to tolerate abuses, real or imaginary, no matter how near to his heart a person or an institution might be. *Sir Stafford Northcote* (afterwards Earl of Iddesleigh) was a painstaking, not particularly brilliant, politician and Devonshire squire. He has been described as 'eminently cautious' by Lord Salisbury, and by Mr. Gladstone, as "a man in whom it was the fixed habit of thought to put himself wholly out of view when he had before him the attainment of great public objects." It could hardly be expected that Lord Lyttelton and Sir Stafford Northcote would be strenuous champions of Eton in her hour of need. Of the other Commissioners, Lord Clarendon had not been to any public school, but more than that he was strongly

187

prejudiced against Eton, as appears from a letter to Henry Reeve, in which he spoke of the Eton article as unanswerable, and the Commission as the proper corollary to it "as so many parents of ill-educated boys appear to think"; Mr. Twisleton was a Civil Service Commissioner, nurtured therefore on red-tape and sealing-wax; the Rev. W. H. Thompson, afterwards the well-known Master of Trinity College, Cambridge, was one of the most fastidious and merciless of critics, especially when matters of scholarship or college administration were concerned; and Mr. Halford Vaughan was a keen lawyer and a professor of history to boot, to whom, as behoved his profession, defects and flaws in an institution were pleasing food for the mind of an active theorist and progressive reformer. It was before such a tribunal, therefore, that the Provost, Fellows, and Head-master of Eton College were bound over to stand up and answer for their sins.

Provost Hawtrey felt the situation deeply. His last speech at the banquet on Founder's Day, December 6, 1861, was mainly devoted to feelings of scorn and mortification, and also of resentment at the wounds inflicted upon the College by two of its *alumni*, Coleridge and Higgins. On the 27th January following Dr. Hawtrey died, and was buried within the chapel, the last person to be laid there. Hawtrey was a great character, a strong individuality. He excelled Dr. Keate in both these respects. His ideas were large and lofty, and so far as public school administration was concerned, of a general nature, and not merely confined to Eton alone. He was a familiar and welcome figure at court, and also in cultivated and literary circles in London, and as a host in his own house, or a guest in those of his friends, he was one of the leaders in a flow of bright and intellectual conversation, characteristic of the age in which he lived. No one could touch on the history of Eton without echoing with enthusiasm Mr. Gladstone's words about Dr. Hawtrey, "It is pleasant to me to speak or write about him."

Dr. Hawtrey's death gave the Fellows an opportunity of asserting, for the last time as it turned out, their time-honoured claim to elect a new Provost themselves. They met and elected Bishop Chapman. The Crown, however, ignored their choice, and promoted the Head-master, Dr. Goodford. The Head-mastership, thus vacated, was anything but an enviable post, since the Head-master had already been summoned for cross-examination by the Commissioners. The loss of Dr. Goodford at such a crisis was particularly unfortunate. It seemed likely to go begging, but was eventually accepted by the Rev. Edward Balston, who had not long before retired from being an Assistant-master for twenty years to the soothing repose of a Fellowship. Dr. Balston was a man of high breeding and fine character. His love for Eton and his belief in the administration of the College and the school, as satisfactory and successful, was deep and genuine. He was hardly, however, the man for the crisis. Having accepted the Head-mastership as a labour of love for the school, rather than from desire of personal aggrandisement, he was subjected to an examination by the Commissioners, which was cruelly wounding to his lofty and sensitive nature.

When the Commissioners met, they had to consider the administration of the College as a Foundation, distinct from the

189

management of the school. The Provost and Fellows had always sheltered themselves behind the statutes, whenever any reform, which they disliked, had been proposed. They now found themselves exposed to distinct charges of wilful neglect of the statutes. One of the charges brought against them, and most strongly pressed, related to the management of the College estates and the profits accruing therefrom. It was the custom on the renewal of a lease, a matter of frequent occurrence, to pay over the 'fine 'to the Fellows, and as the leases were numerous, the sum amassed in this way was often considerable. It was alleged that these profits should have been applied to College purposes, and had been wrongfully appropriated by the Fellows. It did not seem clear when the custom had first grown up, and it was obvious that the Provost and Fellows in appropriating these fines were only doing what their predecessors had done for generations. Public opinion was, however, strongly imbued with the idea that the College had suffered considerably by these appropriations, although the Fellows had always been ready to subscribe handsomely to any additions or alterations in the College, which might be required. It was also alleged that this appropriation was a violation of the statutes, whereby the emoluments of the Fellows were strictly defined and regulated.

Another charge related to the choir. The Founder's statutes provided for the maintenance of a certain number of singing men and choristers, as an integral part of the Foundation. This had fallen so much into neglect, that the services of the chapel were performed by the choir of St. George's Chapel, Windsor, and as the Windsor service followed close upon that at Eton, the choir was forced to leave Eton Chapel before the service was completed. Music had, therefore, in defiance of the Founder's most cherished wish, become almost entirely extinct at Eton.

A third charge was of a more personal nature. It related to a bequest of a large sum of money by Provost Godolphin for the purpose of improving the commons of the Collegers in Hall. It was shown that the improvement had been of the slightest, and it transpired on inquiry that only the dividends had ever been applied in accordance with Provost Godolphin's intention, and that the capital, after accumulating for some little time, had been used to defray the expenses of additional buildings in the College. The bursars rendered no account of the College rents and properties, and deficiencies were usually met by loans.

The evidence all went to show that, however desirable it might be to retain the ecclesiastical foundation of Henry VI., the Fellows, or at all events some portion of them, had become an expensive and unnecessary drain upon the resources of the College.

An inquiry into the accommodation of the King's scholars in College testified to the great improvements carried out by Provost Hodgson and Dr. Hawtrey. There was still something left to be desired in the way of space, food, and cleanliness. The evidence also showed that the result of the improved condition of the 'tugs' had been to lessen, to a certain extent, the contempt felt for them by their more aristocratic comrades among the oppidans. The difference of station was, however, still somewhat accentuated by the 'tugs' being obliged to wear their black gowns during play hours.

The inquiry into the course of instruction was, or was intended to be, very searching. The school was divided into the Upper and Lower School, the former containing the Sixth Form, Fifth Form, and Remove, and the latter the Fourth Form and all below it. In 1861 the Head-master had seventeen assistants to help him in the Upper School, and the Lower-master four for the Lower School. This was a considerable advance upon the days of Dr. Keate, and admitted of a much greater subdivision of forms. As, however, the Assistant-masters were paid by the Head-master or the Lowermaster, every increase of the staff, however desirable, was naturally a tax upon their annual stipends. It has already been stated that the mathematical master was an 'extra' on the list of Assistant-masters, and that his assistants in the mathematical school were employed and paid for by him.

With regard to actual work in school there was great ground for justification of the complaints, that the selections in the *Poetæ Græci, Scriptores Romani,* and other books in general use, were obsolete and an impediment to genuine scholarship. The time-honoured *Eton Latin Grammar,* dating from the fifteenth century, had become an archaism, only excusable by the lack of a proper substitute. This want was shortly supplied by the issue of the *Public Schools Latin Primer,* wherein the *Propria quæ maribus* of Etonian forefathers gave place to the *Psittacus loquitur* of their grandchildren.

It was shown that an excessive amount of time was devoted at Eton to repetition, four mornings a week. Repetition is one of the most valuable forms of mental exercise, and one which strengthens and qualifies the mind for use, much as dumb-bells or Indian clubs do for the muscles of the body. Many Etonians of that time were ready to testify to the immense assistance this exercise had been to them in after life. Repetition, however, if lightly and ineffectively used, is of little value, especially when the number of boys to be heard repeat their lesson is large and the time allotted short. That a master should hear some thirty or forty boys repeat a lesson with little more than about a minute apiece allotted to each boy is in itself evidence that some part, at all events, of this teaching must be time wasted. The quick boy will avail himself of the opportunities afforded by rotation, the idle or stupid boy will merely waste the time of his master and his fellow-pupils. In this, as in other matters of education, it is easier to point at faults than to suggest remedies. The same applies to the making of Latin verses, a form of education loudly decried by those who have either no experience of it themselves, or are ready to acknowledge themselves as complete failures in this respect. That Latin verse was one of the staples of education at Eton was not due to any rooted belief in the efficiency of verse as something indisputable or sacrosanct, but to the tradition, long and honourably maintained, that the best education for a young English gentleman was one which inculcated in him at an early age some knowledge of literary taste and culture, even if it was not found possible to add the power to cultivate it. For this purpose the making of Latin verses is a most admirable exercise, and so long as this Eton tradition shall be maintained, it is difficult, if not impossible, to think of any satisfactory substitute. It was in this way that Wellesley, Canning,

193

Derby, and Gladstone had been trained at Eton, taking an impress which characterised their life up to the very close. The study of Greek can be supported by similar arguments. The charges of neglect in the sphere of mathematics, physical science, history, and foreign languages, were to a great extent ante-dated by the reforms initiated by Dr. Hawtrey, which in so venerable an institution as Eton College had hardly had sufficient time to take root and fructify. The difficulties seemed insuperable, as there must be a limit to the powers of subdividing the hours in one day, as well as the reasoning faculties of the ordinary schoolboy. In some schools of more recent construction the difficulty was met by the complete bi-section of the school into classical and modern sides, a confession in itself that a choice must be made between one or the other. The past history of Eton seemed to justify the authorities in maintaining the predominance of the classical side. The absolute necessity for better teaching accommodation had been met by the College, and a large block of buildings known as the 'New Schools' was erected in 1861, the cost being defrayed as usual partly by the College and partly by private subscriptions.

Another part of the Eton system was evidently a source of weakness. In the Lower School there did not seem to be any fixed minimum of age at which a boy might come to Eton. Some came as early as five or six years old, and remained in the school for twelve or fourteen years. The smaller boys of this kind were all boarded in one house kept by the Rev. John Hawtrey, a cousin of the Provost, and brother of the mathematical master. It was obvious that to try and make the scope of a school *curriculum* wide enough to embrace the requirements of boys of nineteen and boys of six or seven years of age was a task beyond the powers of any single organisation, except at a very great expense and subdivision of labour. The education of boys under twelve or thirteen is now a department by itself, as is exemplified by the immense increase in the number of private and preparatory schools throughout the country. Mr. Hawtrey's house was practically a private school in itself, and to further enhance this he built in 1862 a large house at the end of Common Lane, to which he removed his colony of small boys, relinquishing at the same time his post as Assistant-master. As the numbers, however, of the school increased, the advantages to the small boys became less, and the risks of the situation were distinctly increased. With the consent of all parties concerned, Mr. Hawtrey removed his boys to new premises at Aldin House, Slough, where he established a new and perfectly independent preparatory school. With these boys disappeared all the Lower Forms of the school, Sense and Nonsense, Upper Greek and Lower Greek, First and Second Forms, since it was understood in future that the minimum standard of admission to the school would be that of the Third Form.

The Commissioners inquired fully into the boardinghouse system, the tutorial system, and the discipline exercised over and among the boys.

The growth of the school had been gradual, and liable to periodical fluctuations. The accommodation for the oppidans was, therefore, of correspondingly casual growth. The College as a corporation was not compelled to provide accommodation for the oppidans, although, as their number increased, it had become necessary to observe some rules of discipline and control. In this way a somewhat haphazard system of boarding-houses had grown up, whereby some houses were rented, partly from the College, partly from neighbouring landlords, by Assistant-masters, who also acted as tutors, by others who had no tutorial authority, or by the wives, widows, and other female relatives of College or school officials. After Dr. Hawtrey's abolition of private tutors, the boarding-houses became divided into two classes—those kept by a classical master, who was qualified to act as tutor to the boys in the house, and those kept by an extra master or a Dame, in which cases every boy was allotted to a tutor among the classical masters. The house masters who were not also tutors were and are still invariably called 'Dames,' the old name of 'Dominie' having entirely dropped out of use.

Discipline, as might have been expected, was exercised with greater ease in a tutor's house than in a Dame's, although an attempt was made by Dr. Hawtrey to secure a better discipline in the latter by making a Dame's house subject to inspection by one of the Assistant-masters.

The whole system was not very satisfactory, but very difficult to avoid or improve. The rights of private ownership were such as the College was never willing, even if it was able, to interfere with. Moreover, there seemed to be something advantageous in leaving the questions of board, food, &c., a question between the parents and the

Head-master or Dame, to whom they might think fit to entrust their boys.

On the other hand, the amount of work and responsibility thrown upon a classical tutor had been greatly increased by the changes under Dr. Hawtrey. In addition to the ordinary work in school, a classical tutor was responsible for the preparation of a large number of pupils of varying ages and varying positions in the school. Besides a large share in the ordinary Formwork of each boy, he had to contribute a certain amount of private tuition on his own account. He thus, as it were, worked a school within a school, and that single-handed, having but scanty opportunities for giving attention either to the special requirements of his more accomplished pupils or to the difficulties and blunders of those who might be younger or inferior in intellect.

With regard to the tone of the school itself, the inquiries of the Commissioners may be said to have produced a very satisfactory and hopeful result. In every public school of any great size there must ever be dark spots and difficult places to get over, chiefly caused by those vices and weaknesses which are inherent in human nature, especially in the young, and which can only be controlled by a firm and wholesome treatment, or, if necessary, as in disease, by judicious excision or amputation. The result of the Commissioners' inquiries, extended not only to Masters and parents, but even to boys at the school or who had just left it, showed that the general tone of the school was good, and

197

that in certain details, which had been severely called into question, there was a steady and natural improvement.

The great improvements in College, and a corresponding raising of the standard of comfort in boarding-houses, had removed from the time-honoured practice of 'fagging' much that might have been considered offensive and degrading. The charges of 'bullying,' too, were proved to be special rather than general, and, apart from the natural callousness to suffering in others, both physical and mental, shown by the average boy in every station of life, the whole tone of the school appeared opposed to anything like systematic ill-treatment of one boy by another. The Commission lasted for two and a half years. Although its inquiries were extended to the nine schools mentioned before, it is impossible to escape from the idea that Eton was the main object of the Commissioners' inquiries, and that had it not been for Eton there would have been no Public Schools Commission at all. The Report of the Commissioners was not issued until 1865. It was evident from the Report that, so far as Eton was concerned, the reforms suggested were of such a nature as could only be carried out by a total or partial destruction of the ancient fabric of education at Eton. The inquiry had been long and searching, and the whole mass of evidence collected must always remain one of the most important historical documents in the history of this country.

Various reforms suggested by the Report were carried out at Eton with little difficulty. The changes, however, into the administration of the College were of a very sweeping nature. Two years or more elapsed before Parliament took any action in the matter. In 1868 an Act was passed appointing Commissioners to draw up new statutes for the leading schools, and it became generally known that the old Foundation at Eton was doomed. The Head-master, Dr. Balston, had bitterly resented the tone adopted by the Commissioners in their inquiry into the administration and efficiency of Eton. When Parliament took action he resigned, rather than be forced into any agreement with the changes proposed. The appointment of a successor showed a disposition on the part of the College to meet public opinion. In spite of long tradition, the Provost and Fellows appointed the *Rev. James John Hornby*, who had been an oppidan, and, moreover, at Oxford, and at the moment was second-master at Winchester.

Dr. Hornby became Head-master at a critical moment for himself and the school. He was on the threshold of great changes, the exact extent of which was as yet unknown. While it would naturally have been his duty as an old Etonian to defend the traditions of his old school, he was looked to by a large section of the public outside as intended to inaugurate a new regime. Dr. Hornby found a staff of some twenty masters, all, with the exception of a few of the mathematical and extra masters, old Etonians. The rule that appointments should be given by preference to King's men, which had been broken so successfully in the cases of Mr. Coleridge and Mr. Pickering, was again broken in 1860, when the *Rev.Edmond Warre*, a former oppidan and scholar of Balliol College, Oxford, was appointed an Assistant-master. Subsequently other distinguished Oxonians have been admitted, such as *Henry Elford Luxmoore*, *Francis Tarver*, and *R. A. H. Mitchell*, all appointments fraught with the greatest importance to the school. Dr. Hornby at once set himself to work to supply some deficiencies by increasing the staff of mathematical masters, and admitting them to the same rank and dignity, although without their privileges, as the classical masters. Foreign languages were also cared for, the instruction of the boys in French being entrusted to Mr. Francis Tarver and his brother, Mr. Henry Tarver, assisted by a Frenchman, M. Roublot. German had been provided for by a resident, though extra, master; and an Italian gentleman was attached to the staff, who was seldom without a small class of pupils. Dr. Hornby aimed at a large and carefully selected increase to the staff of classical masters; but it must be admitted that the appointments made during the first seven or eight years of his Head-mastership were, with a few notable exceptions, far from being successful.

The whole day's and week's work, however, and the laws for compulsory chapel service as well, were revised and regulated.

The bolt fell in 1870, when a new "Governing Body" was appointed, intended to contain a large ingredient of non-Etonian members. It consisted of the Provosts of Eton and King's, ex officio, and of five members to be nominated by the two Universities, the Royal Society, the Lord Chief-Justice, and the Assistant masters. These seven members were empowered to nominate two, three, and four additional members, according to their discretion.

The original members of the new Governing Body were the Provost of Eton (Dr. Goodford), the Provost of King's (Dr. Okes), the Dean of

Rochester (Dr. Scott), the Master of Trinity College, Cambridge (Dr. W. H. Thompson), Professor George Gabriel Stokes, Sir Roundell Palmer (afterwards Earl of Selborne and Lord Chancellor), Canon Lightfoot (afterwards Bishop of Durham), the Right Hon. Spencer Walpole, M.P., the Rev. William A. Carter, Lord Lyttelton, and the Earl of Morley. Four of these—Thompson, Stokes, Palmer, and Lightfoot— were non-Etonians.

The new Governing Body then proceeded to draw up new statutes for the College and school, whereby the whole of the original Foundation of Henry VI. was, after four hundred and thirty years, entirely abolished and destroyed.

X

ETON UNDER THE NEW STATUTES

The new statutes drawn up by the new Governing Body of Eton College were, although incased in the rind or shell, so to speak, of the old Foundation, a complete revolution, as compared with the statutes drawn up by the royal Founder of the College. By the latter the College consisted of a Provost, seventy-four scholars, ten Priest-Fellows, ten chaplains, ten clerks, sixteen choristers, a Head-master, an Usher, and thirteen poor infirm men. By the new statutes it was to consist of a Provost and ten Fellows, a Head-master of the school and a Lowermaster, at least seventy scholars, and not more than two chaplains or conducts. It will be seen at once that the whole basis of the College as an ecclesiastical corporation has been swept away, and its statutory connection with the Church limited to the services of two chaplains or conducts (*capellani conductitii*).

Taking the Provost first: formerly he was ordered by statute to be a Master or Bachelor in Divinity, or a Doctor of the Common Law and Master of Arts, a priest born in England, thirty years old, and educated at the Foundation of Eton. Part of this statute had been evaded from time to time, but for two hundred years it had been strictly observed. By the new statute the Provost need only be a member of the Church of England, and not necessarily in Holy Orders, and a Master of Arts, or of some equal or superior degree at one or other of the old Universities. The long-standing dispute as to the right of election was determined once for all by the new statute, that the appointment to the Provostship shall be vested in the Crown.

The Provost of Eton College had up to this date enjoyed precedence and plenary authority over the whole College. These powers were reduced by the new statutes to a general superintendence over the affairs of the College, and a responsibility for seeing that the statutes were duly observed. The Provost had been ex officio Rector of the parish of Eton, and, by special license from the Bishop of Lincoln, had, since 1443, exercised archidiaconal functions in Eton, quite independently of the Archdeacon of Buckinghamshire.

It was obvious that the Provost, if a layman were elected, could not perform these parochial and archidiaconal duties. He was therefore relieved of them, and two or three years later the parish of Eton was constituted into a vicarage, independent of the College, and the Church of St. John the Evangelist, which had been erected as a chapel of ease to the College chapel, was converted into the parish church of Eton. The Collie chapel ceased to have any parochial interest, and became merely a school chapel, served by two paid chaplains on the staff of the school.

Thus perished the religious Foundation of Henry VI. Could it have been saved? Probably not, for the ideas of the country as well as the needs of the community had become greatly changed. Though the College was intended by Henry VI. to be anti-monastic in its general character, lapse of time had brought it into line with other institutions, more monastic in their account, and thereby the object of the most jealous scrutiny by an age in which such ecclesiastical institutions had become obsolete.

The Provost, shorn of his authority (*nominis umbra*), has become little more than the titular head of the College, and the chairman of the Governing Body, and the sole remnant of his once great power would seem to be the casting-vote, which he is entitled to give in the case of an equality of votes at a College meeting.

By the old statutes there were to be ten Fellows, secular priests, elected by the Provost and Fellows jointly, from members or former members of either Foundation. The Fellows of Eton were entirely abolished by the new statutes. It is true that the members of the Governing Body, other than the Provost, were invested with the title of Fellows, but this must have been done simply from a wish to retain the outer semblance of the original Foundation. The existing Fellows were allowed to retain their posts and privileges, and this permission was extended to the then Lower Master, the Rev. F. E. Dumford. At the present day (1899), the sole survivor is the Bursar, the Rev. W. A. Carter, with whom will disappear the last living representative of Henry VI.'s Foundation.

The post of Vice-Provost was retained, and the duties assigned to him were explained by his designation. The Vice-Provost is not *ex officio* a member of the Governing Body. Moreover, by a curious construction of the statutes, the Vice-Provost does not, in event of the Provost being incapacitated, *ipso facto* take his place, for provision is made for the election of a Pro-Provost, whereby it seems possible that the College might enjoy the services of a Provost (incapacitated), a Pro-Provost, and a Vice-Provost, without any one of the three taking part in the meetings of the Governing Body.

The total abolition of the old chapter of Fellows, and the sequestration of their emoluments, has been the subject of much adverse criticism. It has been shown that certain charges of maladministration had been brought against the College, and to a certain extent substantiated, but the sum total of the charges was a very small one, and in no ways commensurate with the benefits that might and did accrue to the school from the presence of a body of men, devoted mind and soul to the welfare and interests of Eton. The Fellowships afforded a convenient set of pensions for some of the Assistant-masters on their retirement, and there have always been some whose services and interests were sufficiently valuable to be retained in this way. Their emoluments were not of such an extent as to allow of the accumulation of great wealth, and they had always been willing and generous contributors to any scheme for the improvement of the College. There were many points about their constitution, such as their monopoly of the preaching in the College chapel, which called for reform, but hardly any argument, save the potent and perhaps sufficient one of economy, would seem to support so strong a step as their total abolition.

Out of the wreck of the old Foundation the one person who emerged triumphant was the Head-master. The kernel of the whole controversy had been the rival interests of the school and the College.

The *Commensales* and other *oppidani*, for whom Henry VI.'s forethought had provided, had swelled in numbers, ebbing and flowing like the ocean tide, and had increased in the last hundred and fifty years from about two hundred to nine hundred. The requisite provisions, however, for the maintenance and education of this enormous number of boys had not increased in any corresponding rate. The supply of Assistant-masters was dependent upon the Head-master, and had been shown to have been ludicrously insufficient in the days of Dr. Keate and Dr. Hawtrey. An increase was necessary in the staff of classical masters, to say nothing of the mathematical masters, and teachers in physical science, foreign languages, history, and other subjects, recommended by the Commission. With an increase of the teaching staff came, as a matter of course, the need for a great increase in the class-rooms and laboratories.

The emoluments of the College were for the most part devoted to the maintenance of the Provost, Fellows, scholars, and other members of the Foundation, and were therefore not available for the purposes of the school. It required an act of violence, therefore, sheltered under the form of an Act of Parliament, to divert these emoluments from the original intention of the Founder. It was obvious, however, that the school must in course of time swallow up the College, and when the 'happy despatch' was effected, even those who most regretted the disappearance of the old Foundation found it difficult to gainsay the necessity and utility of the change.

By the new statutes the Head-master is appointed by the Governing Body, who have the right of dismissing him, and to whom he is answerable for all his actions. He need not be in Holy Orders, but must be a member of the Church of England. He retains the privilege of appointing and dismissing all the Assistant-masters, but their number, rank, and emoluments are under the control of the Governing Body. In this way the Head-master has been relieved from the control of any personal influence, and his position is one of much greater dignity and importance than heretofore. The Lower-master (*ostiarius*) was retained by the new statutes, but as the Lower School has practically disappeared, the position occupied by him with regard to the Head-master is really analogous to that of the Vice-Provost.

The obvious difficulty caused by the abolition of the paid Fellowships was met in the new statutes by the institution of a Pension Fund for the Assistant-masters. By this statute pensions not exceeding £400 per annum might be awarded to the Head-master or any Master who had served for fifteen years and was considered deserving, provided that the total sum awarded in pensions did not exceed £4000 per annum. The Masters also had the first right of presentation to any vacant benefice in the patronage of the College. It is obvious, however, that with an increased staff of Masters, but few of them could ever hope to draw the full pension of £400 a year. One however remarkable result of the secularisation of Eton College and other similar institutions was to relieve the junior members of the staff from the duty, formerly unavoidable, of taking Holy Orders. This has not been from any desire to avoid identification of themselves with the doctrines of the Church of England, for Eton is in itself a striking example of a distinct increase in religious feeling and observance during the last few years, although at the present day only eight Masters out of fifty-six are clerks in Holy Orders. There is a prevailing idea among modern churchmen that no man should take Holy Orders who is not prepared to devote some portion of his life at all events to the actual service of the Church. This idea prevents many high-minded young schoolmasters from taking Orders merely as a means to an end, although they are aware that the existing prejudices of the greater part of the British nation are in favour of entrusting the administration of the great public schools to clergymen.

Turning to the scholars on the Foundation, the new statutes provided for at least seventy, assuming thereby the possibility of an increase in the numbers. The old election by the united authorities of the Colleges of Eton and King's was done away with, with all its picturesque appurtenances. The Founder's restrictions, too, were abolished. The election was vested in the Governing Body, the Examiners appointed by them, and the scholarships were open to all British subjects between the ages of twelve and fifteen, upon a certificate of good character.

In this statute nothing is said about the scholars being poor and indigent, no suggestion is made of any charitable intention on the part of the Governing Body. Henceforward it was an open prize examination, and the successful candidates could hold the scholarship, whatever his rank or the means of his parents. The King's scholars have therefore become a select body, qualified by a severe examination, and are naturally the elite of the school with regard to distinctions in school-work and examinations. Nearly all the discomforts and disadvantages of College, social and domestic, have disappeared, and beyond the wearing of a black cloth gown in school and a surplice in chapel, the main distinction between a colleger and an oppidan is that the former is certified to be a clever boy, and the latter is not. This change is perhaps the one most open to question in the new statutes. The pious and charitable intentions of the Founder were thereby not merely amended, but wholly frustrated. It is one thing to increase and throw open to the world at large an endowment like that of Eton College; it is another to thereby destroy, perhaps in favour of the rich, the few and rapidly diminishing privileges of the poor.

King's College, Cambridge, has on its own account divested itself of its purely Etonian character, and thrown itself open to the world at large. A few scholarships are reserved for Etonians, and form, apart from traditions of love and affection, the sole link between the Colleges which Henry VI. united in his original Foundation. The ties between the Colleges of King's and Eton, though greatly loosened, are still maintained; and it is noteworthy that in a Bill introduced in 1899 for the control of secondary education, the schools of Eton and Winchester were alone exempted from supervision, and are still treated as part of one or other of the two Universities.

The above is but a short summary of the changes brought about by the new statutes of the Governing Body. It can be said for these statutes, that on the whole they have worked well. The constitution of the Governing Body itself has shown, that the safeguards supposed to be instituted by allotting four seats to the nomination of the two Universities, the Royal Society, and the Lord Chief-Justice have not proved very stable, for in each of these cases it is difficult to find persons of eminence and authority who, while at their prime, are able to give much time and attention to matters outside their immediate sphere of influence. Many matters, moreover, pertaining to Eton are of purely local interest, and peculiar to the school. The great source of nourishment for a public school is its traditions, and in the monthly meetings of a Committee like the Governing Body, with a more or less fixed agenda for each meeting, there must always be some danger that these traditions may be neglected. One great difficulty was not foreseen by the Governing Body in framing the statutes. It was assumed by the Commissioners of 1864 that the endowments of Eton College were not only large, but increasing in value. This was one of the arguments used against the retention of paid Fellows. The endowments of Eton College, however, like those of its sister college. King's College, Cambridge, and other similar institutions, especially at Cambridge, were chiefly land, or revenues derived from land. Since the issue of the new statutes the value of the College estates has been gradually declining, and it is with difficulty that the Governing Body can meet the ever-growing demands upon the resources of the College. There are no more individuals or institutions to be plucked, and it is difficult to see from what quarter any increase of revenue is to be obtained. It was not, therefore, to a post of ease and comfort that Dr. Hornby succeeded in 1868. The history of his administration of the school, and that of his successor. Dr. Warre, is so recent and so fresh in the minds of living Etonians, that it would seem presumptuous to criticise or praise them in so short a sketch as the present volume. It will be sufficient to say that Dr. Hornby occupied the post of Head-master with dignity and success at perhaps the most difficult moment in the history of Eton, and that when he succeeded to the Provostship in 1884, upon the death of Dr. Goodford, his work was carried on with additional vigour and success by Dr. Edmond Warre, who still holds the post.

One of the most obvious signs of the raising of the standard of education in the school is the gradual shrinkage of the Lower School. Whereas in former days the Lower School contained about one -half the whole school, it now contains but one-sixth. In fact, by the new statutes the Lower School in its old sense was abolished altogether, and the Lower-master, no longer an Usher, is in reality the *locum tenens* of the Headmaster. Dr. Hornby was successful in organising a scheme whereby the ordinary routine of classics and mathematics was varied by a series of extra studies, selected at choice by boys on attaining one of the higher divisions of the school. In this way teaching was introduced in French and German, history, physics, chemistry, zoology, and other branches of natural science. Dr. Hornby was ably seconded in his efforts to widen the scope of teaching by Dr. Edmond Warre, who was easily marked out as his successor. As Head-master, Dr. Warre has elaborated a system of teaching, in which no charge can again be brought against Eton of narrowness or convention within the scope of education. In mathematics progress was evident by the attainment of a Senior Wrangler, Philip Cowell, in 1892, and a Second Wrangler, G. J. H. Hurst, in 1893. An extension and remodelling of the army class, originally established by Dr. Hawtrey, has been successful in enabling boys to

proceed direct to Sandhurst or Woolwich without the intervention of a "crammer." By way of an experiment a navy class has also been formed to enable boys to proceed straight from Eton into the navy.

All scholarships and exhibitions, except where otherwise specified, are open to be competed for by any boy in the school. As, however, the King's scholars are a specially selected, and to a certain extent specially trained, body, it is not surprising that the majority of the prizes are carried off by them. The more credit, therefore, is due to any oppidan who shows himself a match for them in the school or prize examinations.

By a judicious pruning and transplanting among the staff of Assistant masters. Dr. Hornby was latterly successful in procuring the services of a remarkably high class of men. Dr. Warre has continued this with conspicuous success. Mere scholarship and University distinctions have ceased to be the sole qualification for the post of

Assistant-master at Eton. High character, and in many cases experience of teaching elsewhere, have been the chief causes of selection in the last few years. The position of schoolmaster has been raised in the social scale. Young men of gentle birth and refined breeding are no longer ashamed to join the ranks of teacher. The change has been of incalculable advantage to schools, for there is no faculty so generally inherent in the English boy, and so readily employed by him, as that of discerning at once whether his teacher or his comrade is or is not a 'gentleman.'

To this cause may also be attributed, at all events to a considerable extent, the improvement in discipline which has been manifest in the school during the last twenty years or more. There were times during Dr. Hornby's tenure of Head-mastership when, without any disrespect to him, his authority seemed more latent than apparent. Dr. Hornby had in consequence more than one awkward episode in school discipline which called for the hand of a wise and firm administrator. The change, however, in the general social position of schoolmasters has enabled them to meet the boys on a broader basis of sympathy and affection. The boy no longer feels that the schoolmaster is a race apart, created for the affliction and mortification of the youthful mind and body. He learns how to find in his master not only a teacher and admonisher, but also a friend, both out of school and in school, in the playing-fields as well as in the pupil-room, in fact, in many cases an expanded and improved edition of himself. The moral effect of friendship and sympathy is more potent with the boyish mind than a thousand birch-

213

rods or other forms of physical punishment. There are probably few ties of affection so strong as those which bind many an Eton tutor to the majority of his pupils.

The new regime at Eton had one distinct effect, that of exciting the confidence of the aristocratic or moneyed parent. The number of boys in the school had in 1871 just reached nine hundred, and had risen to its highest point under Dr. Hornby in 1877, when it totalled nine hundred and sixty-two. A few years' decline ensued until 1884, when the appointment of Dr. Warre was the signal for a recrudescence of parental confidence. From that date the numbers have steadily increased. In 1891 they exceeded one thousand, and the question has become urgent whether any further increase in the numbers of the school will not be disadvantageous to the welfare of the whole.

This increase in the numbers of the school has, moreover, taken place in spite of a steady and inevitable increase in the expense of maintaining a boy at Eton. The general comfort of boys in the various boarding-houses has been increased to an extent which would have made their grandfathers smile. Food, clothes, pocket-money are now supplied to the boys in profusion, and the Spartan life of the early years of the nineteenth century has given place to, in comparison, a perfect Capua at its close. This change has been due to some extent to a great increase in the standard of comfort at home and to a large infusion of the classes who owe their position to wealth rather than to rank or distinction of birth.

Eton, as the nursery of the well born and the wealthy, has in these democratic days met with many detractors. It is easy to point to the evils and difficulties which must always arise from the herding together of any number of boys at the age of puberty, well born or otherwise. It should be remembered, on the other hand, that Eton gets a larger share than any other school of those who may without any disrespect be called the wastrels of the aristocracy. There are few fates more cruel than that of a boy, the younger son of a peer or landowner, who may be brought up in a home where every luxury is provided and many faults condoned or ignored, whose existence is but of secondary importance to that of his eldest brother, and who is destined very often to face the world on the scantiest of pittances, and with all the tastes and habits derived from a life of plenty and luxury. Many such boys are sent to Eton, and it reflects honour on the school whenever, as they frequently do, they owe to Eton the moral stamina which enables them later on to overcome the difficulties of their position.

The duties of parents to their children have been insisted upon lately by many educational authorities. In no school are they shown to such advantage or disadvantage as they are at Eton. Many cases of youthful misdemeanour can be traced to careless supervision, if not to actual vices learnt, and not observed or discouraged, at home. The moral training, too, required at Eton is one quite dissociated from religion.

Eton, although a foundation dedicated to Mother Church, has never been a college for the dissemination of ecclesiastical doctrine. Even the influence of Dr. Arnold, so paramount in the educational world of his day, hardly affected Eton at all. It may be perhaps fairly alleged against the old foundation that religion had been almost entirely neglected. The services in chapel were much too frequent, and had become little more than a tiresome routine. These services were hurried through, and the Fellows had, and clung to, a monopoly of the preaching. Sermons veered between dulness and eccentricity. The behaviour of the boys in chapel was very irregular, and under very inadequate control.

It is a curious paradox that after the almost complete secularisation of the Eton foundation, there has arisen in the school a distinct advance in the feeling and reverence for religion. Although comparatively few of the teaching staff are now in holy orders, it may be said without hesitation that the influence of the masters in the sphere of religion has greatly increased, and is felt and understood by the boys. This is well illustrated by the ease with which the school was persuaded to lend its name and identify itself with a great missionary work in the East End of London. The services in chapel are now regulated by a system, so as to be no longer wearisome or annoying. Certain time-honoured disorderly practices, such as 'Church Sock,' have entirely disappeared. The revival of the choral services, so lovingly insisted upon by the royal Founder, has no doubt led to greater decorum among the boys in school. Music, ever since Plato's time, has been recognised as a potent factor in education. Henry VI. was aware of this, and his directions for the choral services are very explicit. From this arose the school of musicians under Provost Bost, mentioned in a previous chapter. But in later years the practice of music had almost entirely died out. The choir, at first an integral part of the Foundation, had almost, if not quite, ceased to exist. The services were conducted by the choir of St. George's Chapel in Windsor, those at Eton being considered as of quite secondary importance. Music ceased to be taught in the school. The Commission of 1860 called attention to this defect. A separate choir was formed for the service of Eton Chapel, supported by the College, although it is no longer actually provided for by the statutes.

In 1864 a further step was taken by the appointment of John Foster, one of the singing-men in Westminster Abbey, to come down to Eton once a week to teach music to such pupils as might present themselves. The event would have been unimportant itself had it not been that Foster numbered among his few pupils a boy who has since become not only the greatest musician educated at Eton, but even, perhaps, the greatest produced by England at any time—Sir Charles Hubert Hastings Parry. In 1870 a residential music-master was appointed in the person of the Rev. Leighton George Hayne, who built himself a house and large music-room at the bottom of Keate's Lane. Dr. Hayne was succeeded by Mr. C. D. Maclean; but music took a more considerable stride under the management of the late Sir Joseph Barnby and the present organist. Dr. Charles Harford Lloyd. There may be said now to be quite a flourishing school of music at Eton, and among the ranks of recent Etonians there has been more than one who in musical composition is likely to make a name for himself, even if he cannot aspire to rivalry with Sir Hubert Parry.

217

XI

SPORTS AND PASTIMES

One important factor in the school life at Eton has hitherto remained unnoticed—the sports and games with which Eton boys have for generations made their boyhood varied, happy, and often famous. The relation borne by games to the ordinary routine of school-work has for long been a subject of diverse opinions. The scholars and divines of the Middle Ages thought little of physical health as an ingredient in education. The churchmen either mortified the flesh with asceticism, or pandered to it by good cheer and luxury. Such sports as the youth of England might indulge in to keep the eye clear and straight, and the muscles strong and ready for use, were of a nature hardly compatible with schoolwork, being chiefly riding, hunting, hawking, tilting, or the like. In the statutes of the older public schools there is no suggestion of any time being given up for actual play or recreation. Such intervals as occurred between the school hours, where not occupied by meals, were left free to the boys for games, but they were few and far between.

By the end of the sixteenth century the rivalry between work and pastime had already become a familiar topic, for in his famous *Scholemaster* Roger Ascham, writing at Windsor, within sight of Eton College, and prompted to his treatise by his friend. Sir Richard Sackville, an old Etonian, makes deliberately the following assertion: "I do not meene, by all this my taulke, that yong Jentlemen should alwaies be poring on a booke, and by using good studies, shold lease honest pleasure and haunt no good pastime. I meene nothing lesse: For it is well knowne, that I both like and love and have alwaies, and do yet still use, all exercises and pastimes that be fitte for my nature and habilitie. And beside naturall disposition, in judgement, also, I was never, either Stoick in doctrine, or Anabaptist in Religion to mislike a merie, pleasant, and plaifull nature, if no outrage be committed against lawe, mesure and good order. Therefore I woud wishe, that, beside some good time, fitlie appointed, and constantlie kepte, to encrease by readinge the knowledge of the tonges and learning, yong gentlemen shold use, and delite in all Courtelie exercises and Jentlemanlike pastimes."

Further on Ascham enumerates the following pastimes, saying, "to ride cumlie: to run faire at the tilte or ring: to plaie at all weapons: to shote faire in bow, or surelie in gon: to vaut lustely: to runne: to leape: to wrestle: to swimme: to daunce cumlie: to sing and playe of instrumentes cunnyngly: to hawke: to hunte: to playe at tennes, and all pastimes generally, which be joyned with labor, used in open place, and on the day light, conteining either some fitte exercise for warre, or some pleasant pastime for peace, be not onelie cumlie and decent, but also verie necessarie, for a Courtlie Jentleman to use."

When the Founder, King Henry VI., bought up the houses, gardens, and fields in the parish of Eton necessary for the foundation of his college, he acquired a considerable tract of open ground known as the

'Kinges Werde.' This piece of ground extended from the College on the north as far as the brook, then known as Colenorton Brook, which runs into the river Thames, and was bounded on the west by the road to Slough, and on the east by the river Thames. This corresponds to what was afterwards known for generations as 'The Playing-Fields.' Beyond the brook were two large fields, then (in 1443) the property of the Prior and Convent of Merton. These fields were acquired by the Founder a little later, and were at an early date known as the 'Upper and Lower Shooting-Fields.' It has been surmised that archery butts were set up here, and perhaps used by the boys. Archery was a popular pastime among high and low. The Founder himself was an archer, and a bracer of his has been preserved. In the days of the Tudor sovereigns archery was a favourite pastime at Court, and Henry VIII. and Elizabeth both excelled in it. Roger Ascham wrote a treatise on it, besides including it in the list of 'cumlie' pastimes for young gentlemen. When Harrow School was founded by John Lyon at the end of the sixteenth century, parents were expected to provide their boys with 'bowshafts, bow-strings, and a bracer,' in addition to pens, ink, and paper. The shooting for the 'Silver Arrow' at Harrow was an annual festival akin to the Eton 'Montem,' and its abolition was due to a similar cause. The playing-fields and shooting -fields were united by a brick bridge, known as Sheep's Bridge, built in 1563-64.

There are but few notices of the playing-fields in the early history of Eton College. In Malim's *Consuetudinarium*, compiled in 1560, there is no mention of them. The only hour in the day allotted for play was between four and five in the afternoon, an extra hour being allowed during the summer, between seven and eight o'clock. The boys did not return home at Christmas or Easter; and though the hours for work were partly or entirely relaxed during these holidays, the boys seem to have been always confined within the precincts of the College when not in school, chapel, or hall, except on the days on which they were given special leave to go out into the fields and neighbouring country.

In 1563, when the French ambassador and his suite were lodged in the College, and produced much discomfort and disorder thereby, one of the complaints made against them was, that they "spoyled a great manie of the Colledge bricks lying on the back side of ther kytchin, wch they threw at the Schollers as they passed between the Schole and the fields." As these obnoxious Frenchmen used also "daily to kill fesants, heronshawes, mallards, teeles, and doves wth their hand gonnes," it is possible that the 'Shooting-Fields' were at that date nothing more than a preserve for such game on land and water. This seems the more likely, inasmuch as it would appear that it was in 1583-84 that the playing-fields were first laid out and planted as they remain at present.

In 1590, on the occasion of a visit by Queen Elizabeth to Eton, a charge is made in the accounts: "To Holdernes for 3 dayes dressinge of the playing-filde by the garden when the Quene came, 18d."

There is but scanty record of the playing-fields, and indeed of the games and pastimes at Eton for the next fifty years, until the days of Provost Rous, who is credited with having planted some of the fine trees in the shooting-fields. This tradition seems due to the fact that the estimated age of some of the large trees would place the date of their plantation during the lifetime of Rous, rather than to any actual evidence that he had a hand in planting them. Pepys on his visit to Eton in 1666 "went into the back fields to see the scholars play." The next notice of the playing-fields at Eton occurs in a letter from Horace Walpole at Cambridge in 1736 to George Montagu. Walpole writes:—

"DEAR GEORGE,—Were not the playing-fields at Eton food for all manner of flights? No old maid's gown, though it had been tormented into all the fashions from King James to King George, ever underwent so many transformations as those poor plains have in my idea. At first I was contented with tending a visionary flock, and sighing some pastoral name to the echo of the cascade under the bridge. How happy should I have been to have had a kingdom only for the pleasure of being driven from it and living disguised in an humble vale! As I got further into Virgil and Clelia, I found myself transported from Arcadia to the garden of Italy; and saw Windsor Castle in no other view than the *Capitoli immobile saxum,* I wish a committee of the House of Commons may ever seem to be the senate; or a bill appear half so agreeable as a billet-doux. You see how deep you have carried me into old stories; I write of them with pleasure, but shall talk of them with more to you. I can't say I am sorry I was never quite a schoolboy; an expedition against bargemen, or a match at cricket, may be very pretty things to recollect; but, thank my stars, I can remember things that are very near as pretty."

Another side-light is thrown by Walpole's friend and contemporary, Thomas Gray, in his famous poem 'On a Distant View of Eton College,' in which he says—

> Say, Father Thames, for thou hast seen
> Full many a sprightly Race
> Disporting on thy Margent green
> The Paths of Pleasure trace.
> Who foremost now delight to cleave
> With pliant Arm thy glassy Wave?
> The captive Linnet which enthrall?
> What Idle Progeny succeed
> To chase the rolling Circle's speed.
> Or urge the flying Ball?
> While some on earnest Business bent
> Their murmuring Labours ply,
> 'Gainst graver Hours, that bring Constraint
> To sweeten Liberty:
> Some bold Adventurers disdain
> The limits of their little Reign,
> And unknown Regions dare descry:
> Still as they run they look behind,
> They hear a Voice in every Wind,
> And snatch a fearful Joy.

Not long after the date of this poem there was compiled the interesting manuscript account of Eton games, entitled *Nugæ*

Etonenses, from which Sir H. Maxwell-Lyte quotes the following list of games:—

Cricket, Fives, Shirking Walls, Scrambling Walls, Bally Cally, Battledores, Peg-top, Peg in the ring, Goals, Hopscotch, Headimy, Conquering Lobs, Hoops, Marbles, Trapball, Steal baggage, Puss in the corner, Cut gallows. Kites, Cloyster and Flyer Gigs, Tops, Humming-tops, Hunt the hare, Hunt the dark lanthorn, Chuck, Sinks, Starecaps, Hustlecap, Football, Slides in School, Leaping Poles, &c.

Now it is noteworthy that of all this miscellaneous list of games there is hardly one, so far as the game can be identified, cricket included, which could not be played within the precincts of the school-yard. Battledores, peg-tops, hop-scotch, hoops, marbles, trapball, and other games on the list are familiar names, even if it be difficult to imagine a modern Eton boy indulging in these somewhat vulgar amusements. Bowling, hoops, and even marbles have from time to time asserted a fleeting fascination at Eton, and there are few Etonians who cannot recall an outbreak of mania for tops at some time or another, though invariably a shortlived one. 'Peg in the ring' appears to be a combination of the peg-top with the volatile button, so dear to the boy in the street. The game of 'Goals' has usually been understood as football, but without good reason, for it would seem as likely to have been some game similar to that of pall-mall, where a ball was driven with a club through a goal. That football was played at an early date is shown by Horman in his *Vulgaria*, who speaks of playing with a "ball full of wynde." But as played, it was probably a kick-about in the school-yard, similar to that played by the Blue-Coat boys at Christ's Hospital.

Gray's "urge the flying Ball" could be understood equally of cricket as football. Walpole mentions cricket as a regular institution, and even then, as at the present day, the source of many 'old-boy' reminiscences. As far back as 1706 cricket was sufficiently popular to be celebrated in Latin verse by a Fellow of Eton, William Goldwin.

These pages are not the place in which to trace the rise and progress of cricket at Eton. The subject has been treated elsewhere, and antiquarian research has collected every scrap of information concerning a game which grew gradually in popular estimation, until after due development it has become the typical pastime of the English race. In the oldest known cricket club, the Hambledon Club, the chief performer was an Etonian, the eighth Earl of Winchilsea. The famous statesman, John Montagu, fourth Earl of Sandwich, was an enthusiastic cricketer, and varied his assiduous duties at the Admiralty with music, theatricals, cricket, and other sports at Hinchinbroke. In 1791 an eleven of old Etonians made their first appearance in London in a match against the Grentlemen of England at the old 'Lord's' cricket-ground.

The first recorded match took place in 1797 against an Oldfield Club. Other early antagonists were the Epsom Club and the Bullingdon from Oxford. The first recorded public school matches were in 1799 and 1800, when Eton played Westminster on the old 'Lord's' ground. The first recorded match between Eton and Harrow took place on the same ground on August 2, 1805. On this occasion Stratford Canning (afterwards Lord Stratford de Redcliffe) played for Eton, and Lord Byron for Harrow. Of this match Byron writes to his friend Charles Gordon, "We have played the Eton, and were most confoundedly beat; however, it was some comfort to me that I got 11 notches the first innings and 7 the second, which was more than any of our side except Brockman and Ipswich could contrive to hit. After the match we dined together and were extremely friendly, not a single discordant word was uttered by either party." The first recorded match between Eton and Winchester took place at Lord's on August 4, 1826, Winchester being victorious in spite of the presence in the Eton eleven of such formidable cricketers as E. H. Pickering and Henry Snow. From these dates the rivalry between these two schools and ton on the cricket-field has been continuous and well sustained, and continues to form one of the central and most exciting episodes in a schoolboy's life.

At Eton there are certain striking episodes in the history and progress of cricket in the school. No one studying the scores of the early cricket matches can fail to be struck by the prevalence of 'tugs' in the Eton eleven. Was this due to the superior athletic training inculcated by the severe discipline in College, or perhaps was it an illustration how brains and athletics are more often to be found in unison than not? Or was it not perhaps due to the fact that, out of the limited accommodation in the playing-fields, one part was always set apart for the College game, leaving the remaining six hundred boys, or such portion of them as called themselves 'dry-bobs,' to compete for the remainder. At all events, many members of the early Eton elevens were tugs, including such well-known cricketers as John Barnard, Henry Snow, John Henry Kirwan, and Thomas Anchitel Anson. Among the oppidan cricketers the most famous were George Osbaldeston, afterwards the famous huntsman, Herbert Jenner, Roger Kynaston, Charles G. Taylor, and William Pickering. It is interesting to note that the match against Winchester in 1829 was mainly won by the efforts of John Henry Parnell, father of the late Irish leader; that John Charles Ryle, the present Bishop of Liverpool, played for Eton in 1833, when Bishop Abraham was also in the eleven, and again in 1834, when he was captain; that Dr. Balston, afterwards Head-master, played in 1836, as his successor, Dr. Hornby, did in 1845.

The first great score made in the Eton and Harrow match was that of 152, made in 1841 by Emilius Bayley, who played no less than four years in succession; his score remains to this present day unsurpassed in this particular match. 1841 was a memorable year, owing to the presence at Eton of three famous fast bowlers, Walter Marcon, George Yonge, and Harvey Fellowes. John Coleridge Patteson, the martyr-bishop, played in 1843, and again in 1844, in which year also played Joseph W. Chitty, one of the most renowned Etonians, and afterwards Lord Justice of Appeal. In 1848 Edward W. Blore, afterwards a popular Fellow and Tutor of Trinity College, Cambridge, made his first appearance, and in 1846 the brothers Aitken. Blore played three years, and took in all 35 wickets against Winchester, and 33 against Harrow. In 1850 there played Charles Loyd Norman, the first member of a large

Eton cricketing family, who were afterwards specially identified with the West Kent Cricket Club.

From 1850 a wave of ill-luck came over Eton in the annual match with Harrow. A new era of cricket, however, was commencing at Eton, which was destined to be fruitful of remarkable results. This was a great deal due to the efforts of two Etonians, G. R. Dupuis (who played first at Lord's in 1851) and R. A. H. Mitchell, the finest amateur cricketer of his day, who made his first appearance in 1858.

Mitchell, one of the finest exponents of the game of cricket, and Dupuis, one of its most learned professors, both became Assistant-masters at Eton, and from that date cricket at Eton became a serious pleasure, resulting in a great development of the game. The period synchronised with the advance of cricket to be not only a great game at schools, but a popular game throughout the country. At Eton the progress of the game was greatly due to the influence of several sets of brothers, who carried on a great tradition in ever-increasing repute. Early among these were the brothers Austen Leigh, of whom the younger, Augustus, is now Provost of King's, and the elder, Edward, is Lowermaster of Eton; they were indeed brands snatched from the burning, or sinners reclaimed, inasmuch as their elder brothers had played for Harrow, one of whom, Spencer Austen Leigh, distinguished himself particularly in the Eton and Harrow match. It may be said, however, that the high-water mark of Eton cricket was reached by the brothers Lyttelton. Lord Lyttelton, mentioned in a previous chapter, himself a Newcastle medallist, sent eight sons to Eton, of whom seven played in the eleven, including three, Charles (now Viscount Cobham), Edward (now Head-master of Haileybury), and Alfred (Recorder of Oxford, and M.P. for Leamington), who are reckoned in the highest rank of amateur cricketers. Another great family of cricketers was the Lubbocks, of whom Alfred Lubbock was the hero of the Eton and Winchester match in 1863, when he made 174 not out, while E. W. Tritton made 130 in the same innings. The Normans, Barnards, Pelhams, Tollemaches, and others are instances of family influence in cricket. In later years the same notoriety was gained by the Studds, and still later by the Pilkingtons. In these pages little more than mention can be made of such famous public-school cricketers as James Round, T. E. Bagge, C. J. Ottaway, C. I. Thornton (the mighty hitter, 'Bloomin' 'igh, bloomin' 'ard, and bloomin' hoften,' to the delight of the spectators), Lord Harris, A. W. Ridley, F. M. Buckland, W. F. Forbes, Hon. Ivo Bligh, Lord Hawke, H. W. Bainbridge, F. Marchant, H. Philipson, H. B. Chinnery, and F. H. E. Cunliffe. Their deeds are duly chronicled in many books of cricket, for histories of the game abound, and hardly any score in a match of any repute has escaped being recorded therein. The annual struggles between Eton and Harrow, and Eton and Winchester, have been very evenly balanced, Harrow having a slight lead in the former case, and Eton a good lead in the latter. The Eton and Winchester match was played at Lord's early in August, at the beginning of the holidays, until 1856, when the date was changed to June, and the place to one or other of the two schools alternately. The Eton and Harrow match continues to be played at Lord's; but now that it has degenerated into something between Barnum's Show and a gigantic picnic, there are not wanting lovers of cricket who would gladly see the match fought out alternately at Eton or Harrow.

For some reason or another during the last ten years Eton cricket seems to have lost something of its dash and sting. This may be due to the decline of the family influence alluded to before, or perhaps to an undue prolongation of some one form of cricket drill. Probably the true cause lies in the difficulty of procuring good wickets in fields where football is played during the winter. Rough wickets are a bad training for boys who may be destined to wield the bat on such a billiard table as Lord's Cricket Ground. This defect, however, will, it is hoped, be shortly remedied. For some time the only cricket-grounds were those in the playing-fields and shooting-fields. The ground in the Upper Shooting-Fields is the best ground, where the school eleven plays and practises, and is known as 'Upper Club.' The ground in the Lower Shooting-Fields was lately occupied by 'Middle Club.' In the playing-fields there were three or four games possible, the best known being 'Sixpenny,' apparently so called in true Etonian fashion because the subscription to it was a shilling. The corner formed by the wall along the Slough Road, and that of the house at the corner of Weston's Yard, known as 'Sixpenny Corner,' was the historic spot for pugilistic encounters. Here the Duke of Wellington fought 'Bobus' Smith, and if the Duke's often-quoted and much-contested remark is right, that the battle of Waterloo was won in the playing-fields at Eton, he was probably alluding to the mills at Sixpenny Corner, rather than to the more civilised contests at cricket and football.

The other pitches in the playing-fields were given to the collegers and to 'Aquatics,' where the 'wet bobs' disported themselves on dry land. When the demand increased for more cricket pitches, 'Sixpenny' was moved to the great field, known as the Timbralls (or Timbrehawe), which became the recognised cricket-field of the Lower Boys. In more recent years further extensions have been made across the Chalvey brook, and in 1897 an immense addition was made to the cricket accommodation by the purchase of the large tract of land extending towards Slough, known as 'Agar's Plough' or 'Dutchman's Farm.' Here new grounds have been laid out, and it will be possible to relieve these and the playing-fields from the strain and damage caused by the winter football.

Football is an ancient game, and has been played at Eton for generations, but its annals, like those of the poor, are 'short and simple.' Every public school has its own set of football rules, drawn up gradually and in direct relation to the spot in which the game is played. There are two games at Eton, the 'Field-game' and the 'Wall-game.' They are really but different varieties of the same game, as played in the open field, or in a long narrow strip against the wall. The 'Field-game' also derives its rules from the limitations under which it was played. The 'bully,' like the 'scrummage' in Rugby football, is the centre of the game, and gives scope for the employment of any number of boys on the same side. It is a fast game, leading to much brilliancy of play, especially behind the bully. As the ball may only be played with the foot, the Eton game is in distinct contrast to that played at Rugby or Harrow. The game at the Wall is at first sight difficult to understand, but it is really the 'Field-game' played in a narrow space. As the narrow space in which the game is played would not admit of the erection of a goal at either end, a variety is introduced by the desire of one side to drive the ball down to the rival end beyond a certain chalk line (whence the names 'good calx' and 'bad calx,' and to get a 'shy,' *i.e.* to be allowed to throw the ball at a goal, marked by a door in the wall at the southern end, and the branch of a tree on the opposite side. The annual struggle on St. Andrew's Day between collegers and oppidans is a famous event at Eton. Owing to the vicinity of the College to the playing-fields, and to the fact of this particular field being their private football field, the youthful 'tug' is brought into contact with the 'Wall-game' at an earlier age than the ordinary oppidan. The collegers, therefore, though so much fewer in number, start with an advantage in the knowledge of the game, an advantage which puts them easily on a par, if not a superiority to the picked eleven of oppidans.

At the present day, now that football has become a public pastime like cricket, the football world is divided into great sections, those who play according to the rules of Rugby School, and those who play the rules drawn up by a Football Association some twenty years ago or more. As Eton, Harrow, and Winchester continue to adhere to their own time-honoured rules of football, they are not unfrequently hindered thereby from joining in the University matches and obtaining a coveted

'Blue.' Suggestions have been made as to the abolition of the special public school games in favour of the uniform Association Rules. It is a matter of consolation to think that the Eton 'Field-game' shows strength enough to resist all such insidious machinations. In fact the training of the Eton game is for sheer dexterity and brilliancy of play the best school for a boy's mind and limb, and the best preparation for the 'bullies' and 'rouges' of after life. The 'house-matches,' moreover, whenever the strength is evenly balanced, are productive of the keenest and hardest fought form of mimic warfare.

Another game, which, though not originally so, has become a purely Eton product, is that of Fives. The game of Fives in its original form was little more than knocking up a ball against the wall in a court enclosed on three sides, either with the hand or with a kind of racquet. At Eton, chance led to a further development of the game. In 1694-95 a new flight of steps was built leading down from the north door of the chapel into the school-yard. It had been the habit for the boys to play fives between the great perpendicular buttresses upon a sort of raised platform. The new steps projected across one of these bays, forming a second platform upon a slightly different level. This afforded an extended compass for the game, which was further complicated by the fact of the side wall of the staircase crossing immediately under the projecting part of the chapel buttress. The eccentricities shown by the ball in striking these differently shaped projections produced an agreeable diversity in the game. A quick eye and good head became as necessary as a strong arm and untiring muscles. There was, however, only one court among the chapel buttresses similarly provided, so that in 1840 a subscription was raised to build some additional and regular fives courts, exactly modelled upon the accidental court against the chapel. In 1847 a set of fives courts was built on the Eton back road. As these proved after some years to be quite inadequate in number for those wishing to play the game, a set of eight more courts was built in 1870, of an improved description. Since then so popular has the game become, that the number of fives courts has been very greatly increased, each house having one or two courts allotted to its own use. In this way several hundreds of boys can play the game, originally played by two or four only between the chapel buttresses. The Eton game has, moreover, spread to other schools, and there is hardly a school of any importance in England, public or private, which does not possess one or two, if not more, fives courts on the Eton model. Few players, however, have any idea of how the eccentric and apparently unreasonable obstructions in the court first came into existence.

That there was a tennis court in Eton in the last years of the reign of Elizabeth, is shown by entries in the Eton Audit books for 'making the tennis-court side,' 1600-1, and 'tiling' the court in 1602-3. Horman also alludes, besides football, to "tennys playe." Tennis, mentioned at Eton as late as 1767, is, however, a game better adapted for grown-up men than for growing boys.

Racquets, in the modern sense, received a new development by the building of two new covered courts in 1866. For many years the Eton racquet-players held their own, even against such formidable antagonists as the champions from Harrow, where racquets is included among the serious games of the school. During the last ten years or so the interest in racquets at Eton has shown an inclination to wane, partly, perhaps, owing to the expenses of playing, and to the fact of there being only two courts. Latterly the game has shown signs of revival, and as Eton proved victorious in the Public School Competition for 1899, it is hoped that players may now arise to emulate the palmy days of Alfred Lyttelton, Ivo Bligh, and other racquet-champions of Eton.

Of other games on land few have taken root and become popular at Eton. Lawn-tennis has never flourished; golf is an impossibility; hockey has had one or two fitful periods of patronage, but is now impossible for Eton boys, since it has become the cherished pastime of the wives and daughters of their masters. During the half terminating at Easter a pack of beagles, kept up by subscription, is hunted, and forms a source of great attraction for the longer-limbed and longer-winded boys in the school, besides being an excellent training school for future Masters of Hounds. Boys of insufficient size or standing, or deficient in cash or enterprise, solace themselves with paper-chases or impromptu steeplechases known as 'jumping.' During this half, too, take place the annual races, the school steeplechase, the mile race, the walking race, and the miscellaneous athletic sports, all of which excite the keenest competition and enthusiasm. Each house has its separate athletic sports as well. Many well-known racers and athletes have made their first appearance in the sports at Eton, among whom may be mentioned the Hon. A. L. Pelham, who won the Open Championship for the half-mile while still an Eton boy; Robert H. Benson, the hero of the sensational dead-heat with E. M. Hawtrey for the three miles at the University Sports in 1872; W. P. Phillips, the sprinter, who died not long after leaving Eton; R. H. Macaulay, the high jumper and quarter-miler; and many others. Fishing during the summer half was at one time a favourite pastime, but has now fallen out of favour, partly, perhaps, through the decease, natural or otherwise, of the legendary monsters who were reputed to have defied the efforts at capture of successive generations of Eton boys. In former days a game of billiards in a tavern seems not only to have been recognised as lawful, but was even shared in by the masters. In these days, however, when the tavern has been degraded into a drinkshop, and the billiard-room into a gambling-hell, both taverns and billiards have had to be put under a most stringent taboo. Before the days of railways riding was often permitted; but as the facilities for travelling increased, the restrictions on locomotion became more severe, until at last horses, carriages, and even the all-pervading bicycle are forbidden without special leave to all Eton boys.

One pastime, however, remains to be mentioned, to some eyes, perhaps, the most important of all, namely, boating. The River Thames flowing past and embracing Eton, which is in fact situated upon the ancient bed of the river, has ever been the source to Eton of an advantage shared by no other school in the land. Westminster School is in truth situated on the banks of the same river, but the pressure of civilisation and the growth of traffic long ago made the Thames at Westminster unfit for navigation by slender craft.

Boating, however, though by no means objected to in itself, except for the danger incurred and sadly illustrated on more than one occasion by boys who could not swim, was still a matter of difficulty owing to the river being out of bounds. A boy might go on the river, but he was not allowed to go to the river; at least he could only go at the risk of infringing a curious rule, which was prevalent at Eton until quite recent days. Every place outside the precincts was 'out of bounds.' It was not supposed that Eton boys would be thus cribbed or confined; but it was necessary for a boy 'out of bounds' to 'shirk' or avoid being seen by a passing master. 'Shirking' could be effected by diving into a shop, or down a back street, or even by dodging behind the imaginary shelter of a lamp-post; but if a boy was unlucky enough to pass across the field of vision in a master's eye, which was not by any means invariably on the alert to perceive him, the one and only punishment was a flogging. The curious part of it was that boating went on uninterruptedly, it being apparently a code of honour among the masters not to walk by the river for fear of seeing the boys on it.

Longboats were in use as far back as 1762, when there were three, which went by the names of the *Snake*, the *Piper's Green*, and *My Guinea's Lion*. Those boys rowing in the longboats were formed into a kind of club, ruled over by the Captain of the Boats, who, by virtue of this dignity, gradually became the most important and the greatest 'swell' in the school. The boats were divided into two divisions, Upper

Boats and Lower Boats. Quite early in the century the ten-oared boat, the Monarchy appears as the first on the list, stroked by the Captain of the Boats. The other boats have borne various names, those of the *Dreadnought* and *Defiance* seeming to be the oldest. By degrees the number of boats has been fixed at nine or ten, the three Upper Boats being now *Monarch*, *Victory*, and *Prince of Wales* (or Third Upper), and the Lower Boats *Britannia*, *Dreadnought*, *Thetis*, *Hibernia* (originally manned by Irish boys only), *St. George*, and *Defiance*, with Alexandra added on occasions, when the number of qualified candidates for boating honours require the addition. On the great festivals in the summer half of the Fourth of June and Election Saturday the boats rowed up in procession to Surly Hall, some two and a half miles above Windsor, where they disembarked on the opposite bank and partook of a champagne supper, returning afterwards in procession to the Brocas, where a display of fireworks took place on the eyot near the Windsor shore. At first the boys wore fantastic dresses, as galley slaves or something similar, but since 1814 a kind of uniform has been adopted, which, combined with the separate colours and emblems of each boat, and floral decorations to the hat, the cockswains being attired in naval uniforms, makes the spectacle and grouping one of the most attractive sights in the summer season. Even those pageants were supposed to be unknown to the authorities, as they took place out of bounds, and Provost Goodall and Dr. Keate always professed entire ignorance of such events.

239

On every alternate Saturday after the Fourth of June, during the summer half, the boats rowed up in procession, the Upper Boats proceeding to Surly Hall, where they dined off ducks and green peas and champagne, while the Lower Boats returned to the rafts, where they indulged in the champagne without the solid food. These events were known as 'check nights,' though there seems to be a diversity of opinion as to the origin of the name, one explanation being that on these nights the faults of rowing were checked, another not attributing it to a higher origin than the check shirts worn by the boys on such occasions.

The festivities on check nights, to say nothing of the Fourth of June and Election Saturday, were not unfrequently the cause of some disorder and not a little scandal. A similar charge was brought against an institution known as 'oppidan dinner,' a banquet held in the White Hart Hotel at Windsor, and of which the authorities felt themselves obliged to profess ignorance. Dr. Keate, in fact, kept himself so duly uninformed of the practice of boating at Eton, that when Eton rowed against Westminster at Maidenhead in 1831, and was victorious, he did not hear of it until the news was forced upon him. Dr. Hawtrey was the first Head-master to recognise boating as an authorised institution; but even he did not remove the anomaly of its being out of bounds to go to the river. Dr. Goodford was very much alive to the abuses of check nights, and in 1860 he succeeded, with the help among the boys of the Hon. C. G. Lyttelton, Captain of the Eleven, and R. H. Blake-Humfrey, Captain of the Boats, in putting an end to both check nights and oppidan dinner. In return. Dr. Goodford allowed boys to go down to the boats without 'shirking,' but only during the summer half. This privilege, once bestowed, was not long in extending itself to the whole school all the year round. The boys, however, were, and are still, required to touch their hats by way of salute to any master whom they may meet. Election Saturday was a cause also of some disregard of school discipline. In former days the school always broke up for the holidays on a Monday, and all work and duty practically terminated on Saturday afternoon. To remedy this the day of breaking up was changed to Friday, and the work continued up to the early school on that day. Election Saturday had long ceased to be a festivity connected with the election of new 'tugs,' and had become a carousal. It was finally abolished in 1867, when the Fourth of June remained as the only real festival of the year.

A selected 'Eight' for racing seems to have been first formed in 1820, but the first race against Westminster took place at Putney in 1829, when Eton was victorious. A contemporary account describes the Etonians as racing in broad blue-striped Guernsey frocks and dark straw hats, like sailors. The two schools only met at intervals. Westminster beat Eton for the first time at Datchet in 1837. The first meeting with Radley took place in 1858, and for the best part of forty years the latter plucky little school has aspired, but in vain, to lower the Eton flag. In 1861 the Eton Eight was allowed to appear for the first time at Henley Regatta. Eton won the Ladies' Plate for the first time in 1864, and from 1866 was successful five years in succession. Several years of ill-luck then ensued, but the honour of Eton has been strikingly vindicated by winning the Ladies' Plate seven years running from 1892 to 1898.

For many years the collegers were not allowed to boat on the upper reach of the river with the oppidans, and were therefore debarred from places in the Eight, although they were able to figure in the cricket Eleven. A colleger, R. G. Marsden, was first allowed to row in the Eight in 1864, the first year Eton won the Ladies' Plate.

The various Eton boat-races and the chronicles of its 'wet-bob' heroes are all set forth in the *Eton Boating Book* by R. H. Blake-Humfrey, and cannot be detailed here. Mention must, however, be made of the prominent part taken by the present Head-master, Dr. Edmond Warre, himself an old University oar, in encouraging and supervising the boating arrangements, not only for the Eight, but also for the smallest wet-bobs. He was ably succeeded as a coach by the Rev. Stuart A. Donaldson, who rowed in the Eton Eight for 1873, who in his turn gave way to Mr. R. S. de Havilland, an Eton and Oxford oar. Of Mr. de Havilland's success little need be said than that under his tuition the Eton Eight has for seven years running won the Ladies' Plate at Henley Regatta. Latterly the general control of the boating for Eton boys has been in the capable hands of Mr. Walter Dumford.

Eton has, in fact, become the chief nursery for rowing in England. The boys are now taken in hand at an early age and taught what rowing really is. The Universities, therefore, look to Eton for the pick of their oarsmen. No greater tribute can be paid to Eton rowing than the fact that some years ago a feud took place in the Cambridge University Boat Club owing to a supposed favouring of Eton oarsmen. This led to a disinclination of Eton oarsmen for Cambridge, and a dearth of Etonians in the Cambridge Eight. Since this date Oxford, with six or seven Etonians on board, won the University Boat Race with unbroken regularity until 1899, when a return of Etonian oarsmen to the Cambridge flag synchronised with a brilliant victory over Oxford.

The Thames cannot be quitted without mention of bathing, one of the most justly popular of Eton pastimes, and one in which Eton is singularly privileged in comparison with other public schools. The Collegers, being confined to the lower river, were allowed to bathe in the river off the playing-fields, and as early as 1549 a scholar, Robert Sacheverell, was drowned off the 'playing-lease' at 'le bathing-place,' being carried away to 'a whirlpole.' The oppidans bathed in the upper river, and in the middle of the eighteenth century the bathing-places were known as Sandy Hole, Cuckoo Ware, Dead Pile, Pope's Hole, Cotton's Hole, South Hope, and Dickson's Hole. Of these Cuckoo Weir is still the bathing-place for the lower boys. South Hope is probably what was in later days called Lower Hope. In 1794 the fifth Earl Waldegrave was accidentally drowned. In 1840 a boy, Charles Montagu, was drowned near Windsor Bridge, and it was in consequence of this that Mr. William Evans, the drawing-master, and the Rev. George Augustus Selwyn, afterwards Bishop of Lichfield, persuaded Dr. Hawtrey to recognise boating under a stringent rule that no boy should be allowed on the river until he had passed an examination in swimming. The well-known bathing-places at 'Athens,' 'Upper Hope,' and 'Cuckoo Weir' were then constructed. Since the passing of this admirable rule a fatal accident from drowning at Eton has been of the rarest occurrence.

It is a matter for the deepest regret that the great increase in the use of the river as a highway by the general public has proved a serious check upon the liberty of bathing at Eton. Should the free use of the river for bathing ever be restricted, one of the pleasantest and most health-giving exercises for youth will be taken away from Eton.

Some obscurity hangs over the original adoption of a pale shade of light-blue as the colour or badge of Eton. There does not seem to be any record of its use before the race against Westminster in 1831, when the news was communicated to the Head-master through the agency of a large dog profusely decked out with light-blue ribbons. It is possible that the battles of the 'Blues' date from the Eton and Westminster races, for the Universities, at all events Cambridge, seem to have only borrowed the idea of a distinctive colour. Distinctive colours and badges had probably been worn by the crews of the various boats. When the light-blue was once adopted as the Eton colour, it was naturally soon worn by the Eleven. In 1860 the 'Field' or Football Eleven were allowed to wear a colour of Eton blue and scarlet quarterly. The adoption of a football colour led in 1862 to the use of distinctive colours for each house football eleven. After this the various 'colours' have increased and multiplied to an extent which renders them only intelligible to Etonians on the spot.

Another innovation under Dr. Goodford in 1860 was the formation of a Volunteer Rifle Corps, which, under the zealous and capable command of Dr. Warre and other Assistant-masters, has become one of the most important institutions in the school. The numbers in the corps became sufficient to admit of its being enrolled as a separate auxiliary battalion of the Buckinghamshire Regiment, but the corps is now known as the 4th Volunteer Battalion of the Oxfordshire Light Infantry. Good drill rather than marksmanship is aimed at, for the rival attractions of cricket and boating render it difficult for many of the most likely shots to practise at the butts during the summer half. The advantages of systematic drilling for boys are now generally recognised, provided that there be no excess in the direction of military precision. That it affects the whole school was well shown by the ease and complete success with which the Eton boys executed the complicated manoeuvres of a torchlight serenade to the Queen in Windsor Castle on the occasion of the Jubilees in 1887 and 1897.

XII

ETON AT THE PRESENT DAY

It must not be supposed from the last chapter that the only antidote to the ordinary routine of work in or out of school was to be found in games. A more serious interlude was often performed by the leading boys in the school. In 1811 Charles Fox Townshend, a member of a family renowned at Eton and in the annals of the State, founded a debating society, known as 'The Eton Society.' At first its members were known as 'Literati.' The name, however, by which the Eton Society is most widely known is that of 'Pop,' the origin of the name being traced on fairly certain grounds to the fact that the Society met for some years in a room over a confectioner's shop, or popina, kept by Mrs. Hatton. In 1846, on the abolition of the old Christopher Inn, 'Pop' removed itself to part of these premises, where it has remained until the present day, although the old inn building is now at the time of writing doomed to destruction.

The Society at first consisted of twenty members, a number afterwards increased to twenty-eight. Most of the brilliant Etonians of the early part of the century— Gladstone, Selwyn, Derby, Sir Francis Doyle, and others—made their *début* as orators in 'Pop,' and the high tone of the debates was kept up until quite recently.

In later years, however, when the qualifications of a boy for 'Pop' became due more to his social weight in the school than to his personal talents, the quality of the debates began to decline, and at the present day debates have nearly, if not altogether, ceased to take place at all, 'Pops' being merely a select clique of chosen 'swells.' It is greatly to be hoped that some effort may be made to revive the drooping glory of 'Pop' as a famous Etonian institution, and that the familiar rules encased in Eton blue on the walls of a 'swell's' room may denote something other than skill in rowing, cricket, or football. It is noteworthy that the five most famous rhetoricians in Parliament—Chatham, Fox, Canning, Derby, and Gladstone—have been Etonians. It is interesting therefore to note that the decline of 'Pop' as a school of oratory synchronises with the decline or disuse of oratory in the House of Commons, and to conjecture, whether the decay of oratory at Westminster has damped the ardour of 'Pop,' or the decline of the debates in 'Pop' has exercised a deleterious effect on the eloquence of public men. 'Pop,' however, was the parent of several similar institutions. A debating society was instituted in College, which has been, and remains, very successful. About 1875 a similar debating society was instituted in each of the most important boardinghouses. Though a marked increase of eloquence has not been so evident in the school as might have been hoped for, the house debating societies afforded to the boys many opportunities of collecting and putting into form their thoughts, and some practice in expressing them.

247

Literature has always been a favourite field of exercise for a budding intellect. It was not, however, until 1786 that it entered the field at Eton as a rival to cricket and football. In that year three Eton boys, George Canning, John Hookham Frere, and 'Bobus' Smith started a magazine called *The Microcosm*, mainly a collection of essays with occasional verse. This magazine, the first published by school-boys, excited great curiosity and interest. It was carried on up to Election 1787. It was the first of a long and varied series of periodicals edited by Eton boys, of which it would be impossible to give a complete list in these pages. 'Gregory Grifiin of the College of Eton, the supposed editor of *The Microcosm*, met with a rival in 1804 in the shape of one 'Solomon Grildrig,' who edited a similar magazine called *The Miniature*. This was chiefly edited by Stratford Canning, who was assisted by Thomas Rennell, Henry Gally Knight, and Richard and Gerald Wellesley, the two sons of the Marquess. The latter magazine ran for about twelve months and then suddenly became of historical importance. The boy-editors found a difficulty in the matter of ways and means. From this they were saved by the enterprise of a young almost unknown publisher, John Murray. Murray was in this way brought in contact with George Canning, and from this incident rose *The Quarterly Review*, the Tory rival of the famous *Edinburgh Review*.

The next literary ventures at Eton are connected with the names of two Etonian writers, who can never be forgotten by their old school, Winthrop Mackworth Praed and John Moultrie. After some attempts at magazines, issued only in manuscript, such as *The College Magazine*,

Horœ Otiosœ, Apis Matina, and others, Praed, assisted by Walter Blunt, a colleger, published in 1820 a magazine called *The Etonian,* the supposed editor being one 'Peregrine Courtenay, King of Clubs.' Among its contributors were boys of marked literary genius, such as Moultrie, under the pseudonym of 'Gerard Montgomery,' Sidney Walker, and Henry Nelson Coleridge. The magazine, which only lasted till Election 1821, when Praed left Eton, had a most remarkable success, and several imitations quickly ensued. In 1827 *The Eton Miscellany* appeared, among the contributors to which were W. E. Gladstone, Bishop Selwyn, Sir Francis H. Doyle, Frederick Rogers (Lord Blachford), and Arthur Hallam. Other rivals of ephemeral existence sprang up along with *The Miscellany,* among the contributors to which were Sir John Wickens, Lord Lyttelton, Dean Goulbum, and others, afterwards to have prominent careers.

The literary productions of public schools have a tendency to become ephemeral, a fate perhaps inevitable through the fact of their being originated by and dependent on the zeal and interest of one boy or a group of boys, at whose departure the enterprise languishes and dies. Such was the fate of all the many spasmodic effusions which hardly any generation of Etonians failed to produce. Some were serious, some funny, but all were ephemeral. Mention may be made of *The Observer,* edited by Vincent Coles, Vincent Cracroft-Amcotts, and W. H. C. Nation in 1859, and its immediate successor, under Coles and Amcotts, *The Phoenix;* also of another, *The Etonian,* supported about 1876 by G. N. Curzon, J. K. Stephen, C. A. Spring-Rice, and others. No later periodical at Eton, however, came up to the level reached in the older days by Canning, Gladstone, Praed, and Moultrie. Perhaps an exception should be made for the verses of James Kenneth Stephen, a genius of the most remarkable promise, who was prevented by a premature death from attaining the full maturity of his powers.

One periodical publication, however, has survived, and shows signs of a prosperous existence for an indefinite period. This is *The Eton Chronicle*, a fortnightly publication, founded in 1863 by W. Wightman Wood, J. E. Tinné, Ashley Pochin, and Henry Nevile Sherbrooke. The *Chronicle* does not pretend to do more than its name suggests. It is probably just the absence of any literary flavour which has caused the Chronicle to flourish for so many years.

Winthrop Mackworth Praed was also the originator of a scheme which was to prove fruitful of much good to the school. At some of the other public schools, like Harrow and Charterhouse, which had begun to challenge with success the supremacy of Eton among schools, a library, or more than one, was provided for the use of the boys. Praed, feeling the want of such a library at Eton, planned one for 'Pop,' but afterwards enlarged his scheme to one open to the whole school. This library was first started in 1821, supported by subscriptions among the upper boys, and located in a room of the Eton bookseller, Edward Pote Williams, who, as his name denotes, had inherited the business and prestige of the Pote family. Dr. Hawtrey encouraged the scheme. A kind of library had existed in a cupboard in Upper School, but was quite useless. When, however, the new College Buildings were erected in

1844 in Weston's Yard, a fine spacious library was erected in them, to which all boys who had reached the middle division of Fifth Form were admitted. To this library that founded by Praed was removed. It was one of the most charming spots in the whole of Eton, and admirably calculated for the purpose of quiet study and reading. It is a matter for the deepest regret that the further extension of the College buildings in 1887 should have involved the destruction of this beautiful room. Upon this sad event the library was removed to a very large room in the New Schools, where it has increased greatly, to a large extent owing to private donations by old Etonians, such as those of Major Myers, the present adjutant of the Eton Volunteers. There is, however, serious need for a proper school library, and in this respect Eton has fallen sadly behind other public schools. It must be remembered that the library in the College belonged to the College, and not to the school. Its contents, moreover, are somewhat of an antiquarian nature, so that it would be quite unsuitable to make any attempt to merge it in a school library.

Many additions have been made to the school buildings during the last quarter of the nineteenth century. The chapel, restored in the base Gothic of the early Victorian era, has been further beautified by the addition of a new organ-screen, to commemorate the Etonians who lost their lives in the Afghan and South African campaigns. Eton Chapel was not much more fortunate in this addition than it had been in the case of former benefactions. Of a more satisfactory nature, if less obvious in their import, have been the beautiful tapestry of 'The Star of

Bethelem,' designed by Sir E. Burne-Jones, executed by William Morris, and presented by Mr. H. E. Luxmoore, and the large painting of 'Sir Galahad,' painted and presented by Mr. G. F. Watts, R.A., both of which works of art are a distinct adornment to the chapel. The chapel had, however, long ceased to be able to accommodate the whole school. For a time the Lower School was forced to attend service in the large music-room, erected at the bottom of Keate's Lane by the Rev. L. G. Hayne. At last, however, a new chapel was erected close by this site, in which about a third of the school are now accommodated.

New class-rooms also became a necessity, and not only was a new block added to the 'New Schools' in 1876, but a new set of class-rooms, including a lecture-theatre, was built on the site of the old mathematical schools, adjoining the new Lower Chapel. The cry, however, for new buildings has been incessant, and new laboratories, workshops, a drill-hall, &c., have proved severe taxes on the resources of the Governing Body. A proper school library is, however, a great need, and also a speech-room, large enough to enable the whole or the greater part of the school to be assembled together if required, although for this purpose 'Upper School' has for generations proved efficacious.

'Speeches' have ever been a special feature of Eton life. They have taken the place of the theatricals, once so much encouraged, of which Mr. Francis Tarver is the recent and sympathetic historian, and also of the dissertations or declamations which the elder boys used at one time to compose. Speeches are the sole relic of these customs. They are usually delivered in Upper School, and on the principal occasion of

'Speeches,' the Fourth of June, the old schoolroom is bright with the faces of parents, relatives, and distinguished visitors. Upper School has, however, shown a want of elasticity with regard to the growth and requirements of Eton. It has for some years ceased to be used as a class-room, except for examination in trials, and now is thought by many to be inadequate even for the purpose of speeches. A new Speech Room is therefore urgently required, and it is probable that the want may have been supplied before the nineteenth century absolutely comes to its end.

With the increase, also, of the numbers in the school, and the raising of the standard of comfort, some addition has been necessary to the boarding-house accommodation. Some of the old houses, including the old building of the Christopher Inn, have been found to be entirely unsuited to modern requirements, and in some cases it is to be feared that these picturesque relics of the past may have to give way to buildings constructed from a more ornate and mercantile point of view. Nothing illustrates so well the difficulty of any systematic form of government for a great public school as the haphazard way in which the boarding-houses have been allowed to grow up. A little vigilance and foresight on the part of the Provost and Fellows in bygone days might have secured to the College the properties within or neighbouring to its precincts, in order to provide for the accommodation of the oppidans. The Fellows, however, clung to their statutes, which they neglected, and their revenues, of which they had no idea of making a profitable use. The oppidans, being only regarded as an extra in the school under the old statutes, had to shift for themselves, and good, bad, or indifferent as the lodging-house accommodation might be in the neighbourhood, it was of no concern to the College authorities, provided that some kind of order and discipline was maintained. Hence the keepers of boardinghouses, male or female, had to rent the houses themselves, some at exorbitant rates from the College itself, or if they had money enough, to buy land and build a house to hold as many boys as possible, which they might hope to dispose of with profit to a successor. In this way it was possible for such a house to be erected as that built by the late Bishop Chapman, and since occupied by Mr. Wolley-Dod and Mr. Daman, an eyesore and a terror to the lover of the picturesque, of which so much still remains at Eton. The same want of foresight prevailed with regard to the security of the lands surrounding Eton College. One of the paramount requirements of a great school like Eton is that it should, as far as possible, be surrounded by open land, free if possible for the boys to indulge in their games of cricket, football, shooting, or jumping, and forming a barrier to the ever-advancing surf that is thrown forward by the ever-billowing metropolis. And yet little had been done to secure this inestimable benefit. Some of the surrounding fields are fortunately protected by Lammas and other Common rights, but on the London side the College was defenceless. Slough and Datchet slowly developed into suburbs of London without the danger being noticed by the Eton authorities. Harrow had been engulfed by the pitiless flood, but, though *proximus ardet Ucalegon,* Eton made no sign, and it might be said almost invited the attention of the jerry-builder and other enemies of the soil. At last the danger threatened became immediate. Some land adjoining the College property on the west side of the Slough road was sold to a speculative builder, with a prospect of adding the popular amenities of workmen's dwellings. At this point some old Etonians interfered, and a subscription having been raised, the land was purchased and handed over to the College as a gift. It then became known that the huge tract of land on the other side of the road, known as 'Agar's or 'Dutchman's' Plough, could be acquired. This news seems to have surprised the Governing Body into action, and now there is plenty of room for new playing-fields; and future generations will walk beneath the shade of elms or limes from the gates of the College almost as far as Slough itself. More, however, remains to be done. The river, the sacred Thames, the artery of life, which makes Eton without a rival among public schools, and has made its name famous in the annals of all who love the water, this river is within measurable distance of becoming intolerable, if not quite inaccessible, for the Eton boys to boat on or bathe in. Year by year the metropolis extrudes upon the neighbouring country increased numbers of its antlike inhabitants. Some are shot out for the day in noisy belching steamers, some more permanently in the more innocent, if not less really obnoxious form of riparian residents. Already the field along the river 'between the Hopes' has been acquired by a Windsor tradesman for the purpose of erecting villas or bungalows; and the time may come when the whole river from Windsor to Maidenhead will present the same appearance as that of the well-known reaches of the river between Putney and Mortlake, the Windsor race-course, elevated to the rank of a suburban meeting, being as it were the key of the situation. Eton on *terra firma* has been to a certain extent secured against the invader, but nothing has as yet been done to assert its rights on the all-precious water-way.

At the close of the nineteenth century, when Eton College has existed for more than four hundred and fifty years, it is astonishing—in fact it almost takes away the breath—to think how much of the advance and progress of Eton has taken place during the century which is now drawing towards its end, it might almost be said during the reign of her present Majesty, the age known as the Victorian era. Allusion has been made to the reforms in the systems and subjects of schoolwork, as well as to the gradual rise and establishment of athletics as an indispensable factor in education. The tendency of the age to arrive at some definite convention of existence, to eliminate prejudice and fancy in favour of some accepted compromise, to find the *auream mediocritatem*, is well exemplified by the changes which have come over the dress of Eton boys during the nineteenth century.

At the beginning of the century trousers had not yet become a universal article of dress. Boys wore shorts, loose at the ankles, white stockings, and often low shoes, like the Blue Coat boys. The little boys wore broad turn-down cambric collars. Starch had not yet enthroned itself on the cuff and shirtfront. Wearing trousers was at first surreptitious, a 'fearful joy,' disguised by artifice at 'absence' or on similar public occasions. Collegers might not wear them without some dread of instant execution. In 1814, however, trousers became adopted everywhere, and Eton boys followed the example of their fathers and cousins. One reads, however, of tight nankeen pantaloons with Hessian boots adorned with tassels, or duck and jean trousers strapped tightly to the instep. At one time the trousers were yellow and baggy, in imitation of the 'navigators' or 'navvies' who were employed in making the new railway. No regular system of dress was enforced. The coat was the regular 'swallow-tail' or dress-coat, the Eton jacket being the same coat without the tails; 'a coat under age,' as it has been well described. By degrees the rigidity of this coat was relaxed, and the tails reduced in importance, until they developed themselves into the present black morning coat. Eton was thus spared the survival of the dress-coat which is still worn at Harrow.

These pages are not the place to trace the genesis of the white tie from the clerical and academical bands, or to follow out the history of the tall silk hat from the conical hats of 1600 to the rough beaver hats of 1800, and on to the shiny silk hat, the 'chimney-pot,' the 'topper,' 'top hat' (in Germany, cylinder), or whatever name it is known by in different places. The adoption of the plain black coat, white or black tie, and silk hat, has proved a happy medium between the military costume of a French *lycée* and the antiquated fashion of a school like Harrow. The dress is necessarily respectable and gentlemanly, and attracts little though sufficient notice. It inculcates habits of cleanliness and tidiness, lapses from these being quickly evident in the dress of an Eton boy. As it entails some expense, the dress calls for some care, and therefore is laid aside for lighter or rougher garments when at play, or for easier and more comfortable clothes when the formalities of school life are relaxed.

Many writers have attempted to describe an Eton boy's life, but few have succeeded. Collections of reminiscences such as those of the Rev. W. Lucas Collins, A. D. Coleridge, the Rev. W. Hill Tucker, Charles Allix Wilkinson, James Brinsley-Richards, or Alfred Lubbock, will bring back to many minds incidents of their past lives, or those of their fathers and forebears: incidents sanctified by the quasi-religious halo of a happy past. To describe a schoolboy's life is well-nigh impossible. Those who have tried to do so have been compelled, for the sake of their book, to make their boy into a hero, to place him in the unsuitable 'choice of Hercules' between the conflicting powers of good and evil, and to bring him through triumphantly at the end, like a hero of melodrama. Boys are seldom so dramatic in their careers. The incidents in their life are numerous, petty, and commonplace, the memory of them for the most part fleeting; and among the thousand boys at Eton, it is obvious that the prizes in work or athletics must be to the few, and that the many must live through a course of unclassed, unnoted, though by no means unhappy insignificance. Such a life is most happily described in the little books *A Day of my Life at Eton*, and *About Some Fellows,* published by G. Nugent-Bankes, while still a boy at Eton. But to the general reader, not being an Etonian, these books, however fascinating, can be little else than a rather wearisome chronicle of small-beer, in which heroism, ambition, and all the magnificent qualities which are supposed to animate the heart of an English boy are to all appearances entirely lacking. Schools are, however, for boys, not heroes; and proud as a school may be of its champions in the lists of scholarships and games, or of their success in after life, the bulk of a schoolmaster's time, the hardest and least sympathetic side of his work, is the charge of the innumerable unknown, the illustrious obscure, who pass in battalions through his hands.

It is a commonplace among parents of Eton boys, and among the unsparing critics of the school, to comment on the little apparent progress made by the boys in their studies at school, and the comparative uselessness in after life of such knowledge as they acquire at Eton. This is an unfair view of a schoolmaster"s duty, which is not to cram knowledge into a boy, like fattening a beast for a cattle show, but to induce him not only to acquire some knowledge, but also to put it, no matter how small it may be, to some material use. A former Eton master, William Johnson (*multis ille bonis flebilis*) has well said that "Eton is not a mere place of residence for people working avowedly for an examination, a place which one is to leave as soon as one ceases to acquire fresh knowledge. It is a place which contains its own remedies for idleness, if people will only apply them; a place in which there is charity as well as selfish prudence, that goes on hoping and looks to a distant point."

A great public school may be compared to a fair garden; such a garden as the memory connects with an old English home, a deep-red brick manor house, a grey-stoned crumbling castle or grange. Such a garden is described by Bacon, with its three parts—"A *Greene* in the

259

Entrance, a *Heath* or *Desart* in the Going forth, and the Maine Garden in the midst, besides Alleys on both sides." It is easy to trace these divisions in a public school—the Green, 'finely shome' and 'pleasant to the eye'; the Heath "framed, as much as may be, to a Naturall Wildness"; and the Main Garden, "not close, but the Aire open and Free." The Head-master, too, may be compared to the gardener, and he will best succeed who pays as much attention to his ordinary plants and flowers as he does to his exotics and hothouse blooms. Some gardeners may gain repute from the beauty and rarity of these exotics, and the prizes gained by them at flower-shows, but it is not on such flowers that a true garden depends for its charm and fragrance. Such plants may be the more interesting to rear, and bring greater obvious glory and reward, but it is often the case with them, that the richer and more highly scented the blossom, the more noisome its decay.

A good gardener should attend even to his hardy annuals, for without due care they may present but a sorry appearance to the eye, and as he cannot turn all his flowers into roses, lilies, or carnations, he should take a pride and interest in his violets and primroses as well as in his peonies, marigolds, or wall-flowers. Nor will a good gardener try to cut or prune his shrubs into one particular shape, forcing his laurels and lilacs into the same semblance as his hedges of box or yew, even though, like Bacon, he may have a liking for "Little low Hedges, Round, like Welts, with some Pretty Pyramides."

Then again a schoolmaster will have a herbaceous border in his athletes—strong lusty plants, full of the sap and vigour of life—the backbone, it may be said, of his garden, needing careful supervision to restrain them from exuberance or encroachment.

In such a way may a schoolmaster, like a true and good gardener, gaze upon his garden, rich with flowers and fruit, and by watchful care behold it growing daily in beauty, fragrance, and vitality. And of such gardens there is none more fair than Eton.

In the preceding pages some attempt has been made to describe the great changes wrought in the constitution of Eton College during the later half of the nineteenth century. A question may naturally be raised as to how far the character of the boys themselves has been affected by these changes. Does the school, which under the original Foundation produced a Chatham, a Canning, and a Gladstone, a Wellesley and a Wellington, a Porson, a Praed, or a Shelley, still continue, in spite of the cataclysms in its constitution, to produce boys with the same destiny of fame and supremacy in after life? There is no sign at present that the class or character of the boys has been in any way affected by the somewhat startling development of events described in the last chapters. The Eton boy remains very much the same; and it is difficult to assert with confidence that he is any better or worse for the many reforms in the educational machine whereby his teachers are trying to grind him into shape. This result is perhaps mainly due to that all-pervading element in the Eton system which has done so much to form and maintain the peculiar character of an Eton boy, the almost entire reliance by the masters upon the boys themselves, as the best legislators for their own personal rules of honour and prestige.

A boy on coming to Eton for the first time finds out at once that he has to make and keep a position for himself, however small it may be, and that it is upon the estimation in which he is held by his comrades, rather than upon the protection afforded him by his masters, that he must rely for his happiness and comfort in his school-life. He thus quickly becomes conscious of responsibilities—of duties to perform and unwritten laws to obey. These at last become mere matters of daily routine, until one day he discovers that a great change has taken place in his position, and that where before he was content to obey and follow, he is suddenly called upon to lead and perhaps eventually to govern. This microcosm of authority, watched over and tended with affectionate anxiety by the authorities, is the real nourishing sap of Eton as a school. It is this which makes Eton, as an eminent living Etonian has justly said, 'breed captains.' In every walk of life where a leader is required there is seldom any man better equipped for the purpose than an Etonian, and, more important still, there is seldom any man so willingly followed, be it in peace or war, by his subordinates.

In politics Eton's line of Prime Ministers has been continued from Mr. Gladstone and the Earl of Derby by the Marquess of Salisbury and the Earl of Rosebery, and seems likely to be further continued by the present Leader of the House of Commons, the Right Hon. Arthur James Balfour. Etonians have been conspicuous in the Governments of both great parties in the State. On the Conservative side have been George Ward Hunt, the Earl of Carnarvon, Sir Michael Hicks-Beach, Bart., the present Earl of Derby, the Earl Cadogan, the Marquess of Lansdowne,

Lord Balfour of Burleigh, the Marquess of Lothian, Lord Randolph Churchill, Sir William Walrond, Gerald William Balfour, Aretas Akers-Douglas, the Marquess of Londonderry, Earl Brownlow, Lord Windsor, the Hon. George Nathaniel Curzon (now Lord Curzon of Kedleston), the Hon. W. St. John Brodrick, George Wyndham, and W. G. Ellison-Macartney. On the Liberal side have been the Earl of Kimberley, George J. Shaw-Lefevre, the Earl of Strafford, Sir Arthur Divett Hayter, Bart., C. Seale-Hayne, Earl Carrington, the Earl of Cork, Lord Monkswell, Lord Edmond Fitzmaurice, Herbert J. Gladstone, and before the great Home Rule disruption, John G. Dodson (Lord Monk Bretton), E. Heneage, and the Earl of Morley. To the dignified form of Mr. Brand in the Speaker's chair succeeded another Etonian, perhaps even more dignified still, Arthur Wellesley Peel, the *Peel undecimus* of former days. A tribute to the utility of an Eton training is shown by the large proportion of Etonians chosen to act as Parliamentary Whips for either party during the last fifty or sixty years.

Eton still remains the chief nursery of the peerage, though it would tax the utmost energies of the Lord Chamberlain's department to enumerate the numerous scions of the nobility who have been educated at Eton with varying degrees of success. A mere list, however, of titled *alumni* would be no criterion of Eton's success as a school. Perhaps one of the most striking tributes to Eton is the share it has had in that movement of events which may be described as controlled by the imperial idea. In the administration of the Indian Empire and the Colonies, not only have the highest posts been filled by Etonians, but many of those also which are almost as important if they are less conspicuous and offer but little opportunity for personal distinction. It has been said that the sun never sets on the British Empire; and if this be true, it almost follows as a corollary that the sun never sets on Eton.

The government of India has been to a great extent in the hands of Etonians. Since the days of Cornwallis, Wellesley, and Metcalfe no less than eight Governors-General and Viceroys of India have been Etonians: Lord Auckland, the Earl of Ellenborough, Earl Canning, the Earl of Elgin, the Marquess of Dufferin, the Marquess of Lansdowne, yet another Earl of Elgin—a worthy successor of a great name at a difficult period in the history of India—and the present Viceroy, Lord Curzon of Kedleston, whose distinguished career at Eton foreshadowed, like those of Canning and Gladstone, the prominent part in public life which he has played, and seems destined to continue with increased prestige.

The provinces of India have also been administered by many Etonians. It has been said that a majority of them were at one time governed simultaneously by Etonians who had boarded at the same house when Eton boys. It will be sufficient perhaps to point to the two distinguished brothers, Sir Alfred C. Lyall and Sir James Lyall, to Sir Auckland Colvin, William Mackworth Young, Sir Stewart Colvin Bayley, Sir Lyttelton Holyoake Bayley, Sir Mountstuart Jackson, as examples of those whose Eton training has helped them to administer the affairs of the great dependency, in some cases at the risk or even actual cost of their lives. A similar prominence is shown by Etonians in the administration of the difficult and checkered affairs of the moribund Turkish Empire. Few at Eton could have foreseen the part destined to be played by Sir Edgar Vincent and Sir Vincent Caillard in the history of Turkish finance, or that played in Egypt by Sir Charles Rivers Wilson, or a few years ago by Sir Gerald Portal and at present by Mr. J. L. Gorst, in Crete by Sir Herbert Chermside, in Zanzibar by Sir Arthur Hardinge, in Uganda by the late Major Roderick Owen, and in Rhodesia by the Hon. Arthur Lawley. The Dominion of Canada has also been ruled by Etonians, in the shape of Earl Cathcart, Lord Lisgar, the Marquess of Dufferin, the Marquess of Lansdowne, the Marquess of Lorne, and the present Earl of Derby; and the Viceroy at the present day is a well-known and popular Etonian, the Earl of Minto.

The other colonies too have had their share in Eton as an element of government. New South Wales has had Sir William Denison, Lord Lisgar, and the Earls of Belmore, Carrington, Jersey, and Beauchamp; Victoria, the Earl of Hopetoun; South Australia, the Earl of Kintore; Queensland, Lord Lamington; West Australia, Sir Gerard Smith; New Zealand, the Earl of Onslow; the Cape of Good Hope, Sir Philip Wodehouse.

At home the gift of 'captaincy,' taught at Eton, has been well tested in the Civil Service. In fonner days, when the posts in the Civil Service were either mere sinecures or given by the private patronage of the Ministers in power, it was not surprising that many posts were held by Etonians as scions of the chief governing families in the land. At the close of the nineteenth century, in the more regenerate days when the posts in the Civil Service are thrown open to public competition and promotion is chiefly by merit, it is all the more satisfactory to find that so many of the highest and most responsible posts in the Civil Service are still held by Etonians, and to learn that in a public office no man is so likely to get on well as one who has been an Eton boy.

The following posts held recently or at present by Etonians will be sufficient to indicate their influence:—

The Treasury, Secretary.	Lord Welby.
The Treasury, Assistant-Secretary.	Sir Edward Hamilton.
The Treasury, Principal Clerk and Auditor of the Civil List.	Stephen E. Spring-Rice.
Admiralty, Principal Clerk.	H. F. Vansittart-Neale.
Colonial Office, Permanent Under Secretary of State.	Sir Robert G. W. Herbert.
Council of Education, Secretary.	Sir George W. Kekewich.
Office of Works, Secretary.	Algernon B. Mitford.
Office of Works, Secretary.	Reginald B. Brett (Viscount Esher).
Comptroller and Auditor-General.	Sir Charles Lister Ryan.
Registrar-General.	Sir Brydges P. Henniker.
Privy Council, Registrar.	Edward S. Hope.
India Office, Assistant Under-Secretary.	Sir Horace George Walpole.
India Office, Principal Clerk.	Richmond T. W. Ritchie.
Foreign Office, Permanent Under-Secretary.	Sir Francis B. Alston.
Foreign Office, Permanent Under-Secretary.	Sir Thomas H. Sanderson.
Foreign Office, Chief Clerk.	Sir George E. Dallas.
Foreign Office, Assistant Under-Secretary.	Hon. F. L. Bertie.
Post Office, Secretary.	Sir Stevenson A. Blackwood.

Post Office, Secretary	Sir Spencer Walpole.
Post Office, Financial Secretary	Algernon Turnor.
Board of Trade, Assistant-Secretary	Hon. Thomas H. W. Pelham.
Ordnance Factories, Deputy Director-General	Hay Frederick Donaldson.
Civil Service Commission.	Lord francis Hervey.
Charity Commission.	Sir George Youong, Bart.
Charity Commission.	Richard Durnford.
Prisons Commission, Chairman	Evelyn J. Ruggles-Brise.
Railway and Canal Commissioner.	Viscount Cobham.
British Museum, Keeper of Antiquities. . . .	Sir Augustus Wollaston Franks.
National Portrait Gallery, Director	Lionel Cust.
Record Office, Deputy-Keeper.	Sir Henry C. Maxwell-Lyte.
Woodsand Forests, Commissioner.	John F. Horner.
The Mint, Deputy-Master	Hon. Charles Fremantle.
Crown Office, House of Lords, Chief Clerk . .	Adolphus G. C. Liddell.

The Foreign Office and Diplomatic profession being careers in which the advantages of birth and wealth play a leading part, have ever presented an obvious field for the budding Etonian, and one in which an Eton training is especially valued. It is sufficient to point to the names of Sir Henry G. Elliot, Sir Edward Malet, Sir Edward Monson, Lord Vivian, Lord Currie, Sir Francis Clare Ford, Sir Martin Gosselin, Sir Arthur Hardinge, Sir Edwin Egerton, and the Marquess of Dufferin as instances of the part already played by Etonians in the affairs of Europe, and to look forward to such accomplished diplomats as the Hon. Michael Herbert, Cecil A. Spring-Rice, George H. Barclay, and others to do the same in the future.

Finance is a field in which Etonians might less be expected to succeed. For generations, however, the members of the great banking families in the city of London have been educated at Eton, and it is not therefore surprising that there should be a preponderance of Etonians upon the Board of Directors of the Bank of England.

Under the new statutes Eton has been deprived of many advantages which tended to draw some of its most eminent sons to the Church as a profession. It is therefore satisfactory to find that on the present bench of Bishops four are Etonians: Lord Alwyne Compton (Ely), the Hon. and Rev. Augustus Legge (Lichfield), J. C. Ryle (Liverpool), and G. W. Kennion (Bath and Wells); while the See of Oxford was recently occupied by James F. Mackarness. Among the Suffragan bishops should be noted the Hon. and Rev. Arthur T. Lyttelton (Southampton), and Alfred Earle (Marlborough), and among Colonial bishops Edward Hobhouse, Bishop of New Zealand, and John Coleridge Patteson, the martyred Bishop of Polynesia; John Richardson Selwyn, Bishop of Melanesia; James E. C. Welldon, lately Head-master of Harrow, and now Bishop of Calcutta and Metropolitan of India, and John Reginald Harmer, now Bishop of Adelaide. Eton also has contributed some of its most active workers to the Church in London, such as Henry Scott-Holland, Charles Wellington Furse, Basil Wilberforce, the Hon. and Rev. James G. Adderley, the Hon. and Rev. Algernon G. Lawley, J. H. J. Ellison (now at Windsor), and Stewart Headlam. The Eton Mission at Hackney Wick, under the guidance of the Rev. St. Clair Donaldson, is in itself a tribute to the active interest taken by Eton and Etonians in the cause of religion and charity. Dr. Edward Bouverie Pusey was the leader at Oxford of a High Church revival, which had a most powerful influence on his contemporaries. At the present moment, when another contest of a somewhat critical nature is raging in the Church, it is interesting to note that two of the principal antagonists, Viscount Halifax and Lord Kinnaird, are Etonians. Among other past and present dignitaries of the Church may be noted Canon Venables of Lincoln, the Rev. Rowland Williams, Vice-Principal of Lampeter, Canon the Hon. and Rev. W. H. Fremantle of Ripon, the Rev. Charles B. Scott, Dean of Rochester (formerly Head-master of Westminster, and joint author of *Liddell and Scott's Greek Lexicon*), Vincent Stuckey Coles, Principal of Pusey House, Oxford, Winfrid Burrows, Head of the Clergy School at Leeds, and others, who testify that at Eton religion, if not brought so prominently forward in education as elsewhere, has been far from being neglected or kept in the background.

At the Universities Eton has held its own both in scholarship and its share in the administration; and the names may be mentioned of the Hon. and Rev. George Brodrick, Warden of Merton College, Oxford; Sir William Reynell Anson, President of All Souls' College, Oxford; R. Shute, Tutor of Christ Church, Oxford; Paul F. Willert, Fellow and Tutor of Exeter College; Edward H. Hayes, Fellow and Tutor of New College; William H. Forbes, Fellow and Tutor of Balliol College, Oxford; Norman M. Ferrers, Master of Caius College, Cambridge; Augustus Austen Leigh, Provost of King's College, Cambridge; the Hon. and Rev. Latimer Neville, Master of Magdalene College, Cambridge; Herbert E.

Ryle, President of Queens' College, Cambridge; Henry Bradshaw, Librarian of Cambridge University; John Willis Clark, Registrary of Cambridge University; and Edward W. Blore, Fellow and Tutor of Trinity College, Cambridge. In the ranks of Professors or Schoolmasters are or have been, in addition to Thring of Uppingham and Welldon of Harrow, the Hon. and Rev. Edward Lyttelton, Headmaster of Haileybury; Edward Cams Selwyn, Head-master of Uppingham; Edward Mallet Young, Head-master of Sherborne; Thomas F. Kirby, Bursar of Winchester; Henry C. Goodhart, Professor of Humanity at Edinburgh; George W. Prothero, Professor of History at Edinburgh; Sir Roland Knyvett Wilson, Reader in Indian Law; Francis W. Maitland, Downing Professor of Law at Cambridge; Goldwin Smith, formerly Professor of Modern History at Oxford; Sir Frederick Pollock, Professor of Jurisprudence at Oxford; Lord Rayleigh, Senior Wrangler and Professor of Experimental Physics at Cambridge; Henry A. Miers, Professor of Mineralogy at Oxford; and Gilbert C. Bourne, University Lecturer in Animal Morphology at Oxford.

Public life in the London County Council has brought into prominent notice Willoughby H. Dickinson and Henry P. Harris; while the rival attractions of the London School Board have been profitable to the Hon. Lyulph Stanley, Athelstan Riley, Evelyn Cecil, William C. Bridgeman, and other energetic Etonians.

The Law has afforded several Etonians opportunities for distinction, notably Sir James Fitzjames Stephen, Sir Henry Cotton, Sir Joseph W. Chitty, the Hon. Alfred Thesiger, Sir A. Kekewich, Sir William Rann

Kennedy, who all attained the Bench; Henry J. Bushby and Wyndham Slade, the London magistrates; George H. Urmson, Commissioner in Lunacy; Herbert James Hope, Registrar of the Court of Bankruptcy; and George S. Barnes, Official Receiver of Companies in Liquidation; while among those likely to attain further distinction at the Bar are F. A. Bosanquet, Q.C., Recorder of Wolverhampton, the present Lord Coleridge, the Hon. Alfred Lyttelton, Recorder of Oxford, John F. P. Rawlinson, Recorder of Cambridge, John Eldon Bankes, George P. C. Lawrence, and Lord Robert Cecil.

The Army has ever drawn largely on Eton for its officers, and wherever the flag of England has waved in battle there have many Etonians laid down their lives for their country—in the Crimea, in South Africa, Afghanistan, and the Soudan. The most prominent Etonian in the army is Field-Marshal Lord Roberts, who, like the Duke of Wellington, was not remarkable in any way when at Eton. Close on him comes General Sir Redvers Buller. Other Etonians on the active list are Lieutenant-General Sir Charles Mansfield Clarke, Lieutenant-General Lord Methuen, and Major-General the Hon. Neville G. Lyttelton, Colonel Villiers Hatton of the Grenadier Guards, Sir Henry E. Colvile, V.C., Colonel Francis W. Rhodes, and many others too numerous to reckon here. On the retired list may be noted the names of Lord Chelmsford, Sir George Higginson, and many others, who have done their duty (*rude donati*) and earned their leisure.

The Navy, owing to the early age at which cadets must begin their education, is a profession to which Etonians can seldom proceed; but even in this profession Eton can claim Admiral Sir George Tryon, Admiral the Earl of Clanwilliam, Admiral Arthur Knyvett Wilson, and Captain Arthur Moore, the present commander of the *Britannia*. The famous Arctic explorer. Sir Robert Le Mesurier M'Clure, who first discovered the North-West Passage, is also stated to have been at Eton and Sandhurst before joining the navy.

Etonian Literature is proud to recognise as the successor of Shelley the famous poet Algernon C. Swinburne. After him come Robert Bridges, Lord de Tabley, and Arthur C. Benson. Other branches of literature claim Leslie Stephen, both as an author and as first editor of the great *Dictionary of National Biography*; Arthur J. Butler, the brothers Julian and Howard Sturgis, Robert N. Cust, the Orientalist, the late and present Earls of Crawford, and the last EarPs son. Lord Balcarres, Sir John Lubbock, Bart., and Bernard Holland.

Journalism has known in its ranks Thomas Chenery, editor of the *Times*; Mowbray Morris, also of the *Times*; Herbert W. Paul, of the *Daily News*; Henry J. Cust, of the *Pall Mall Gazette*; Walter H. Pollock, of the *Saturday Review*; and Francis C. Burnand, the genial editor of *Punch*. Among printers have been members of the great firms of Spottiswoode and Clowes, while publishing has lately exercised a great fascination for Etonians, the great firms of Murray, Longman, Smith & Elder, and Macmillan, with the more recent firms of Arnold, Duckworth, and others, reckoning Etonians among their principal partners.

Art, for the practice of which Eton affords but few opportunities, has yet produced the Hon. John Collier, Philip Norman, and Arthur J. Ryle among painters; William Eden Nesfield among architects; and George Warrington Taylor, first manager of William Morris's famous art-furnishing firm in London. Mention should also be made of the American brothers, sculptor and painter, Waldo and Julian Story, and of Lord Ronald Sutherland Gower and Charles Bennet Lawes among sculptors. Mention has already been made of the high position attained by Sir Hubert Parry in the domain of Music. As an antiquary no higher position has ever been attained than that of Sir Augustus Wollaston Franks, F.R.S., President of the Society of Antiquaries; and as a Librarian none higher than Henry Bradshaw. Even the Stage counts Etonians among its chief performers, followers of Charles Kean, such as Charles H. Hawtrey, Arthur Bourchier, Stewart Dawson, and William G. Elliot. The founder of the modern 'Polytechnic' institutions was an Etonian, Quintin Hogg.

Of more miscellaneous attainments, the names are worth mentioning of Sir John Dugdale Astley, Bart., John Moyer Heathcote, the tennis champion, Sir Francis Marindin, Lord Edward Pelham-Clinton, Arthur H. Smith-Barry, W. Wightman Wood, Douglas W. Freshfield, Clinton T. Dent, Sir Alfred Dent (of Borneo), William F. Donkin, Sir George Chetwynd, Sir Henry Fletcher, the Hon. Auberon Herbert, Chaloner W. Chute, the Hon. Mark Rolle, Sir W. Brampton Guidon, Edward Denison, James Round, the late and present Earls of Winchilsea, the late and present Lords de L'Isle and Dudley, the late and present Earls of Pembroke, Cecil C. Cotes, Eustace Neville-Rolfe, the two brothers Sir Charles and Sir George Russell, H. E. Chetwynd-Stapylton, compiler of the Eton lists, to which this work is so largely indebted; the Hon. Horace Plunkett, M.P., Sir Algernon West, F. C. Rasch, M.P., H. Cosmo Bonsor, M.P., Sir Denis le Marchant, H. A. Butler-Johnstone, Geoffrey Drage, Lord Wantage, Lord Cottesloe, the late and present Earls of Darnley, the Earl of Ellesmere, Lord Walsingham, the Earl of Wemyss, the Earl of Meath, the Marquess of Waterford, Guy Nickalls, the mighty oarsman, and many others whose names have been brought before the public in some remarkable way.

It may seem an easy way to prove the credit of a school by accumulating statistics of its success in turning out boys capable of obtaining scholarships at the moment, and of attaining to reasonable success in after life. The annals of any large public school could provide similar information. The list given above is not so much for the glorification of Eton as the school to which a majority of those who excel in rank or wealth are wont to send their sons, as to show on how many divers fields Eton boys have met with success in after life. An Etonian on reading the names given above would be struck by the fact that but a small minority of the names mentioned are those of boys who were denoted, earmarked it might be said, when still boys, as likely to succeed in after life. It is the pride of Eton that it trains almost every boy to face the duties in life which may confront him. As an Etonian Prime Minister has said, every day at Eton is forming a great man, and furnishing material for the future history of the country. Eton may be relied upon to produce its Cannings, Coleridges, Wellesleys, Gladstones, Cecils, and Curzons, its Lytteltons and Lubbocks, so long as it maintains its position at the head of English public schools. But it is not upon the success of individuals that the school relies, not merely on scholarships gained at the universities, on centuries made at Lord's, not even on a succession of Etonian Prime Ministers or Etonian Viceroys of India. Eton relies upon its traditions of honour, its self-regulated independence of spirit, and, above all, its power of inspiring a life-long affection and an unseverable bond of union among its boys. Age does little to weaken the love of Eton. Once an Eton boy, always an Eton boy, even, like Horace Walpole, in the sere and yellow leaf of life. When George Augustus Selwyn was consecrated to be bishop of the then almost unknown islands of Melanesia, the parting words to him from the pulpit of St. Paul's Cathedral were, 'Floreat Ecclesia, Floreat Etona,' When Robert Elwes rode to certain death agamst the Boer bullets at Laing's Nek, his cry was not 'Victory or Westminster Abbey!' his thoughts not of home or family, but his last words were 'Floreat Etona.' He is not the only Etonian who has met death with those words in his heart, if not upon his lips.

Above all, there is one result of an Eton training which accompanies a boy through his career in life. Like Chaucer's Knight, who

> from the tyme that he first began
> To ryden out, he lovede chyvalrye,
> Trouthe and honour, fredom and cortesie,

if a boy prove a true son of Eton, he will always be, in Chaucer's words,

A verray perfight gentil knight.

It is easy to point out the faults and weak places of Eton as a school, it is easy to comment on the disadvantages of the old Foundation, or on the somewhat cumbrous mechanism of the new, but it is difficult to suggest new or satisfactory measures for improvement. It is the boys who make Eton, not its Governing Body; not even its Head-master and his staff. Eton is a natural and indigenous product of England, and its existence has for four and a half centuries been part and parcel of England's progress and prosperity.

At the close of the nineteenth century the lines written by the Marquess Wellesley, in 1839, in anticipation of the changes which were then imminent, still remain apposite:—

Incorrupta, precor, maneas atque integra, neu te
    Aura regat populi, neu novitatis amor;
Stet quoque prisca Domus; (neque enim manus impia tangat)
    Floreat in mediis intemerata minis;
Det Patribus Patres, Populoque det inclyta Cives
    Eloquiumque Foro Judiciisque decus,
Concilioque animos magnoeque det ordine Genti
    Immortalem alta cum pietate Fidem;
Floreat, intact per postera secula fama,
    Cura diu Patriae, Cura paterna Dei.

Floreat Etona—Esto Perpetua.

THE END.

Printed in Great Britain
by Amazon